SPANISH NEW YORK NARRATIVES 1898–1936
MODERNIZATION, OTHERNESS AND NATION

LEGENDA

LEGENDA, founded in 1995 by the European Humanities Research Centre of the University of Oxford, is now a joint imprint of the Modern Humanities Research Association and Maney Publishing. Titles range from medieval texts to contemporary cinema and form a widely comparative view of the modern humanities, including works on Arabic, Catalan, English, French, German, Greek, Italian, Portuguese, Russian, Spanish, and Yiddish literature. An Editorial Board of distinguished academic specialists works in collaboration with leading scholarly bodies such as the Society for French Studies, the British Comparative Literature Association and the Association of Hispanists of Great Britain & Ireland.

MHRA

The Modern Humanities Research Association (MHRA) encourages and promotes advanced study and research in the field of the modern humanities, especially modern European languages and literature, including English, and also cinema. It also aims to break down the barriers between scholars working in different disciplines and to maintain the unity of humanistic scholarship in the face of increasing specialization. The Association fulfils this purpose primarily through the publication of journals, bibliographies, monographs and other aids to research.

Maney Publishing is one of the few remaining independent British academic publishers. Founded in 1900 the company has offices both in the UK, in Leeds and London, and in North America, in Philadelphia. Since 1945 Maney Publishing has worked closely with learned societies, their editors, authors, and members, in publishing academic books and journals to the highest traditional standards of materials and production.

STUDIES IN HISPANIC AND LUSOPHONE CULTURES

Studies in Hispanic and Lusophone Cultures are selected and edited by the Association of Hispanists of Great Britain & Ireland. The series seeks to publish the best new research in all areas of the literature, thought, history, culture, film, and languages of Spain, Spanish America, and the Portuguese-speaking world.

The Association of Hispanists of Great Britain & Ireland is a professional association which represents a very diverse discipline, in terms of both geographical coverage and objects of study. Its website showcases new work by members, and publicises jobs, conferences and grants in the field.

Editorial Committee
Chair: Professor Trevor Dadson (Queen Mary, University of London)
Professor Catherine Davies (University of Nottingham)
Professor Andrew Ginger (University of Bristol)
Professor Hilary Owen (University of Manchester)
Professor Christopher Perriam (University of Manchester)
Professor Alison Sinclair (Clare College, Cambridge)
Professor Philip Swanson (University of Sheffield)

Managing Editor
Dr Graham Nelson
41 Wellington Square, Oxford OX1 2JF, UK

www.legendabooks.com/series/shlc

STUDIES IN HISPANIC AND LUSOPHONE CULTURES

1. *Unamuno's Theory of the Novel*, by C. A. Longhurst
2. *Pessoa's Geometry of the Abyss: Modernity and the* Book of Disquiet, by Paulo de Medeiros
3. *Artifice and Invention in the Spanish Golden Age*, edited by Stephen Boyd and Terence O'Reilly
4. *The Latin American Short Story at its Limits: Fragmentation, Hybridity and Intermediality*, by Lucy Bell
5. *Spanish New York Narratives 1898–1936: Modernization, Otherness and Nation*, by David Miranda-Barreiro
6. *The Art of Ana Clavel: Ghosts, Urinals, Dolls, Shadows and Outlaw Desires*, by Jane Elizabeth Lavery
7. *Alejo Carpentier and the Musical Text*, by Katia Chornik

Spanish New York Narratives 1898–1936

Modernization, Otherness and Nation

David Miranda-Barreiro

Studies in Hispanic and Lusophone Culture 5
Modern Humanities Research Association and Maney Publishing
2014

Published by the
Modern Humanities Research Association and Maney Publishing
1 Carlton House Terrace
London SW1Y 5AF
United Kingdom

LEGENDA is an imprint of the
Modern Humanities Research Association and Maney Publishing

Maney Publishing is the trading name of W. S. Maney & Son Ltd,
whose registered office is at Suite 1C, Joseph's Well, Hanover Walk, Leeds LS3 1AB

ISBN 978-1-909662-15-5

First published 2014

All rights reserved. No part of this publication may be reproduced or disseminated or transmitted in any form or by any means, electronic, mechanical, photocopying, recording or otherwise, or stored in any retrieval system, or otherwise used in any manner whatsoever without the express permission of the copyright owner

© Modern Humanities Research Association and W. S. Maney & Son Ltd 2014

Printed in Great Britain

Cover: 875 Design

Copy-Editor: Dr Susan Wharton

CONTENTS

	Acknowledgements	ix
	Preface	x
	Introduction: New York City: a Symbol of Modernization in Early Twentieth-Century Spanish Narrative	1
1	Spanish Narratives of Modernity: Going Beyond Exclusive Definitions of Early Twentieth-Century Spanish Literature	10
2	The Hidalgo against the 'Masses': the Challenge to the Classist Nation	25
3	Images of the Modern Woman: the Challenge to the Patriarchal Nation	67
4	Racialism versus Multiculturalism: the Challenge to the Ethnic Nation	110
	Conclusion	159
	Afterword: New York in Spanish Narrative: A Constant Presence in the Twentieth and Twenty-First Centuries	165
	Bibliography	169
	Index	185

In Memoriam
Nigel Dennis

ACKNOWLEDGEMENTS

The thesis on which this book is based was awarded one of the two AHGBI (Association of Hispanists of Great Britain and Ireland)-Spanish Embassy Postgraduate Prizes for the most distinguished PhD thesis in Hispanic and Luso-Brazilian Studies in 2012. I would like to thank the AHGBI, especially Professor Trevor Dadson, for organizing this award and giving me the honour of being one of its first two winners. In this regard, my gratitude extends to the Spanish Embassy, in particular to Fidel López Álvarez (Minister-Counsellor for Cultural and Scientific Affairs), and to Professor Colin Davis (General Editor of Legenda), for funding and setting up this prize together with the AHGBI.

Two people were instrumental in my receiving this award: my viva examiners Professor Nigel Dennis and Dr Beatriz Barrantes Martín, who kindly supported my candidature. I am truly indebted to both of them. Sadly, Professor Dennis passed away unexpectedly a few months after the verdict was made public. This book is humbly dedicated to him. His generosity and inspiration will always stay with me.

A special thanks to the School of Modern Languages at Bangor University (Wales), which funded my PhD thesis, and in particular to my supervisor, Dr Helena Miguélez-Carballeira, for her close guidance and constant support throughout the process. I would also like to thank Professor Carol Tully and Linda Christine Jones.

Finally, I would like to thank my friends, especially Dr Daniel Arias Mosquera for his big-hearted friendship and Dr Craig Patterson, who kindly helped me by translating the extracts in Spanish quoted in this book; Dr Armelle Blin-Rolland for her inspiring work and her support; and my family: my brother Quique, my sister Gema and my parents, Emerio and Amelia, to whom I owe everything.

Sections of Chapter 4 first appeared in a different form as 'Primitivist Modernism and Imperialist Colonialism: The View of African Americans in José Moreno Villa's *Pruebas de Nueva York* and Julio Camba's *La ciudad automática*' (*Journal of Spanish Cultural Studies*, 14.1 (2013): 52–69). I am grateful to the editors for their permission to include this material.

D.M.-B., June 2014

PREFACE

In 2003, I wrote six titles in a small notebook: *Poeta en Nueva York, Diario de un poeta reciencasado, Pruebas de Nueva York, El hombre que inventó Manhattan, Cuaderno de Nueva York,* and *Ventanas de Manhattan*. As a new graduate in Hispanic studies, the presence of New York City in Spanish contemporary literature struck me as a curious coincidence. I was far from imagining that two years later I would arrive at Bangor University as a Graduate Teaching Assistant, and that I would not only write an MA dissertation on one of these texts (José Hierro's *Cuaderno de Nueva York*) but that I would also include José Moreno Villa's *Pruebas de Nueva York* in a PhD thesis in which I studied this phenomenon more extensively. Originally, I set myself an extremely ambitious goal: to provide an exhaustive view of the role played by New York in Spanish literature from the beginning of the twentieth century to the present day. As soon as the preliminary research unfolded, it became obvious that such a task was highly unrealistic: New York had a constant and abundant presence in Spanish letters. It was necessary to rethink the scope of the study, and the appearance of a series of patterns in the narrative renditions of this city written by Spanish authors in the first three decades of the twentieth century made me realize that the texts published in this period showed a commonality of discourse shared by similar texts written in other European countries. These thematic parallels became the core of my study, and reflect not only the image of New York (and by extension of the United States) that Spanish writers and travellers had at the time, but also their views about the reality of their own country and the reactions brought about by modernization throughout Europe. More than ten years after my first timid approach to this rich corpus, and thanks to Bangor University, the AHGBI, the Spanish Embassy, and Legenda, this book is the final result of that endeavour.

INTRODUCTION

> Too often literature and culture are presumed to be politically, even historically innocent; it has regularly seemed otherwise to me [...] society and literary culture can only be understood and studied together
>
> EDWARD SAID

New York City: a Symbol of Modernization in Early Twentieth-Century Spanish Narrative

When in 1932 the Spanish journalist and travel writer Julio Camba argued that 'nuestra época sólo Nueva York ha acertado a encarnarla' [only New York has succeeded in embodying our epoch] (1960: 11), he was tapping into a well-established trope of European modernity. Camba's statement condenses the widespread, early twentieth-century perception of New York as the modern metropolis *par excellence*. By the time of Camba's writing, the city had in fact become a fashionable literary topic in Spanish literature, as Federico García Lorca acknowledged in his *Conferencia-recital*, where he presented *Poeta en Nueva York* (written between 1929 and 1930, published posthumously in 1940): 'no os voy a decir lo que es Nueva York por fuera, porque, juntamente con Moscú, son las dos ciudades antagónicas sobre las cuales se vierte ahora un río de libros descriptivos' [I am not going to tell you what New York is like on the outside, because both it and Moscow are opposing cities upon which a deluge of descriptive books now descends] (1997: 111–12). Curiosity about the United States and its increasing influence in Europe was also reflected in texts such as *V Amerike* (1906) by Maxim Gorky, *The Man who Disappeared (America)* (1927) by Franz Kafka, *New York* (1929) by Paul Morand, *America the Menace: Scenes from the Life of the Future* (1930) by Georges Duhamel, and H. G. Wells's *The Future in America: A Search After Realities* (1906), which includes a chapter on New York, and *The New America, the New World* (1935), amongst others.[1] In their works, European thinkers and writers developed a twofold view of the United States as 'the future'. On the one hand, America represented an innovative architecture, a new social organization, and the site of astonishing technological developments. On the other, the same modernization not only posed a threat to the hegemony traditionally held by European powers worldwide, but also reflected the crisis of modernity that the Old Continent was undergoing at the turn of the century.

This book will look at New York City's recurrent role as a symbol of modernization in early twentieth-century Spanish narrative. Taking the representations of this city in a range of literary texts as a departing point, I will explore the connections between the often contradictory reactions to modernization and the crisis of Spanish national identity triggered by the so-called 'Desastre del 98'. Furthermore, the book addresses the similarities between the reactions to US modernization in European and Spanish texts of the period, which often revolve around three main recurrent themes: mechanization and mass society, women's emancipation, and multiculturalism. Modernization processes intensified in the early twentieth century, precisely when the United States started its rise as a world power. This process of acceleration coincided with the questioning of the values promoted by modernity in Europe. A key text of the time, Oswald Spengler's *The Decline of the West* (1926, 1928), captured the sense of disenchantment that invaded Europe, especially after the First World War. The reaction of the arts to such a crisis — in the form of modernism — denounced the decadence of modern life, as Marshall Berman points out, 'in the name of values that modernity itself has created' (1999: 23). Ironically, modernization was regarded as a threat to the values of Western liberalism, since economic, technological, and political change favoured the rise and visibility of the 'Others' of European modernity: the 'masses'[2] (as opposed to bourgeois elitism), women (as opposed to patriarchy), and non-white peoples (as opposed to white colonial power). At the same time, the increasing influence of US-capitalist modernization in Europe fostered the image of this country as a 'Big Other' that imperilled European values (Wagner 2001: 111). Under this view, the United States of America was seen as the embodiment of a potentially threatening future in which mass democracy, mass production, women's emancipation and multiculturalism challenged the principles of Western civilization.

While Europe was facing, in Spengler's words, 'the early winter of full Civilization' (1926: 44), Spain was also immersed in a domestic crisis. The year 1898 has been seen as a turning point in Spanish history, when the final fall of the Spanish Empire and subsequent regionalist claims for independence from Catalonia, the Basque Country, and Galicia not only questioned the social and political structures of the Restoration system, but also posed the daunting question of how to solve the so-called 'problema de España'. Similarly to the European case, Spain was perceived by its intellectual elite as a nation in decay. It is, then, not surprising that 'regeneration' became the catchword for a group of polymaths concerned with the perceived weaknesses of their country. The solutions for the 'regeneration' of Spain were, however, not homogeneous. As Helen Graham and Jo Labanyi have pointed out, in Spain 'fin de siècle European anxieties about the decadence of Western civilization were experienced in a particular complex form', with intellectuals divided 'as to whether or not Spain should follow the European modernizing model, and as to whether the problem in Spain's case was modernity or a lack of modernization' (1995c: 21). For conservative sectors, the country would be regenerated through the recovery of traditional values and by the restoration of Spain's imperial past. Conversely, liberal positions, inspired mainly by the French Enlightenment and the ideas of the German philosopher Friedrich Krause, argued for the Europeanization of Spain as the solution for the country's backwardness and stagnation. These two opposing positions — at least theoretically — also involved two distinct conceptions of national identity: two different views of the nation that led to the division of Spanish society and eventually to the Civil War. The clash between different political views of the nation was not exclusive to the Spanish case, however. Rather, the Spanish crisis was 'a regional variant of a crisis that had rocked most of Europe since the First World War in which three opposing projects for the reconstruction of the post-war state — liberal democracy, fascism and revolutionary socialism — had vied for hegemony' (Balfour 2000: 246).

Nevertheless, the modernization of Spanish society seemed to progress independently of the controversies about national identity. In spite of being 'highly uneven, concentrated mainly in the north, north-east, and the Levant' (Balfour 2000: 246), such modernization prompted what Balfour has defined as 'a long-term crisis', since 'in many parts of Spain, industrialisation, urbanisation, migration and the spread of communication networks were undermining the social and ideological structures of the Restoration system' (Balfour 1996: 113). In the 1920s, under the 'regenerationist' dictatorship of Miguel Primo de Rivera, the country's progress towards modernization became particularly visible. Despite the political repression exerted by the regime, Spain saw the increasing presence of the 'masses' and women in the public arena. Later on, at the beginning of the 1930s, and after Primo's administration failed to provide the solution for the 'Spanish malady', the arrival of the Second Republic was perceived as an opportunity for change. It seemed that Spain was finally going to be Europeanized. During these two decades, Spain's half-hearted entry into the realm of modernization was seen with suspicion not only by traditionalist sectors, but also by liberal ones. On the one hand, reactions against modernizing processes from conservative positions mirrored their distrust of foreign values. Modernization posed a threat to the restoration of 'true Spanishness'. On the other hand, cautious attitudes towards modernization from liberal positions were in tune with the ambivalence of modernist responses to change in the rest of Europe. Spanish Republican and liberal intellectuals aimed to create a modern Spanish nation-state inspired by the values of the French Enlightenment (education, democracy, and secularization). However, whereas Spain was initiating its struggle towards modernity, calls for Europeanization clashed with the rise of the 'masses', women's claims for civil equality, and postcolonial debates arising from the country's loss of its hold in America. As John A. McCulloch argues, Spain was facing a cultural dilemma: 'its ideological "tug-of-war" between a historical tendency for extreme introversion, whilst simultaneously striving to be outward looking on a par with her European neighbours' (2007: 3).

In the midst of this turmoil, New York emerges in Spanish literature as the symbol of modern times. In this regard, the intersections between the representation of New York in Spanish and European literature, and the role played by this city, not only in travel literature but also in narrative fiction, have not been sufficiently examined. The case studies chosen for the present book — the travelogues *Pruebas de Nueva York* [*Proofs of New York*] (1927) by José Moreno Villa and *La ciudad automática* [*The Automatic City*] (1932) by Julio Camba, the novel *Anticípolis* [*The City of Anticipation*] (1931) by Luis de Oteyza and the novella *El crisol de las razas* [*The Melting Pot*] (1929) by Teresa de Escoriaza — capture some of the widespread opinions about this city in European and Spanish modernism[3] and the reactions to modernizing processes at the time.[4] Although these texts cannot be classified as modernist owing to their lack of literary experimentation, they are indeed modern inasmuch as they share similar reactions towards modernity to the ones found in the canonical texts of Spanish 'high modernism'. The thematic similarities between 'high' and 'low' texts of the modern period blur the clear-cut distinction between modernism and mass culture, and remind us of the need to grant more attention to genres and texts traditionally dismissed from studies of literary modernity.

Spanish New York Narratives (1898–1936)

This book will examine a corpus of early twentieth-century narrative texts about New York, published between 1898 and 1936, with special focus on the 1920s and 1930s. Although the chosen case studies were published in these two decades, I consider that a restrictive contextualization of the narrative representations of New York published between 1920 and 1936 would offer a fragmented account of this phenomenon, since the texts written in this period must be inscribed within the extensive literary interest on New York and the United States arising in Spain since the end of the nineteenth century. An example of this vast bibliography is Isabel García-Montón's *Viaje a la modernidad: la visión de los Estados Unidos en la España finisecular* [*A Journey to Modernity: The View of the United States in Fin-de-Siècle Spain*] (2002), an anthology of narrative texts published between 1875 and 1931. The corpus selected by García-Montón is mainly based on excerpts taken from late nineteenth-century and early twentieth-century travelogues (the only exception being *Anticípolis* by Luis de Oteyza), a fact that highlights the early curiosity awakened in Spanish writers and travellers by the United States, and the continuity of this theme during the decades prior to the Spanish Civil War. The curiosity of Spanish writers and travellers towards the United States did not diminish in the opening decades of the twentieth century and, as García Lorca indicated in the first public reading of his New York poems, the city gained special relevance during this period. Some examples of Spanish travelogues set (partially or fully) in New York published between 1900 and 1936 include: Eduardo Zamacois, *Dos años en América: impresiones de un viaje por Buenos Aires, Montevideo, Chile, Brasil, New-York y Cuba* [*Two Years in America: Impressions of a Journey through Buenos Aires, Montevideo, Chile, Brasil, New York and Cuba*] (1912), Mariano Alarcón, *Impresiones de un viaje a New-York* [*Impressions of a Journey to New York*] (1918), Eduardo Criado Requena, *La ciudad de los rascacielos* [*The City of Skyscrapers*] (1919), Luis Araquistáin, *El peligro yanqui* [*The Yankee Danger*] (1921), Vicente Blasco Ibáñez, *La vuelta al mundo de un novelista* [*A Novelist around the World*] (Chapter 2: 'La ciudad que venció a la noche' [The City that Defeated the Night]) (1924), Joaquín Belda, *En el país del bluff. Veinte días en Nueva York* [*In the Country of the Bluff. Twenty Years in New York*] (1926), Jacinto Miquelarena, *... Pero ellos no tienen bananas [El viaje a Nueva York]* (*... But they Don't Have Bananas [The Journey to New York]*) (1930), Pedro Segura, *Nueva York 1935: impresiones de un viaje a los Estados Unidos* [*New York: 1935: Impressions of a Journey to the United States*] (1935), as well as the two travelogues by José Moreno Villa and Julio Camba analysed in this book. In addition, New York was the setting for some works of narrative fiction, although in smaller numbers, as in the case of the novel *Los cauces. Novela de la vida norteamericana* [*The Channels. A Novel about Life in North*

America] (1922) by Rómulo de Mora, the novella *El crisol de las razas* (1929) by Teresa de Escoriaza, the novel *Don Clorato de Potasa* (1929) — whose second part is located in New York — by Edgar Neville, the novel *Anticípolis* (1931) by Luis de Oteyza and his collection of short stories *Picaresca Puritana* [*Puritan Picaresque*] (1931). As it will be discussed more in detail in the first chapter, many of these texts and their authors have remained mostly forgotten or, as in the case of Luis de Oteyza, have only recently been rescued from oblivion, thanks to the re-issue of some of his works.

In spite of the flurry of Spanish New York narratives published during this period, the study of the literary relationship between Spain and New York in the opening decades of the twentieth century has remained almost exclusively focused on the canonical texts of Spanish high modernism: Juan Ramón Jiménez's *Diario de un poeta reciencasado* [*Diary of a Newly-Wed Poet*] (1917) and Federico García Lorca's *Poeta en Nueva York*. Both texts have received extensive critical attention. However, they have mostly been considered in isolation from the considerable number of literary texts about New York also published during this period. Following a wider perspective, the interest of this city for Spanish writers in the early twentieth century has also been the focus of two studies of the poetic representation of New York in Hispanic literature: *El poeta y la ciudad. Nueva York y los escritores hispanos* [*The Poet and the City. New York and the Hispanic Writers*] (1994) by Dionisio Cañas, and the comprehensive *Historia poética de Nueva York en la España contemporánea* [*Poetic History of New York in Contemporary Spain*] (2012) by Julio Neira. These two scholars have drawn attention to the existence of an extensive corpus of Hispanic poetic works about New York. Cañas's study also includes a short 'Apéndice Histórico' which offers an overview of New York's presence in Hispanic letters (1994: 143–72), and pays special attention to Moreno Villa's travelogue, which is briefly analysed in relation to Lorca's *Poeta en Nueva York*. This brief examination focuses on the similarities between Moreno Villa's and Lorca's discourses regarding the situation of black people in US society, the opposition between nature (spiritualism)/civilization (materialism, capitalism), as well as other topics such as commercialism and the reactions of both poets towards the urban 'masses'. Cañas highlights that many of Moreno Villa's opinions are very similar to the ones expressed by Lorca years later. Such similarity is explained by the possibility that Lorca was familiar with Moreno Villa's book, but Cañas does not consider the influence of other narrative works also published before Lorca's stay in New York:

> unos años después vendrá Lorca a Manhattan y, aunque no sabemos si leyó el libro de Moreno Villa — posiblemente tuvo acceso a los artículos conforme fueron saliendo en la prensa –, las coincidencias en la actitud de Lorca frente a Nueva York son tantas que es difícil no pensar que ciertas "ideas hechas", respecto a la ciudad, no provienen ya del texto del primero. (Cañas 1994: 158)

> [some years later Lorca would come to Manhattan, and although we do not know if he read Morena Villa's book (he might have had access to the articles as they were published), the coincidences in Lorca's attitude towards New York are so numerous that it is hard not to think that certain preconceived ideas concerning the city have their source in the latter's text.]

In spite of its focus on poetry, Neira's study also provides a reference to Spanish narrative works inspired by New York, and states that:

> tampoco debe olvidarse que la fascinación literaria de los españoles por la ciudad no es patrimonio exclusivo de los poetas. También los prosistas, novelistas, periodistas, humoristas, se ocuparon de reflejar el impulso emergente de Nueva York como símbolo de la postcontemporaneidad nacida como resultado de los movimientos de vanguardia. (2012: 26)
>
> [it should not be forgotten either that the Spanish literary fascination with the city is not the exclusive realm of poets. Prose writers, novelists, journalists, and humorists also engaged in reflecting the emerging impulse of New York as a reflection of postcontemporaneity born as a result of avant-garde movements.]

By contrast, the examination of the narrative representation of New York and the United States in Spanish literature has been limited generally to less exhaustive studies, namely: 'Agentes de una aproximación cultural: viajeros españoles en los Estados Unidos tras la Guerra Finisecular' [Agents of a Cultural Approach: Spanish Travellers in the United States after the Fin-de-Siècle War] (2000) by Isabel García-Montón, 'Some 20th Century Spanish Views on the U.S' (2000) by Carmen González López-Briones, *Nueva York en los escritores españoles del siglo XX* [*New York in Twentieth-Century Spanish Writers*] (2003) by Emilio José Álvarez Castaño (2003), and Eloy Navarro Domínguez's introduction to *La ciudad de los rascacielos* by Eduardo Criado Requena (2004). García-Montón brings to the fore a very specific group of travelogues, written between 1899 and 1914. The depiction of the United States given in these books is directed to restore a more balanced view of US society after the 1898 war (García-Montón 2000: 238). For her part, González López-Briones (2000) refers to a wide range of texts published from the early twentieth century to the 1990s. This broad review is nevertheless restricted to a brief approach to the books. For example, in relation to Camba's view of New York, González López-Briones argues that the writer 'reflects a city full of activity and energy, yet Camba did not fail to transmit its idiosyncrasies and some of the problems he perceived' (2000: 274). The questions of what these 'idiosyncrasies' and 'problems' were, and most importantly, why these 'problems' were perceived as such by Camba, are not addressed. *Nueva York en los escritores españoles del siglo XX* (2003), by Álvarez Castaño, defines New York as the first modern metropolis (2003: 7) and provides a list of common themes present in the corpus, including the crowds, the accelerated pace of urban life, multiculturalism, and jazz music. Together with Jiménez and García Lorca's collections of poems, two of the texts chosen for analysis by Álvarez Castaño are precisely *Pruebas de Nueva York* and *La ciudad automática*. Although his analysis suggests some potentially interesting points for debate, his approach to the texts is — especially in the case of Moreno Villa's chronicles — highly dependent on the authors' biographical details. On the contrary, Navarro's preliminary study to *La ciudad de los rascacielos* highlights that this text must be contextualized within the prominent awakening of interest in Spanish journalism and literature in the nineteenth and twentieth centuries by the United States. Navarro refers to New York as an image that captures European anxieties towards modernization:

> los europeos empezarán [...] a interrogar a la gran ciudad norteamericana acerca

de su propio futuro, ante las evidentes señales (presentes tanto en el urbanismo como en los modos de vida de las grandes capitales europeas) de que el modelo económico y social que representa esa misma ciudad está destinado a extenderse por todo Occidente. En este sentido, la consideración de los Estados Unidos y de la gran metrópolis norteamericana como símbolo del futuro y espejo del presente experimentará aún distintas oscilaciones a lo largo del siglo XX en función de los cambios que se dan en los valores éticos y estéticos de la propia sociedad europea occidental y en la relación del continente con los Estados Unidos. (2004: 39–40)

[Europeans will begin [...] to examine the great North American city as regards their own future, before such evident signs (present in urban development as much as in the lifestyle of the great European cities) that the economic and social model which this very city represents is destined to be extended throughout the West in its entirety. In this sense, the consideration of the United States and of the great North American metropolis as a symbol of the future and mirror of the present will undergo different variations during the twentieth century, based on the changes that occur in ethical and aesthetic values of Western European society itself, and in the Continent's relationship with the United States.]

The image of New York as a 'symbol of the future and mirror of the present' argued by Navarro will be essential for the examination of the representation of this city in early twentieth-century Spanish narrative that is the focus of this book. Titles such as *Anticípolis* and *La ciudad automática* show at first glance the futuristic character given to the metropolis. Early twentieth-century Spain was at the crossroads between capitalism, industrialism and mass democracy — social processes which are indeed the product of modernization — and the traditionalism of the Restoration system. As the present book aims to demonstrate, Spanish writers also 'interrogated' New York about the destabilizing effects that modernization could trigger in their own country. The recurrent literary presence of this city in a historical period when modernity and modernization became a recurrent theme in the debates on Spanish national identity raises a series of questions: why did New York capture the attention of Spanish writers at the time? In what ways do these authors' views of New York reflect the anxieties and contradictions brought about by the Spanish crisis of modernization and national identity? Why is there such a persistent focus on mass society and mechanization, women's emancipation, and New York's polyethnicity in these texts? By addressing these questions, this study aims not only to contribute to current research on Spanish literary modernity, but also to highlight and reassess the presence of New York in Spanish early twentieth-century narrative.

A Note on Methodology

The book follows a thematic approach, as opposed to a book- or author-based one, for various reasons. Structurally, this modus operandi helps avoid repetition, since these four texts share similar themes and are driven by analogous anxieties. Moreover, from an analytic point of view, a thematic approach will highlight the concomitances between the discourses expressed in the texts and their connections to the crisis of Spanish national identity. The book is organized in four chapters, three of them (2, 3 and 4) devoted to the analysis of each of the main thematic aspects that recur in Spanish New York narratives of this period: mass society and mechanization, women's emancipation, and US incipient multiculturalism. However, these three different aspects cannot be considered in isolation. In order to highlight the similarities between Spanish New York narratives and other European texts either inspired by or set in this city, each of these chapters will start with an introductory section which will provide a historical context as well as a theoretical framework for the subsequent analysis of the case studies.

Chapter 1 will examine recent reassessments of the Spanish narrative written in this period, which have challenged generational categorizations in favour of a wider and less restrictive view. In this regard, I propose a fresher and more overarching approach, which highlights the importance of the study of mass-produced and travel narratives for a complete understanding of early twentieth-century Spanish literature. I will also include a brief overview of recent developments in the study of these two genres and a brief introduction to the authors and the texts chosen as case studies.

The second chapter, 'The Hidalgo against the "Masses": the Challenge to the Classist Nation', offers an analysis of the responses to mass society and mechanization in *Pruebas de Nueva York*, *La ciudad automática*, and *Anticípolis* (exceptionally in this chapter, *El crisol de las razas* is excluded from the analysis, owing to the scarce references to this theme in the novella). I will look at the recurrent and contradictory view of the United States — of which New York works as metonymy — as a simultaneously futuristic and primitive society, in contrast with a self-perception of Spain and Europe as the repository of civilization. The reactions against technology, capitalism, and mass society reflect the ambivalent responses to modernizing processes in early twentieth-century Spain, especially with regards to the concerns expressed by leading intellectuals such as José Ortega y Gasset about the threat posed by the increasing power of the 'masses' to Western civilization.

The view of women's emancipation in New York offered in the case studies will be the focus of Chapter 3, 'Images of the Modern Woman: the Challenge to the Patriarchal Nation'. I will examine the negative reactions against the 'modern woman' shown in *Pruebas de Nueva York* and *La ciudad automática*, suggesting that such discontent unveils the strength of patriarchal discourses in the formation of Western modernity as well as in the conception of Spanish national identity proposed by both conservative and liberal stances. The increasing presence of American women in public life challenged Spanish male-centred views of the nation, in which women were relegated to a submissive role. On the contrary, *Anticípolis* and *El crisol de las razas* contribute to the debate in a more productive manner. The opposition between modern and traditional models of womanhood carried out in these texts stresses the important role played by women in the struggle for modernization in Spain.

The fourth and final chapter, 'Racialism versus Multiculturalism: the Challenge to the Ethnic Nation', will turn to the attitudes towards New York's polyethnicity developed in all four texts, by focusing on references to the black and Jewish communities. Recurrent racist attitudes expressed in *Pruebas de Nueva York*, *La ciudad automática*, and *El crisol de las razas* reveal, on the one hand, essentialist views of the nation as a community constructed as 'racially' homogeneous. The nature of the United States as a nation based on political citizenship rather than kinship of blood challenged Western conceptions of nationhood. Racialist theories in vogue in Europe at the time will be found in the case studies, in the form of stereotypes aimed at strengthening the opposition between primitivism and civilization. Moreover, colonialist attitudes to former colonies such as Cuba and Puerto Rico convey a sense of nostalgia for the Spanish colonial past. Once more, *Anticípolis* involves an innovative response, by developing a counter-discourse that empowers the colonial 'Other' and also explores the possibilities of a transnational concept of identity.

Through a close scrutiny of these three recurrent themes in the texts chosen for analysis, I aim to provide an innovative understanding of the tensions and anxieties around views of class, gender, and 'race' that were at the core of the redefinition of Spanish national identity in the first decades of the twentieth century. Following similar reactions in other European countries, the challenges posed by the entrance of modernization into Spain were reflected in the view of New York and US society provided by these writers. The examination of early twentieth-century Spanish New York narratives will therefore shed new light on the literature published in this period, as well as on the clash between tradition and modernization taking place in Spain at the time.

Notes to the Introduction

1. For more examples, see William T. Spoerri's *The Old World and the New: A Synopsis of Current European Views on American Civilization* (1937, first published in 1936), Olga Peters Hasty and Susanne Fusso's *America through Russian Eyes, 1874–1926* (1988) and the series 'Foreign Travellers in America (1810–1935)' published by Arno Press (New York) in the 1970s.
2. Throughout this book I will place terms such as 'masses' and 'race' in inverted commas, to highlight their nature as social constructs.
3. The use of the term 'modernism' in this book will refer to the so-called international modernism and not to the Hispanic literary movement known as *modernismo*.
4. Here I refer to the first edition of the texts; the editions I will follow are *Pruebas de Nueva York* (1989), *El crisol de las razas* (1929), *Anticípolis* (2006), and *La ciudad automática* (1960).

CHAPTER 1

Spanish Narratives of Modernity: Going Beyond Exclusive Definitions of Early Twentieth-Century Spanish Literature

> Esos conceptos de 'generación' [...] y de 'genialidad individual' [...] han sido claves y determinantes a la hora de construir el canon de la literatura española. Pero, ¿dónde quedan autores y obras que iban a contracorriente o que, simplemente, no respondían fielmente a esos postulados?
>
> [These two concepts of 'generation' [...] and of 'individual genius' [...] have been crucial and decisive when constructing the canon of Spanish literature. But where does that leave authors and works who went against the tide or who simply did not respond faithfully to these positions?]
>
> BEATRIZ BARRANTES MARTÍN

In this chapter, I will contextualize my analysis of early twentieth-century Spanish New York narratives within the theoretical reassessment of the Spanish literature written in the period 1898–1936, which has been the focus of much critical work within Hispanic literary and cultural studies since the 1990s. Although this book is indebted to the new and innovative perspectives developed in recent decades, this study will argue for an even more inclusive view of modern Spanish narrative, by highlighting the similarities shared by texts traditionally characterized as 'high modernism' and those labelled as mass-produced and travel narratives, often neglected by literary studies due to their alleged lack of aesthetic qualities. To borrow Andreas Huyssen's term (1988 [1986]), the 'Great Divide' between high and low culture will be challenged in favour of a more permeable relationship between these texts, going beyond fixed and rigid literary categories. As it will be shown throughout this book, both 'high' and 'low' works share analogous views on the impact that modernization had on Spanish national identity at the time.

In order to offer a more complete understanding of the chosen case studies, this first chapter will also provide a brief biographical note on the authors (some of them probably unknown to the reader) as well as a short insight into previous critical approaches to these texts. Furthermore, to avoid repetition in subsequent chapters, I will give a synopsis of the novella *El crisol de las razas* and the novel *Anticípolis*, as well as a summary of the publishing history behind the travelogues *Pruebas de Nueva York* and *La ciudad automática*.

In the seminal volume *Spanish Cultural Studies: An Introduction: The Struggle for Modernity* (1995), scholars such as Helen Graham, Jo Labanyi, Sebastian Balfour, José Álvarez Junco, and Sue Frenk bring to the fore the contradictions posed by modernizing processes to the redefinition of Spanish national identity after the crisis triggered by the end of the Spanish Empire in 1898. The volume revolves around 'the role that culture has played in constructing – and resisting — modernity', and stresses 'the notion that culture is – as the Civil War would show so dramatically – a form of struggle' (Graham and Labanyi 1995b: vii). This path was also followed subsequently in the collection of essays edited by David T. Gies (1999), which contains similar studies by Gies, Inman Fox, Álvarez Junco, and Thomas Mermall. Furthermore, Balfour (1997) and Fox (1998) have also worked on the examination of Spanish national identity in the decades prior to the Civil War.

A number of studies have focused on the attitudes towards modernity and modernization in early twentieth-century Spanish narrative, going beyond the traditional dichotomy between the so-called Generation of 98 and Spanish *Modernismo*, as well as the division of the period into a series of different 'Generations' (1898, 1914, 1927). Scholars such as Helen Graham and Jo Labanyi (1995a), David T. Gies (1999), Anthony Geist and José B. Monleón (1999), Carlos Blanco Aguinaga (1999), Mary Lee Bretz (2001), Susan Larson and Eva Woods (2005), Elena Delgado, Jordana Mendelson and Óscar Vázquez (2007) and Christopher Soufas (2007, 2010) have challenged a monolithic notion of Spanish modernism as 'a collection of set texts' (Graham and Labanyi 1995b: vi–vii), thus arguing for the superseding of generational classifications which fostered 'the idea that contemporary Spanish literature remains fundamentally different from contemporary literature of the rest of Europe' (Soufas 2007: 22). Soufas points out that the tradition of dividing literature into generations 'has created a situation in Spanish literature in which the part defines the whole', and therefore, 'writers who do not fit the generational pigeonhole do not fare well' (2007: 48). In her comprehensive study of Spanish modernism, Bretz examines the role played by 'Francoist reappropiation and redefinition of early twentieth-century criticism' in works such as Pedro Laín Entralgo's *La generación del noventa y ocho* [*The Generation of 98*] (1993 [1945]) and Guillermo Díaz-Plaja's *Modernismo frente a noventa y ocho* [*Modernism versus 98*] (1979 [1951]) that established the opposition between the Generation of 98 as 'virile, energetic, socially and politically committed, governed by reason, in search of precise forms and categories, architectural, metaphysical, Castilian, classical, allied with Velázquez, ethical, and obsessed with time and temporality', and *Modernismo* as 'feminine, passive, governed by sensibility, individualistic, escapist, ivory tower, vegetable, sensual, allied with El Greco, amoral, a mixture of disparate elements, and concerned with instantaneity and the moment' (Bretz 2001: 67). As Bretz shows, traditional critical paradigms have been challenged more recently by Germán Gullón (1992) and Christopher Soufas (2010), who 'argue for the need to view Spanish literature of the period within the context of international modernism' (Bretz 2001: 21). Likewise, the volume edited by Anthony Geist and José B. Monleón (1999) aims precisely to show how Spanish modernism has been left out of the European modernist canon. In this vein, Carlos Blanco Aguinaga

(1999) proposes to include in this canon both works by writers from the Generation of 98/*Modernismo* such as Unamuno, as well as those Spanish writers ascribed to 'high modernism' (the Generation of 27). In the latter case, Lorca's *Poeta en Nueva York* would be the main exponent, since his poems represent 'not only the so-called alienation of modern urban life — one of the characteristics of modernism [...] but also the relationship of *that* to peripheral life' (Blanco Aguinaga 1999: 10). Larson and Woods also go against the distinction between Spanish and European modernism, arguing that 'the specificity of Spanish modernity does not mean that it lies outside of a larger European modernity (France, Germany, England), or that Spain arrives "late" to modernity, as is so often assumed' (2005: 5). Similarly, in his examination of Ramón Gómez de la Serna's narrative works, John McCulloch has argued for an understanding of novels such as *El novelista* [*The Novelist*] (1923) 'within the context of modernist fiction at large', therefore connecting Ramón 'with contemporary international literary figures such as Joyce or Woolf in the way traditional notions of literature are subjected to questioning' (2007: 90). Finally, Delgado, Mendelson, and Vázquez have highlighted the 'misperception of the participation of the country's artists and writers in the formation of cultural modernism' (2007: 108). In contrast with terminologies such as 'alternative' or 'peripheral' modernisms, they propose the adjective 'recalcitrant', which captures 'the conflictive relationship between modernity and Spain' (2007: 109). Importantly for this book, Delgado, Mendelson and Vázquez suggest that:

> a crucial archive that deserves further study is that of the little studied (though widely popular in its time) pulp fiction written in the first quarter of the twentieth century. It is in those texts where a different side of Spanish cultural modernity can be found: one in which we discover an unabashed exploration of sexuality and pleasure, in contrast to the stark denial of both found in the so-called *noventayochistas*. (2007: 113)

It seems that the authors above are referring mainly to early twentieth-century erotic novellas, since they allude to Pura Fernández's essay (2002) on *fin de siècle* Spanish literary eroticism. However, pulp fiction or mass-produced literature published in Spain in the first decades of the last century also presents a strong focus on other anxieties brought about by modernization in relation to mechanization and mass society, women's emancipation, and multiculturalism. As a matter of fact, two of the four texts chosen for this book (*Anticípolis* and *El crisol de las razas*) sit comfortably with the definition of mass-produced literary works. In contrast with the extensive attention given to the Generation of 98/*Modernismo*, the avant-garde novel and the Generation of 27, texts and authors that do not fall neatly into these categories have often been catalogued as 'raros y olvidados' [strange and forgotten] (Sainz de Robles 1971, 1975 and Alonso 2008). As Cecilio Alonso argues:

> escritores muy difundidos que habían alcanzado gran popularidad sobre todo en la narrativa breve y en el teatro, fueron ingresados sin más en la cofradía de la rareza y el olvido a partir de 1939. Y contra las previsiones de recuperación que cabía suponer antes de 1975, lo cierto es que muy pocos de aquellos raros han dejado de serlo y menos todavía el número de los que han salido del olvido por la vía editorial. (2008: 11)

[quite well-known writers who had achieved great popularity, above all in short narrative and theatre, were consigned without further ado to the fraternity of oddity and oblivion after 1939. And against forecasts of the recovery that were expected before 1975, what is certain is that very few of those oddballs have stopped being precisely that and even less the number of those who emerged from oblivion through the route of publishing.]

Alonso proposes to delineate an alternative canon, in order to fill the void caused by the destruction of the cultural network that culminated in the Second Spanish Republic (Alonso 2008: 11). In this vein, this book highlights the productivity of the study of literary genres such as the travel book and popular narratives for a more comprehensive understanding of Spanish literary modernity, and pits the notion of culture as a continuous process of negotiation against a fixed and static division into different 'groups' or 'generations'. The present study is inspired by the pioneering work of Beatriz Barrantes, who argues for a more inclusive view of Spanish narrative of the 1920s and 1930s, since:

> la interconexión durante estas dos décadas de diferentes manifestaciones artísticas, diferentes grupos generacionales y diferentes tendencias políticas terminó cristalizando en una compleja red cultural que queda totalmente desvirtuada si se estudia a la luz de binarismos pedagógicos. (2007: 104)

> [the interconnection during these two decades of different artistic manifestations, different generational groupings and different political tendencies ended up crystallising in a complex cultural network, which becomes completely distorted if it is studied in the light of pedagogical, binary oppositions.]

Furthermore, Barrantes emphasizes the multiplicity of literary genres coexisting in these two decades, 'desde el folletín romántico populista, hasta la más pura experimentación vanguardista minoritaria, pasando por el relato de viajes o la novela proletaria', which, in spite of their differences, 'todos pertenecen a un mismo contexto moderno y sus producciones culturales, "vanguardistas" o no, constituyen excelentes catalizadores de lo que era ya una realidad incuestionable, la modernidad' [from the populist Romantic feuilleton, to the purest minority avante-garde experimentation, including the travelogue or proletarian novel, all belong to the same modern context and its cultural productions, "avant-garde" or not, and constitute excellent catalysts of what was already an unquestionable reality: modernity] (Barrantes 2007: 104). The case studies brought together in this book certainly confirm Barrantes's criteria. A close look at those literary works that have been dismissed for their alleged lack of literary value demonstrates that they share similar concerns and attitudes towards modernizing processes with modernist narrative. In order to overcome previous reductive views, Barrantes proposes a new term, 'novela de la modernidad', which encompasses:

> tanto la tradicionalmente considerada 'novela de vanguardia', como toda una serie de manifestaciones que, a pesar de no ser consideradas 'vanguardistas' *sensu estrictu*, comparten buena parte de esa estética preocupada por los fenómenos urbanísticos, el recalentamiento político del país o los novedosos patrones de las relaciones interpersonales de esas dos décadas. (2007: 105)

> [the traditionally-regarded 'avant-garde novel', as well as an entire series of

elements which, in spite of not being considered 'avant-garde' *sensu stricto*, share a great deal of that aesthetic concerned with urban phenomena, growing national political tensions or innovative paradigms of interpersonal relationships during these two decades.]

Taking Barrantes's definition one step further, this book proposes an even more overarching concept, that of *narrativas de la modernidad* or 'narratives of modernity', which comprises narrative genres other than the novel, such as the travel book and the novella. It is not the aim of this book, however, to incorporate early twentieth-century New York Spanish narratives into an 'alternative canon' of forgotten works or to judge the aesthetic or artistic qualities of these texts. Popular narratives and personal testimonies of the modern metropolis provided in journalistic chronicles and travel narratives offer an enriching perspective on the reactions to modernizing processes in early twentieth-century Spanish literature, and the study of the narrative of this period would be incomplete without taking them into account.

New York in Spanish Mass-Produced Popular Narratives: *El crisol de las razas* and *Anticípolis*

In the main, criticism of early twentieth-century Spanish popular literary texts has focused on two types of narratives: women-authored texts and the novella published serially in collections such as *El Cuento Semanal* [*The Weekly Story*] (1907–1912), *Los Contemporáneos* [*The Contemporaries*] (1909–1926), *La Novela Corta* [*The Novella*] (1916–1925), *La Novela Semanal* [*The Weekly Novel*] (1921–1925), and *La Novela de Hoy* [*Today's Novel*] (1922–1932).[1] Significantly, these two paths often converge, since the publication of women's writing was usually limited to mass-produced popular literature (Johnson 2003a: 24), confirming the modernist identification between 'low' culture and women which Andreas Huyssen identified in his influential study *After the Great Divide* (1988: 47). While the presence of women in the avant-garde was extremely small — and restricted to a secondary role –, 'the marked increase in popular newspapers and magazines and, above all, commercial publishers, resulting in numerous series of novellas or short stories produced cheaply for mass consumption, provided great opportunities for women writers' (Davies 1998: 109). The alleged lack of literary experimentation in these texts has been the main reason traditionally argued to exclude female writers from studies of Spanish modernist literature (Johnson 2003b: 160). However, the 'Great Divide' between male/elitist and female/mass-produced literature must be clarified. Far from being mere cheap and light entertainment, these genres tapped into the same cultural debates raised by those texts traditionally defined as 'high literature', voicing concerns about modernization, and sometimes resorting to subversive discourses which challenged traditional conceptions of national, class, and gender identity. As Alberto Sánchez Álvarez-Insúa points out, the novellas published in the first decades of the twentieth century in collections such as *El Cuento Semanal* (1907–1912):

> convierten la literatura y aledaños en palestra política, replantean costumbres y formas de vida, introducen nuevos modelos morales y de comportamiento, inciden directamente sobre aspectos tan importantes como la sexualidad

y consiguen por fin que la lectura se convierta en la forma más barata y fundamental de ocio y cultura. (2007: 91)

[they turn literature and its limits into political arena, rethink customs and ways of life, introduce new models of morality and behaviour, impact directly upon aspects as important as sexuality, and ultimately succeed in turning reading into the cheapest and most fundamental form of leisure and culture.]

Two of the case studies that will be analysed in this book can be classified as examples of mass-produced popular narratives. First of all, Teresa de Escoriaza's novella *El crisol de las razas* (1929), published within the collection *Los novelistas* (Prensa Moderna). Escoriaza (San Sebastián, 1891–San Sebastián, 1968) was a representative of the 'New Woman' who, together with other contemporary Spanish women writers:

utilizan la narración para proyectar las inquietudes sociales de todo tipo que les preocupan. Son las primeras periodistas y corresponsales de guerra como Carmen de Burgos y Sofía Casanova; críticas literarias como Blanca de los Ríos y Pardo Bazán, conferenciantes, ensayistas, traductoras y, sobre todo, divulgadoras de unas ideas e inquietudes que tenían como uno de los ejes principales la incorporación de la mujer a la vida pública española. (Muñoz Olivares 2000: 96)

[employ narrative to project all kinds of social preoccupations with which they are concerned. They are the first journalists and war correspondents, like Carmen de Burgos and Sofía Casanova; literary critics like Blanca de los Ríos and Pardo Bazán; conference speakers, essayists, translators and, above all, promoters of ideas and concerns which they held as one of the principal bases of the incorporation of woman into Spanish public life.]

She obtained a university degree and worked as a journalist and a lecturer in Spanish in the United States (Palenque 2006: 364). Interestingly for the present study, Escoriaza collaborated on the newspaper *La Libertad* founded in 1919 and directed by Luis de Oteyza. From 1919 to 1921, she published (under the male pseudonym Félix de Haro) a section entitled 'Desde Nueva York' [From New York], where she gave her opinions about this city. These articles can be considered the prelude for her novella, since some of the main themes of *El crisol de las razas* (women's emancipation and the connection between capitalism and Judaism) are already outlined in her journalistic contributions from the United States. In 1921, she was sent by *La Libertad* to Morocco as a war correspondent, and her chronicles were subsequently gathered in the volume *Del dolor de la guerra (crónicas de la campaña de Marruecos)* [*On the Pain of War (Chronicles of the Campaign in Morocco*] (1921). Escoriaza's journalistic activities were not limited to the printed press. She also participated in the first radio broadcasts in Spain, in which she gave the so-called 'Primera Conferencia Feminista' [First Feminist Lecture] in this medium (Escoriaza 1924).

The most complete approach to her life and work to date is Marta Palenque's article 'Ni ofelias ni amazonas, sino seres completos: aproximación a Teresa de Escoriaza' [Neither Ophelias nor Amazons but incomplete beings: A study about Teresa de Escoriaza] (2006). Palenque provides an extensive biographical note in which she mentions Escoriaza's friendship with Luis de Oteyza and her contributions to *La Libertad*. Moreover, she includes the only reference, to the best of my knowledge, to Escoriaza's novella. Palenque points out that *El crisol de las razas* had never been included in the list of Spanish texts with a focus on New York published at the time (2006: 372). By contrast, it seems that Escoriaza enjoyed certain popularity as a writer and journalist during her lifetime. Rafael Cansinos Assens, for instance, mentions her in his memoirs when alluding to the feminist Isabel Oyarzábal, of whom he says:

> pertenece a ese número de nobles mujeres, de ideología moderna, desligadas de la tradición clerical, libres, pero no libertinas, en que figuran Teresa de Escoriaza, Clara Campoamor y otras menos célebres, que continúan la línea de Carmen de Burgos y las llamadas damas rojas de principios de siglo. (1995: 271)

> [she belongs to that group of noble women which was modern in ideology, freed from clerical tradition, free but not libertines, and in which are present Teresa de Escoriaza, Clara Campoamor and other lesser figures who continue the line of Carmen de Burgos and the so-called red ladies from the beginning of the century.]

Escoriaza is here seen as the equal of well-known literary and political figures such as Carmen de Burgos and Clara Campoamor. The press also echoed Escoriaza's popularity. In *T.S.H. (Revista Semanal, Órgano de Radio Madrid)*, she is referred to as a 'distinguished writer' (Escoriaza 1924: 13). Similarly, a piece of news in the republican newspaper *El Radical* covering the celebration of the anniversary of the Republic in New York includes Escoriaza in the group of Spanish celebrities who attended the event, and alludes to her as a 'prominent writer' (Anonymous 1933: 1). In spite of such recognition, Escoriaza's fame and her contributions to Spanish feminism have been overlooked in reassessments of modern Spanish narrative. By contrast, her figure has been recently celebrated by the *Academia Española de la Radio* [Spanish Radio Academy], which has organized the *Premio de Radio Teresa de Escoriaza* [Teresa de Escoriaza Radio Award] in 2014 as part of UNESCO'S World Radio Day.[2]

Placing the emphasis on a race-oriented discourse, her novella *El crisol de las razas* depicts New York as a shambolic urban experiment in which the coexistence of different cultures and 'races' results in chaos. As Palenque argues, the text

> conecta con la visión amarga del futuro de la civilización que la misma ciudad representa a ojos de los que la visitan. Nueva York es aquí la gran urbe de los años 20, con casi seis millones de habitantes, a la que acuden personas de todos los continentes y razas en busca de una vida mejor; es la promesa de una civilización sin límites raciales o ideológicos, lo que a Escoriaza (una de esas personas) le parece imposible. (2006: 372–74)

> [links with the bitter version of the future of civilization which the same city represents in the eyes of those who visit it. New York is in this case the great city of the 1920s, with almost six million inhabitants, where people from all continents and races arrive in search of a better life; it is the promise of a civilization without racial or ideological limits, which seems impossible to Escoriaza (one of those people).]

The novella tells the story of Helen Waters, an Anglo-Saxon American woman married to a Russian-Jewish tycoon, Boris Zinovief. When Boris becomes interested in Sonia, a Russian singer, Helen decides to fight for her marriage and recover her husband. The narrative concludes with Helen being accidentally killed. The moral of the story is directed to show the alleged menace provoked by the coexistence of different 'races' in the same nation, and the novella presents the supposedly conflictive character of polyethnicity precisely through the failed marriage between Helen and Boris. Escoriaza's text repudiates the idea of a country with a multi-ethnic population, in contrast with the concept of nationhood promoted by European nationalisms at the time, often identified with 'racial' homogeneity. In tune with Western discourses of Otherness, the main threat posed by ethnic heterogeneity comes from the East, in the form of an archetypical 'Jew' described as greedy, lustful and uncivilized, who is in addition blamed for the tragic ending of the story. On the contrary, Helen represents an intrepid and independent American 'modern woman', who has nevertheless compromised her individual freedom by marrying a man from a different 'race' and a different class. Helen's character is in turn juxtaposed with a female counterpart, Sonia, who is doomed to remain subdued to patriarchy owing to her economic difficulties. Class, gender, and 'race' are therefore at the core of an ambivalent view of the United States that condemns miscegenation but can also be interpreted as a feminist plea for women's liberation from patriarchy.

The second case study that can be classified as an example of mass-produced popular narrative is *Anticípolis* (1931) by Luis de Oteyza. The novel was issued by 'Renacimiento', a publishing house which included in its catalogue both prestigious authors (such as Benito Pérez Galdós and Emilia Pardo Bazán) and writers of 'cheap' literature who were economically more profitable. Whereas established authors such as Unamuno complained about the lack of readers and commercial success of his works, writers such as Oteyza enjoyed a great deal of popularity with the Spanish readership (Martínez Martín 2001: 201). However, in spite of his successful career as a journalist, the popularity of his novels and even his political career as ambassador of the Republican government in Venezuela, the life and work of Luis de Oteyza (Zafra, 1883 — Caracas, 1961), has until recently been largely forgotten by Spanish literary studies. His name has been at most mentioned in passing, as Barrantes points out, in lists of 'Otros autores' [Other Authors] or under rather arbitrary classifications (2006: 80). The status of Oteyza as a 'forgotten writer' was in fact highlighted by Luis Antonio de Villena in 'Un moderno muy olvidado: Luis de Oteyza' [A Largely Forgotten Modern Writer: Luis de Oteyza], included in the volume *Oscura turba de los más raros escritores españoles* [*Obscure Throng of the Strangest Spanish Writers*] (1999). Villena refers to the writer's contribution to the struggle for modernity in 1920s and early 1930s Spain, and describes Oteyza as:

> el representante de un periodismo muy moderno en una España [...] en que ésta luchaba por ser moderna, y lo conseguía aparentemente más en sus escritores *menores* (Retama, Oteyza) que en los mayores (Unamuno, Pérez de Ayala), superficialmente más tradicionales, aunque claro es, de muchísimo más peso. (1999: 169)

[the representative of a very modern journalism in a Spain [...] where this country fought to be modern, and achieved this apparently more in its lesser writers (Retama, Oteyza) than in the greater ones (Unamuno, Pérez de Ayala), who were superficially more traditional, although clearly of much more greater bearing.]

Nevertheless, interest in Oteyza's work has increased in recent years, thanks to the re-edition of some of his journalistic and literary publications: *El Diablo Blanco* [*The White Devil*] (1993, 2006), *Abd-El-Krim y los prisioneros* [*Abd-El-Krim and the Prisioners*] (2000), *Obras selectas* [*Selected Works*] (2000), *De España al Japón* [*From Spain to Japan*] (2012), and *En el remoto Cipango* [*In the Faraway Cipango*] (2013). Of particular importance for the present book is the re-edition of *Anticípolis* by Barrantes (2006), who later published a study of the novel (2008).

In her introductory study to *Anticípolis*, Barrantes points out that Oteyza's works feature key elements of a literature envisaged for mass consumption, such as adventure, love stories, action, and exotic locations (2006: 42). His most popular novel, *El Diablo Blanco* (1928) ran to five editions in Spanish and was translated into fourteen languages. Thanks to its international success, the book was almost made into a Hollywood film, in which the main character was to have been played by Lionel Barrymore, but in the end the project did not go ahead (Barrantes 2006: 22–23). *Anticípolis* was re-issued in 1933, this time by a different publisher, Fénix (Barrantes 2006: 79). The fact that the book was reviewed in the United States in the journal *Hispania* (Millard 1932: 307–08) gives the measure of the attention it elicited internationally.

Barrantes argues that *Anticípolis* engages with the most topical issues of its time, namely the clash between progress and traditionalism, the consequences of modernization, feminism, and issues of multiculturalism and immigration (2006: 72). She situates the text within European and Spanish responses to modernity and modernization, by relating it to the work of European modernist authors such as Baudelaire and Dickens, and to Spanish avant-garde texts written in the 1920s, in which the city often becomes the object of criticism towards the effects of modernity in the individual (2006: 46–47). Similarly to European and Spanish modernist texts, Barrantes argues, *Anticípolis* presents a contradictory image of the metropolis. New York embodies the future of civilization, both in a positive and in a negative sense. On the one hand, the presence of the 'masses' and the frantic rhythm of modern life reflects the widespread view of mass society as inevitably alienating and dehumanizing (Barrantes 2006: 63). On the other hand, it also praises progress, especially regarding women's emancipation (Barrantes 2006: 73).

The novel tells the story of a Spanish family that moves from Oviedo to New York in order to fulfil the unrealistic aspirations of the head of the family, Don Antonio, who dreams of becoming a successful inventor. However, Antonio plays a small role in the text, since the novel starts with his funeral and we only know about his life from a series of flashbacks. After his death, Doña Jesusa, his wife, who detests New York and its modernity, decides to take her children back to Oviedo. However, they do not agree with this decision and start a revolt against their mother, since they consider themselves to be New Yorkers and do not want to leave the city and return to a country that they see as backward. Rosa, the elder daughter, is the head of this rebellion and assumes the leading role in the family, even over her brothers. From that moment on, the story revolves around a dialectical battle between the mother and the daughter. New York as 'the city of anticipation' is a concept voiced by a key character in the novel, Dr Jiménez, who describes New York as an avant-garde city, an image of the future awaiting the rest of the world. The opposition between Jesusa — the representation of the traditional woman — and Rosa — the embodiment of the modern woman — reflects the contrast between Spain's stagnation and New York's modernization. Barrantes concludes that:

> Oteyza consigue en *Anticípolis* presentar las dos caras de la modernidad a través de la construcción de personajes metafóricos; parece que lo que el escritor finalmente intentaba explicar era que [...] la modernidad también contenía sus propias contradicciones, pero que, a pesar de ello, el progreso, aun con todos sus efectos negativos, era la única manera de seguir adelante. (Barrantes 2006: 73)
>
> [in *Anticípolis*, Oteyza succeeds in presenting the two faces of modernity through the construction of metaphorical characters; it seems that what this writer ultimately sought to explain was that [...] modernity also contained its own contradictions, but that in spite of this, progress, even with all its negative effects, was the only way of moving forward.]

Barrantes's study will constitute the starting point for my analysis of *Anticípolis*. However, the opposition between traditionalism and modernization inherent in the dichotomy traditional/modern woman must be considered at a deeper level, in relation to the crisis of modernization and of national identity undergone by Spain in the first decades of the twentieth century. As this book will show, the conflict between traditionalism and modernization embodied by the symbolic characters of the novel is embedded in the often contradictory responses to modernity offered by early twentieth-century Spanish writers.

New York in Spanish Travel Literature: *Pruebas de Nueva York* and *La ciudad automática*

In his study of travel writing, Carl Thompson argues that although the genre 'has seen its literary status rise in recent decades' it was 'for much of the twentieth century at least [...] dismissed by literary critics and cultural commentators as a minor, somewhat middle-brow form' (2011: 2). Such indifference did not take into account either its longevity or its influence in the development of other narrative genres, as Percy G. Adams showed in *Travel Literature and the Evolution of the Novel* (1983). Thompson also points out the influence of modernity in the blooming of the genre during the 1920s and 1930s, when 'new technologies contributed significantly to a dramatic increase in what one might label global interconnectedness' (2011: 57). The development and consolidation of new means of transport such as the automobile and the aeroplane had a direct effect on the literary production of the period. Robert Wohl for example has suggested that 'the intellectuals of the war generation [labelled in his study as the Generation of 1914] were fascinated by the image of the traveler' to the extent that 'they viewed themselves as wanderers and vagabonds who traveled without itineraries' (1979: 226). As a consequence of such fascination, and thanks to the possibilities opened by technology, 'some of the most popular literary works of the period were written in the form of a travel reportage, and many authors from the war generation capitalized on the interest in foreign settings to get their careers underway' (Wohl 1979: 227). As was the case in other European countries, Spanish authors cultivated this genre extensively, in which New York became a fashionable literary destination. In some cases, as in José Moreno Villa's *Pruebas de Nueva York* and Julio Camba's *La ciudad automática*, travelogues typically consisted of a series of newspaper articles previously published during the writer's stay in the city.

In comparison with the other writers whose texts have been chosen as case studies for this book, it would be imprecise to locate José Moreno Villa (Málaga 1887 — Ciudad de México 1955) within a list of 'strange' or 'forgotten' authors. For twenty years (1917–1937) the author worked as a member of staff in the *Residencia de Estudiantes*, the famous centre founded in Madrid by the *Institución Libre de Enseñanza* in 1910, and breeding ground for the poets of the Generation of 1927. Despite his contact with the writers of the so-called 'Silver Age' of Spanish letters, his ascription to a literary movement has been often problematic. Guillermo Carnero argues that Moreno Villa had the 'bad luck' to start his literary career in the middle of two well-defined generations (1989: 13). Similarly, Francisco Javier Díez de Revenga defines the author as an 'unclassifiable writer' located between Hispanic modernism and the avant-garde (2001: 129). It is worth noting that literary studies of Moreno Villa's literary production tend to emphasize the avant-garde character of his poetry, and often highlight his relationship to the Generation of 1927.[3] It seems that the study of Moreno Villa's work needs to be justified by the question of literary value which in a sense confirms the elitism of avant-garde experimentalism and its insertion in the canon. Consequently, the vast majority of critical attention given to Moreno Villa's work has been devoted to his poetic production.[4] In contrast, although Moreno Villa's prose has recently been collected in a series of volumes,[5] it has not been the object of much critical scrutiny. One of these few studies is Eduardo Jiménez Urdiales's analysis of Moreno Villa's narrative fiction, consisting of two volumes: *Evoluciones, cuentos, caprichos, bestiario, epitafios y obras paralelas* [*Evolutions, Tales, Capriccios, Bestiary, Epitaphs and Parallel Works*] (1918) and *Patrañas* [*Tall Tales*] (1921). Jiménez Urdiales argues that the author

> acoge y asume todo el saber recibido de las generaciones precedentes, en contra de la actitud, impuesta por la mayoría de las tendencias del vanguardismo artístico y literario europeo, de rechazar la tradición cultural para crear una poética moderna basada en la experiencia propia dentro del nuevo espacio urbano creado a raíz de los progresos industriales y técnicos de principios de siglo. (1998: 18)

> [embraces and assumes all the knowledge received from previous generations, in opposition to the attitude, imposed by most of the European literary and artistic avant-garde trends, of rejecting the cultural tradition in order to create a modern poetics based on their own personal experience in the new urban space created as a result of the industrial and technical progress at the beginning of the century]

This lack of experimentation is possibly the main reason for the scant critical interest his fiction has received, as opposed to the attention given to the documentary value of his memoirs, *Vida en claro* [*Clear Life*] (2006 [1944]).[6] In contrast with the alleged lack of interest in modernity shown by Moreno Villa in previous narrative texts, *Pruebas de Nueva York* revolves around themes such as the modern city, industrialization and mechanization, capitalism, women's emancipation, and multiculturalism. The text was inspired by his stay in New York in 1927. He travelled to the United States in order to meet the family of his American girlfriend, Florence — whom he had met in the *Residencia de Estudiantes*– and to obtain her father's permission to marry her. The experience resulted in failure, since Moreno Villa was rejected by Florence's parents and returned to Madrid, 'recién soltero' as he put it, alluding in a parodic way to Juan Ramón Jimenez's *Diario de un poeta reciencasado* (Ballesteros and Neira 2000: 27). During the time he spent in New York, Moreno Villa wrote a series of articles for the journal *El Sol*, published between 19 May and 24 July 1927, and subsequently gathered in the volume entitled *Pruebas de Nueva York*, which has mostly been regarded as a secondary text of mere documentary interest that complements the love story depicted in the collection of poems *Jacinta la pelirroja* (1929).[7] This widespread view has been promoted in studies such as those by Ballesteros and Neira, who define the travelogue as a mere sentimental chronicle of his love story (2000: 27). Díaz de Castro also argues that references to cosmopolitism, polyethnicity, the 'masses', the American woman, and jazz music help to understand the author's relationship with 'Jacinta' (1989: 35). In such a reading, Moreno Villa's representation of New York is understood as a reaction to the setbacks he suffered in his emotional life. Ballesteros and Neira propose that the writer's portrait of the city as an incarnation of capitalism — which the author relates to the influence of Judaism — is caused by 'the conflict' with his fiancé's Jewish family (2000: 26). In a similar way, they see Moreno Villa's description of the American modern woman as an expression of disappointment in love (Ballesteros and Neira 2000: 26).

In contrast, I propose that the image of New York developed in *Pruebas de Nueva York* is not a mere reflection of Moreno Villa's failed relationship with Florence or simply of his personal circumstances. As a detailed analysis of his travelogue will show, Moreno Villa's view of New York and US society provides an excellent insight into the contradictions brought about by modernization in both Spain and Europe.

Apart from two novellas, *El destierro* [*Exile*] (*El Cuento Semanal*, 1907) and *El matrimonio de Restrepo* [*The Restrepo Marriage*] (*La Novela de Hoy*, 1924), both re-issued by Ediciones del Viento in 2007, Julio Camba's literary career developed mainly in the context of journalism. He wrote for several newspapers (including *ABC* and *El Sol*) and some of his articles were subsequently published as books. Camba was especially renowned for his chronicles from foreign countries, such as *Londres* (1973 [1916]), *Alemania, impresiones de un español* [*Germany, Impressions of a Spaniard*] (1968 [1916]), *Un año en el otro mundo* [*A Year in the Other World*] (2009 [1917]), *Aventuras de una peseta* [*Adventures of a Peseta*] (2007 [1923]) and *La ciudad automática* (1960 [1932]). The success of Camba's articles, as demonstrated by the constant republication of his books, especially by Espasa Calpe, led to his inclusion in some general studies of Spanish literature such as those by Nicolás González (1943: 127), Ángel Valbuena (1950: 527–28), Emiliano Díaz Echarri and José María Roca (1962: 1390–92), and Juan Chabás (2001: 254–55). Mentions of Camba's work, however, have focused on its journalistic and humorous character, and therefore his output has been relegated to categories such as 'escritores humorísticos' [humorous writers] (González Echarri, Valbuena) and 'ensayo y periodismo' [essay and journalism] (Chabás, Bazo and Varcálcel).

Since the 1980s, critical interest in Camba has increased, both from a biographical approach and in studies of his journalistic prose.[8] Critical work on this writer has also engaged with the strict distinction between traditional literary genres and subsidiary ones (i.e. journalism and travel writing). General studies on this matter such as those by José Ortega (1995), Félix Rebollo (1998), and Lluis Albert Chillón (1999) have questioned the downgrading of journalism to a secondary place within literary studies and shown its connections with narrative genres such as the novel. In his study, Ortega includes Camba in a list of canonical writers such as Unamuno, Azorín, and Ortega y Gasset, who actively published in the press. Similarly, Jordi Gracia and Domingo Ródenas have incorporated Camba in their anthology of Spanish essays (2008: 227–33). Efforts to establish the importance of Camba's work have also followed the path of the paradigm of movements and generational divisions, as in the work of Socorro Girón (1984), who defines Camba as 'escritor novecentista' [from the Generation of 1914] (1984: 13). Moreover, public vindications of Camba's figure by writers and journalists such as Juan Bonilla, Antonio Muñoz Molina, and Manuel Rivas — the latter was awarded in 2002 the 23rd Premio Julio Camba [Julio Camba Journalism Award] — as well as the institutional support given by the Xunta de Galicia and Galician universities to research on his life and work seem to have been directed at restoring his reputation. Fermín Galindo, in fact, refers to the 'hostility' towards Camba shown by 'some sectors of Galician society' (2004: 237). Significantly, Galindo does not refer to the reasons for such antagonism, which I infer was prompted by the writer's sympathies for the Fascist uprising against the Republican government in 1936, as well as Camba's criticism of Galician nationalism and disdain for the Galician language. As a matter of fact, Camba's affinity with Franco's regime has often either been toned down (López García 2003: 160–66) or completely erased (Girón 1984: 33).

More recently, in 2012, the *Instituto Cervantes* in New York commemorated the 50th anniversary of Camba's death with a round table entitled '50 años de la muerte de Julio Camba. Un gallego en Nueva York' [50 years since Julio Camba's Death. A Galician in New York]. The press echoed this anniversary with the publication of two articles: 'Julio Camba, el primer distópico' [Julio Camba, the First Dystopian Writer] by Henrique Mariño (*Público*, 23 February 2012) and 'La mirada aguda de Julio Camba resucita medio siglo después' [Julio Camba's Sharp Look Resurrects after Half a Century] by Luís Pousa (*La Voz de Galicia*, 27 February 2012).[9] In these articles, *La ciudad automática* is praised as a work that deserves an important place in universal literature (Mariño), owing to its view of modern society as a dystopian world that precedes similar reactions by authors such as Aldous Huxley, George Orwell, and Ray Bradbury. Camba is also described as one of the best talents of twentieth-century Spanish literature (Pousa). In particular, Mariño's article provides a highly favourable review of the text, in which, however, the controversial depiction of gender and 'racial' issues carried out by the writer are not mentioned. Such oversight is not new; on the contrary, it represents a constant in most academic and journalistic approaches to Camba's legacy. Camba's often ferocious criticism of foreign cultures and his controversial stance in relation to themes such as multiculturalism and women's emancipation has been, at most, alleviated by considering it as an expression of his humorous style (López 2003: 14; Galindo 2002: 44; Girón 1984: 218). Nevertheless, as María Dolores Costa (1996) has shown, a critical analysis of Camba's work should not be reduced to the acknowledgement of the writer's ability to play with words and to satirize other cultures. In her study of Camba's travel writing, which contains several references to *La ciudad automática*, Costa dismantles the view of the writer as mere humorist (1996: 154–65). She points out his recurrent use of stereotypes (1996: 156–57), and his negative reaction against women's emancipation (1996: 161). As she notes, 'Camba's criticism ultimately serves no didactic function. He does not intend to civilize the "barbarians", simply degrade them' (1996: 162). Humour is frequently a defence mechanism, and beneath Camba's wit we often find the anxiety raised by social changes prompted by modernization.

Julio Camba's view of New York revolves around the mechanical nature of the city, as the title of his travelogue indicates. *La ciudad automática* is a compilation of Camba's New York chronicles written between 1931 and 1932 for *ABC*. This was not his first visit to the United States, since in 1916 he had already been sent there by the same newspaper. His articles about US society were subsequently gathered in the volume *Un año en el otro mundo* (1917), in which he provides a general impression of the United States. In *La ciudad automática* he focuses on New York, although he refers to the city as representative of American society. Camba depicts New York as a futuristic metropolis eliciting a series of contradictory reactions, both positive and guarded; as he states: 'nos atrae porque uno no puede vivir al margen del tiempo, y nos rechaza por la estupidez enorme del tiempo en que le ha tocado vivir a uno' [it attracts us because one cannot live outside of time, and we reject it because of the enormous stupidity of the time in which it has befallen one to live.] (1960: 11). This attitude, combined with his focus on themes included under titles such as 'Rascacielos' [Skyscrapers], 'Judíos' [Jews], 'Negros y blancos' [Blacks and Whites], 'La "American Girl"' [The "American Girl"], 'La serie' [Mass Production], and 'La mecanización' [Mechanization], directly connects the book to similar New York narratives produced in Spain at the time. Moreover, the reception of the travelogue confirms the interest raised by New York in Spain; as López García points out, the book captured the attention of the writers of the Generation of 27, and Salvador Dalí was fascinated by the view of the United States offered by Camba (2003: 155).

The representation of New York given in Camba's travelogue is constructed upon a sarcastic approach to modernization, in which sardonic remarks about women's access to the private sphere reveal male anxieties towards the challenge to patriarchal social structures represented by the 'modern woman'. Furthermore, multiculturalism is rendered as problematic, and is based on stereotypical descriptions of Jews and blacks in particular, stemming from Western discourses of 'Otherness'. The text conveys the idea that the progress prompted by modernization does not imply the superiority of the 'New World' over the 'Old Continent'. As will be shown in the next chapter, which analyses the view of US mechanization and mass society in the texts by Moreno Villa, Oteyza, and Camba, *La ciudad automática* strongly rejects the modernization embodied by New York.

Notes to Chapter 1

1. The early twentieth-century Spanish novella has been studied by Federico Carlos Sainz de Robles (1971, 1975), Luis Fernández Cifuentes (1982), Brigitte Magnien (1986), Alberto Sánchez Álvarez-Insúa (1996), Jesús A. Martínez-Martín (2001), Manuel Martínez Arnaldos (2007), and Cecilio Alonso (2008), amongst others.
2. More information about the award can be found on the World Radio Day website: <http://www.diamundialdelaradio.es/escoriaza.html> (Accessed 14 March 2014).
3. Such is the approach taken by José Luis Cano (1970: 49–53), Guillermo Carnero (1977: 368–69, 1989: 15), Luis Izquierdo (1978: 3, 1989: 70), Carmen de Mora (1978: 156), Álvaro Salvador (1978: 353), Margarita Smerdou (1988: 66), Francisco Javier Díez de Castro (1989: 32), Eugenio Carmona (1985: 9), and Humberto Huergo Cardoso (1996: 490).
4. Apart from the essays already mentioned, this is the focus of José Francisco Cirre (1963), María Antonia López Frías (1990), Rosa Romojaro (1991), Ada Salas Moreno (1992), James Valender (1999), and Andrés Romero Jodar (2009).
5. See Moreno Villa (2001), (2010), and (2011).
6. Moreno Villa's autobiography has been studied by José Luis Cano (1976), José María Bermejo (1978), Pura Serrano Acosta and José A. Fortes (1989), Manuel Alberca Serrano (1989), and María José Romero Chamorro (1988).
7. *Jacinta la pelirroja* has been studied by José Servera Baño (1978), Álvaro Salvador (1978), José Ángel Cilleruelo (1988), José de la Calle (1990), Salvador Jiménez Fajardo (1996), Humberto Huergo Cardoso (1996), Rafael Ballesteros and Julio Neira (2000), Rosa Romojaro (1991), and Khemais Jouini (2007).
8. See Benito Leiro (1986), Diego Bernal (1997), Pedro López García (2003), Mariano Gómez-Santos (2003), Juan A. Hernández Les (2006), Jordi Gracia and Domingo Ródenas (2008), Socorro Girón (1984), María Dolores Costa (1996), Almudena Revilla (2002), José Antonio Llera (2002; 2003; 2004), Fermín Galindo (2002), Ofelia Requejo (2003), Ana Rodríguez Fischer (2004), and Rafael Alarcón (2005).
9. The *Instituto Cervantes* in New York announced this event on its website: <http://nyork.cervantes.es/FichasCultura/Ficha80285_27_1.htm> (Accessed 14 March 2014). The articles by Mariño and Pousa can be also consulted online: <http://blogs.publico.es/henrique-marino/2012/02/23/julio-camba-visionario-sociedad-distopica-orwell-huxley-bradbury/>; <http://www.lavozdegalicia.es/noticia/ocioycultura/2012/02/27/mirada-aguda-julio-camba-resucita-medio-siglo-despues-reconocido/0003_201202G27P27992.htm> (Accessed 14 March 2014).

CHAPTER 2

❖

The Hidalgo against the 'Masses': The Challenge to the Classist Nation

> Es una civilización de masas y no de individuos. Es una civilización de grandes estructuras arquitectónicas. Es una civilización de insectos
>
> [It is a civilization of masses and not of individuals. It is a civilization of great architectural structures. It is a civilization of insects]
>
> JULIO CAMBA

In tune with similar images of the United States developed in Europe during the first decades of the twentieth century, the New York narratives by Moreno Villa, Oteyza, and Camba draw strongly on a vehement criticism of mass society and mechanization, presented in these texts as a sign of social regression. Contradictorily, the United States are characterized as a primitive society, where the 'masses' are threatening the moral and cultural authority of the intellectual elites, and Americans are described as a mass of dehumanized individuals, standardized by capitalism, the machine, and mass production. Such fear of regression towards primitivism reflected the widespread belief in the imminent demise of Western civilization. Simultaneously, the power acquired by this menacing internal 'Other' in the United States is contrasted with Spain's elitist social structures, where intellectuals such as José Ortega y Gasset defended the pre-eminence of a leading minority in the task of regenerating the nation.

This chapter will begin with an overview of the reactions in European literature to US mechanization and mass society and their similarities with the Spanish New York narratives published at the time. Next, it will move on to the examination of *Pruebas de Nueva York*, *Anticípolis*, and *La ciudad automática*, focusing especially on the connections between the rise of this threatening 'Other' and the crisis of Spanish national identity. Teresa de Escoriaza's *El crisol de las razas* will not be considered here. Although Escoriaza's novella includes references to technology — in particular, to means of transport such as the automobile and the subway — this text gives greater emphasis to issues of gender and 'race', which I will analyse in Chapters 3 and 4 respectively.

European Reactions to US Mechanization: the Threat of Technology and Mass Society

In the early decades of the twentieth century, Europeans developed a contradictory opinion of the United States as a primitive society in which the influence of technology and mechanization — metaphorically represented by the slaughterhouses in Chicago and the car factories in Detroit — would lead to the disappearance of individuality amid the engulfing, standardized mass. Such negative perceptions echoed European concerns about the decline of Western civilization. The consequences of the First World War had turned the belief in constant progress into distrust of civilization and its technological achievements, encapsulated in Spengler's pessimistic view of 'the decline of that West-European Culture which is now spread over the entire globe' (1926: 50). Similarly, in *The Salvaging of Civilization* (1921), H. G. Wells pondered the effects of the Great War and contemporary concerns about the future of the West (1921: 1–12). This image of decay is one of the key themes addressed by European modernist writers, who gave literary form to the pessimism and disappointment felt towards a civilization that was seen to have brought about the possibility of its own annulment (Punter: 2007: 36).

The sense of decadence was also generated by the unprecedented growth of population produced by industrialism and the rise of the so-called 'masses'. As J. W. Burrow has pointed out, great European cities such as London, Paris, and Berlin became 'the dominant social image of the period: its excitement, its horrors, its threat to social order and decency, its physical and moral squalor and unhealthiness, its dwarfing impersonality' (2000: xi). Since the late nineteenth century, the 'masses' had been seen in Europe as an internal and degenerate 'Other', which threatened the health of Western 'races' (Pick 1989: 21). *Dégénérescence* was in fact a concept originating in nineteenth-century European psychiatry which enjoyed great currency in a vast number of scientific publications on social evolution, degeneration, and perversion. Such concerns were to a great extent motivated by theories of evolution argued by Charles Darwin in *On the Origin of Species* (1859). The interpretation of Darwin's ideas of 'natural selection' as the famous axiom of the 'survival of the fittest' coined by Herbert Spencer, and their application to the physical and psychic deterioration of the 'lower classes', served as the scientific basis for the trope of Europe's degeneration. Darwinism challenged the idea of species as permanent, and therefore the belief in the notion of a universal human nature. The application of evolutionary theories to society — Social Darwinism — introduced the 'struggle for survival' that characterized animal and plant kingdoms to human life. One of the consequences of such theories was the thought that, as well as being in a sense hardwired for evolution, human 'races' were also quite capable of regression (Hawkins 1997: 146). The terminological switch from the 'people' to the 'masses' for the largest portion of the population was accompanied by the development of 'Crowd Psychology'. According to studies such as Gustave Le Bon's *The Crowd* (1895), individuals experienced a regression to a pre-civilized state when part of the 'masses'. The only way to prevent the decadence of Western society, therefore, would be to entrust the control of the population to a rational elite, and to resort to pseudo-scientific disciplines such as Eugenics, pioneered by Darwin's son-in-law Francis Galton (Burrow 2000: 99). In the first decades of the twentieth century, and in tune with concerns about mass society and degeneration, European intellectuals such as T. S. Eliot, Paul Valéry, Oswald Spengler, Julien Benda, and F. R. Leavis (notably in his pamphlet 'Mass Civilization and Minority

Culture', published in 1930), also regarded cultural elitism as the guardian of the values acquired by progress and civilization (Fusi 1997: 110). Following such elitist assumptions, if the order was subverted and the 'masses' overcame the leading minority, Europe ran the risk of degenerating into a pre-civilized state, that is, back to primitivism.

In Spain, debates about the decadence of the country intensified after its defeat in the war against the United States in 1898. However, the pessimistic view of Spain as a nation suffering from a chronic illness developed by writers, intellectuals, and politicians was not only caused by the final demise of the empire, but also sprang from the arrival of modernizing processes in the country (Juliá 2004: 81).[1] The increasing industrialization of Spanish cities such as Bilbao, Madrid, and Barcelona was regarded with distrust by Pío Baroja and Azorín, for example. In *Camino de perfección (Pasión mística)* [*Path of Perfection (Mystic Passion)*] (1901), Baroja describes the industrial city, 'aquella gran capital con sus chimeneas' [that great capital with its chimneys], as 'el monstruo que había de tragar a los hermanos abandonados' [the monster which was to swallow the abandoned brothers] (1972: 13–14). Similarly, in *Diario de un enfermo* [*Diary of a Sick Man*] (1901), Azorín shows his discontent towards Madrid's industrial growth by stating that 'hay una barbarie más hórrida que la barbarie antigua: el industrialismo moderno, el afán de lucro, la explotación colectiva' [there is a barbarism more horrid than ancient barbarism: modern industrialism, the profit motive, collective exploitation'.] (1975: 383). Following the precepts of Social Darwinism, the working class was regarded as degenerate. Spain also felt the strength and the violence of the 'masses', especially in events such as the *Semana Trágica de Barcelona* [Barcelona's Tragic Week] in 1909, the general strike in 1917, the so-called 'Bolshevik triennium' (1918–20) in Andalusia, and the strikes organized by the CNT (*Confederación Nacional de Trabajadores*) [Worker's National Confederation] in Barcelona in 1919. Between 1918 and 1921, 'never had Spain seen so many strikes nor so much violence and terrorism' (Arranz and Cabrera 2000: 199). Despite regenerationist grumblings about the health of the country, few practical solutions were in fact provided, and the proposals to change the political system made by politicians such as Joaquín Costa did not have an effect on the government. Frustration led the intellectuals to blame the people for Spain's condition. Costa, in particular, turned to a desperate solution: if Spain were to avoid the calamity of social revolution, a leader had to emerge, an 'iron surgeon' who would operate on the sick body of the nation and restore its health. The 'iron surgeon' condenses the distrust of Spanish intellectuals in the 'masses'; as Santos Juliá argues, Costa did not put any hope in the 'weak' and 'degenerated' population but rather in the leadership of someone who could educate and 'nourish' the 'masses' (2004: 127).

Elitism and degeneration are also core ideas in Ortega y Gasset's analysis of Spain's decline, articulated in *La España invertebrada* [*Invertebrate Spain*] (1921), where the philosopher declares his intention to outline 'la gran enfermedad' [the great illness] suffered by the country (2007a: 32). Ortega ultimately relates Spain's decadence to 'racial' degeneration; he argues that 'la raíz de la descomposición nacional está, como es lógico, en el alma misma de nuestro pueblo' since 'los pueblos degeneran por defectos íntimos', and he concludes that 'si la raza o razas peninsulares hubiesen producido un gran número de personalidades eminentes, con genialidad contemplativa, o práctica, es posible que tal abundancia hubiera bastado a contrapesar la indocilidad de las masas' [the root of national decomposition lies, naturally, in the very soul of our people', since 'peoples degenerate because of intimate defects [...] if the peninsular race or races had produced a great number of eminent personalities, contemplative or practical in their genius, it is possible that such an abundance would have sufficed as a counterweight to the disobedience of the masses] (2007a: 136). Ortega's project of national regeneration combined Europeanization with elitism: he considered that Spain had drifted from European civilization, and therefore the solution for the so-called 'Spanish problem' was to return to it (Juliá 2004: 145). However, years later, he would show his discontent with the path taken by Western civilization. In *La rebelión de las masas* [*The Rebellion of the Masses*] (1929), he argued that 'muchas cosas parecían ya imposibles en el siglo XIX, firme en su fe progresista. Hoy, de parecernos todo posible, presentimos que es posible también lo peor: el retroceso, la barbarie, la decadencia' [many things seemed impossible in the nineteenth century, firm in its progressive faith. Today, with everything seemingly possible, we foresee that the worst is also possible: depression, barbarism, decadence] (2007b: 111). Such a pessimistic view of civilization was explained by the advent of mass society:

> desde que en el siglo VI empieza la historia europea, hasta el año 1800 — por tanto, en toda la longitud de doce siglos –, Europa no consigue llegar a otra cifra de población que la de 180 millones de habitantes. Pues bien, de 1800 a 1914 — por tanto, en poco más de un siglo — la población europea asciende de 180 a ¡460 millones! (2007b: 116)

> [from the sixth century when European history begins, until 1800 (therefore, throughout the duration of twelve centuries), Europe does not manage to attain a greater population rate than that of 180 million inhabitants. However, from 1800 to 1914 (therefore, in little over a century), the European population rises from 180 to 460 million!]

Echoing similar diagnosis voiced by other European intellectuals, the Spanish philosopher declared that the 'masses' had revolted against the leading elites, 'las minorías selectas' (2007b: 83), and therefore posed a threat to the values of European liberalism.

Ortega's analysis of the decline of the West sheds light on the connection between European and Spanish responses to US modernization, and on the relationship between the Spanish and European crisis. Some of the European literary representations of the United States written in this period drew on similar anxieties in order to convey the paradoxical view of the United States as a 'primitive' country dominated by mechanization, mass society, and cold capitalism. For example, the initial impression left by New York on H. G. Wells, as reflected in *The Future in America* (1906), reproduces contemporary European concerns about mass society:

> They arrive marching afoot by every street in endless procession; crammed trolley-cars disgorge them; the Subway poors them out... The individual counts for nothing [...]. Perhaps they hurry more, perhaps they seem more

eager. But the distinctive effect is the mass, the black torrent, rippled with unmeaning faces, the great, the unprecedented multitudinousness of the thing, the inhuman force of it all. (1906: 36–37)

In his travelogue *America the Menace: Scenes from the Life of the Future* (1930), Georges Duhamel argues that 'no nation has thrown itself into the excess of industrial civilization more deliberately than America' (1974: xiii). The French writer reacts strongly against new forms of mass culture, especially the cinema, which he declares to be

a pastime for slaves, an amusement for the illiterate, for poor creatures stupefied by work and anxiety. It is the skillfully poisoned nourishment of a multitude that the powers of Moloch have judged and condemned, and whose degradation they are finally accomplishing. (1974: 34)

By the same token, in Franz Kafka's first novel *The Man Who Disappeared (America)* (1927), New York's modernity encapsulates the two-fold view of 'Americanization' in the Old Continent as both 'Europe's future and as meaning the destruction of traditional culture by materialism and technology' (Robertson, in Kafka 2012: xiv). Although written in a humorous tone that contrasts with the darkness of his subsequent texts, Kafka's novel reflects contemporary concerns about the effects of technology on the individual, who is subjected to the need of efficiency dictated by capitalism and to the frantic rhythm of modern life. Interestingly, Kafka never visited the United States; as Anne Fuchs (2002: 27) points out, the view of this country given in his novel is highly influenced by contemporary travelogues, especially by Arthur Holitscher's *Amerika heute und morgen* (*America Today and Tomorrow*), which describes 'both the gigantic scale of American life and the exploitation of industrial workers' (Robertson, in Kafka 2012: xiii). Kafka's novel exemplifies the use of the symbol 'America', not to 'denote the American reality mimetically but rather to connote a specifically European version of America' (Fuchs 2002: 26). As Peter Wagner also argues, 'America' worked as 'a counter-image, developed by Europeans for their own social world' (2001: 115).

The threat posed by mechanization to the individual in the United States was also pointed out by writers who criticized the dehumanizing effects that mass production (Taylorism and Fordism) and capitalism had on the working class. In *V Amerike* (1906), Maxim Gorky described New York as 'The City of the Yellow Devil', an image that captures the view of the United States as a materialist society, dominated by 'the power of the Gold' — the Yellow Devil — in which individuals are enslaved by technology and trade:

entering the city is like getting into a stomach of stone and iron, a stomach that has swallowed several million people and is consuming and digesting them. The street is a slippery, greedy throat, in the depths of which float dark bits of the city's food — living people. Everywhere — overhead, underfoot, alongside, iron clangs, exulting in its victory. Awakened to life and animated by the power of Gold, it casts its web about man, strangles him, sucks its blood and brain, devours his muscles and nerves, and grows and grows, resting upon voiceless stone, and spreading the links of its chain ever more widely. (Gorky 2001: 10)

Gorky's description of this city is reminiscent of Baroja's view of the industrial city as 'el monstruo que había de tragar a los hermanos abandonados'; this similarity showcases the shared reactions to modernization voiced by coetaneous writers in different countries. Such reactions did not fade in the following decades, as one can note when comparing Gorky's diatribe against the superficial and materialist entertainment offered on Coney Island (here denominated the 'Realm of Boredom') to García Lorca's poem 'Paisaje de la multitud que vomita (Anochecer en Coney Island)' [Landscape of the Vomiting Crowds (Nightfall in Coney Island)] included in *Poeta en Nueva York*:

> People eating, drinking and smoking. But Man is not heard. The air is filled with the even hissing of the arc lights, ragged fragments of music [...]. All this merges in an irritating hum as of some invisible string, thick and taut, and when a human voice invades this incessant sound it seems like a frightened whisper. Everything glitters insolently, baring its dismal ugliness ... (Gorky 2001: 33–34)[2]

Gorky also devotes a section to 'The Mob', where he describes how mechanization and capitalism turn the working class into a grey 'mass' of hollow individuals, who are reduced to being 'tools' and whose life is dictated by work:

> They were taught to work but not to live, and so the day of rest is hard for them. Tools quite capable of creating machines, cathedrals, great ships and pretty little knickknacks of gold, they do not feel themselves capable of filling in the day by anything except their everyday mechanical work. (2001: 55)

In a similar vein, Louis-Ferdinand Céline's *Voyage au bout de la nuit* [*Journey to the End of the Night*] (1932) criticizes the poor conditions suffered by workers in the Ford factory, who are turned into machines and relentlessly devoured and killed by the mechanism of mass production:

> Everything trembled in the enormous building, and we ourselves, from our ears to the soles of our feet, were gathered into this trembling, which came from the windows, the floor, and all the clanking metal, tremors that shook the whole building from top to bottom. We ourselves became machines, our flesh trembled in the furious din, it gripped us around our heads and in our bowels and rose up to the eyes in quick continuous jolts. The further we went, the more of our companions we lost. In leaving them we gave them bright little smiles, as if all this were just lovely. It was no longer possible to speak to them or hear them. Each time three or four of them stopped at a machine. (2013: 185–86)

In his study of the novel, John Sturrock connects this crude depiction of Fordism to the author's stay in the United States as a League of Nations medical missionary, during which he visited the Ford factory in Detroit. Following this visit, Céline wrote a report in which, according to Sturrock, he 'exaggerates greatly Ford's indifference to the physical conditions of its prospective employees' with the intention of enabling the writer 'to reach a large and tendentious conclusion as to the nature of industrial society'. Céline claims, for example, that

> with the new degree of mechanisation which has been reached at Ford, human operatives on the assembly-line no longer need to be skilled or healthy. They are interchangeable in their functions and so unspecific in their work that the absence of particular individuals is of no account. (Sturrock 1990: 17–18)

Céline's exaggerated view of mass production condenses the distrust in modern society voiced by European modernist writers. Rather than a realistic view of the United States, their depiction of mechanization and their concerns about the loss of individuality work as a projection of the anxieties brought about by modernization in Europe.

Several of the Spanish New York narratives written between 1898 and 1936 show similar reactions to mechanization and mass society. For example, the view of New York given in *Dos años en América* (1911) connects Eduardo Zamacois's text with contemporary diatribes against the effects of capitalism and mechanization in the United States, which according to this travel book turn its population into a greedy and primitive crowd: 'El alma borrascosa de New-York guarda relación apretada con la psicología de sus habitantes; la ciudad de hierro y piedra sólo podía albergar una muchedumbre codiciosa, peleadora, con instintos y rapacidades de pirata y músculos de acero' [The stormy soul of New York retains a close relationship with its inhabitants' psychology; the city of iron and stone could only host a covetous and quarrelsome mob, with pirate-like instincts and rapacity, and steel muscles. Its will is essentially selfish; its individualism, ferocious.] (quoted by Navarro Domínguez 2004: 42). Similarly to Gorky's *V Amerike*, Zamacois refers to Coney Island as 'el símbolo más acabado de la deshumanización que percibe en la ciudad y en la civilización norteamericana' [the most complete symbol of dehumanization that can be perceived in the North American city and civilization] (Navarro Domínguez 2004: 42).

In *El peligro yanqui* (1921), Luis Araquistáin also describes Americans as an 'anonymous mass' (Araquistáin 1921: 16) subjected to the machine:

> la fluidez de la masa sólo puede lograrse a fuerza de máquinas. Todo está aquí mecanizado, sujeto al maquinismo. Es rara la relación humana directa. El hombre apenas puede comunicarse con el hombre sino por el intermedio de una máquina. (Araquistáin 1921: 20)
>
> [the fluidity of the mass can only be achieved by machines. Everything here is mechanized, and subject to machinism. Direct human interaction is rare. Man can hardly communicate with man except through the intermediary of a machine.]

Even in texts which provide a more positive opinion of the city, such as Joaquín Belda's travelogue *En el país del bluff: veinte días en Nueva York* (1926), in which he praises the cleanliness and comfort provided by technology (1926: 220), we find several negative remarks about mass society and mass production. Belda describes New York as a 'human beehive' (1926: 19), where even deceased people are treated as a product of mass consumption, and compares funeral homes to food factories (1926: 210). In a similar way, Eduardo Criado Requena's *La ciudad de los rascacielos* (1919) offers a balanced opinion of the United States, trying to leave behind European prejudices about this country, and suggesting that certain aspects of the US way of life could serve to improve Spanish society. Nevertheless, in his description of New York's hectic lifestyle, a certain criticism of mechanization can be perceived:

> Al llegar a la estación toma precipitadamente el billete [...] y lo echa en un depósito de cristal custodiado por un negro, que no hace otra cosa que dar a una palanca para que el billete caiga a una caja de madera. Todo es automático (hasta el negro). Cuando nuestro hombre llega a la estación, el tren eléctrico ha parado, pero por tan pocos segundos, que, por mucho que corre, llega a las puertas de hierro cuando el conductor las cierra estrepitosamente. Allí todo es matemático: si el encargado de cerrar las puertas ve que a uno le faltan dos pasos para entrar en el coche y la campana de salida ha tocado, cumplirá con su deber, aunque el otro se quede en tierra. Esto es en los elevados, que en los trenes subterráneos las puertas se cierran solas automáticamente. ¡Cuántas veces hemos visto a mujeres y hombres apiñados, cogidos entre las dos puertas, haciendo esfuerzos por entrar o salir! (2004: 132)
>
> [Upon arriving at the station, he hurriedly takes the ticket and puts it in a glass container watched over by a black man, who does nothing else but pull a lever so that the ticket falls into a wooden box. Everything is automatic (even the black man). When our man reaches the station, the electric train has stopped but just for a few seconds and, no matter how fast he goes, he reaches the iron doors when the driver closes them noisily. Everything is mathematical there: if the person in charge of closing the doors sees that someone is two steps away from boarding the carriage and the exit bell has rang, he will do his duty, even though the other person is left stranded. This is in the overhead railways, since in the underground trains doors close automatically. How many times have we seen crowded women and men, caught between the two doors, attempting to board or alight!]

In the travelogue ...*Pero ellos no tienen bananas* (1930) by Jacinto Miquelarena, the metropolis is also depicted as a 'working machine' where sentimentality is 'mechanically produced' through projections (an allusion to cinema) and the gramophone (1930: 158). New York's hospitals are also described by this writer as factories where maternity has been 'Taylorized' (1930: 136).

The reactions towards technology and mass society in Spanish travelogues and popular narratives reflect similar concerns expressed by avant-garde novelists at the time. In spite of being inspired by and reflecting the scientific, technological, and artistic developments of the time, Spanish modernist texts labelled as 'avant-garde' novels also gave expression to negative attitudes towards civilization. Ana Rodríguez Fischer argues that, although Spain did not participate in the First World War, the conflict had a 'spiritual' impact on the country (1999: 17). As in other European states, the aftermath of the war was experienced as 'una devastadora explosión de todo el caudal filosófico amasado durante la etapa anterior al que se unían las múltiples intervenciones mecánicas entonces gestadas y realizadas en el siglo XX — telegrafía sin hilos, navegación aérea, automovilismo...' [a devastating explosion of all the philosophical wealth built up during the period prior to that which united multiple, mechanical interventions at that time conceived and realized in the twentieth century: wireless telegraph, aerial navigation, motoring...] (Fischer 1999: 21). The ideological crisis brought about by the conflict and its influence on daily life had an enormous impact in Spain, leading to economic, political, social, and cultural readjustments. Of Ramón Gómez de la Serna's novel *Cinelandia* (1923), John McCulloch writes:

> despite Gómez de la Serna's fascination with modernity, in *Cinelandia* there is also an underlying sense of despair at the homogenisation of the human form, and the suggestion that human experience is ultimately vacuous. The historian Oswald Spengler wrote about 'The unanchored late man of the megapolis' who inhabited a world of growing commercialism, pervasive materialism, dissonance and fragmentation. The world depicted in *Cinelandia* is not distant from that decried by Spengler, capturing the loneliness of modern man who inhabits a burgeoning city, uprooted and alone. In this sense it is a novel very much of its time. (2007: 54)

Studies of Spanish avant-garde narratives such as those by Buckley and Crispin (1973) and Fuentes (1984) have distinguished between two avant-gardes. Avant-garde novels written in the early 1920s supposedly celebrate modernity and radiate an optimistic praise of technology, whereas later works display increasing concerns related to mechanization, capitalism, and urbanization (Barrantes 2007: 102–03). Contrary to previous positions, Barrantes argues for the existence of a hidden anxiety surrounding materialism, urban space, crowds, and technology in most of the texts ascribed to the avant-garde canon (2007: 103). Among the examples discussed by this critic, we find *Sentimental Dancing* (1925) by Valentín Andrés Álvarez, and *El profesor inútil* [*The Useless Professor*] (1926) by Benjamín Jarnés. Criticism of modernization in the avant-garde narrative became stronger in subsequent years in novels such as *Locura y muerte de nadie* [*Madness and Death of Nobody*] (1929) also by Jarnés, *Luna de copas* [*Glass Moon*] (1929) by Antonio Espina, and *Hermes en la vía pública* [*Hermes in the Street*] (1934) by Antonio de Obregón, in which the city is presented as a dehumanizing and alienating entity. These texts give expression to the tensions and contradictions brought about by the advent of a capitalist mass society dominated by the increasing mechanization of modern life and the presence of the urban crowds. These themes have an especially prominent presence in the New York narratives of Moreno Villa, Oteyza, and Camba.

'Cirujanos de Siempre-Mata y Nunca-Salva': Spain's Modernization Beyond *Regeneracionismo* in *Pruebas de Nueva York*

Pruebas de Nueva York opens with a drawing by Moreno Villa which can be seen as a symbol of the attitudes towards the city found in his travelogue (Moreno Villa 1989: 13). New York's skyline is drawn as an imprecise, almost ghostly silhouette, which creates an impression of distance. A factory, located at the front of the vague outline of the metropolis, dominates the scene. On the other side of a wide river — probably the East River — we find a close-up of a more precise portrayal of dying nature, where leafless and fragile trees look like skeletons but resist disappearing.[3] The picture is therefore dialectic in nature in that it exhibits two opposing realities. On the one hand, the factory is an image of modernization, the symbol of an emerging and powerful new civilization based on technological progress and industrialization. On the other, the dying trees seem to evoke the decadence of Spain, and also perhaps the rough Castilian landscape continuously revived as the essence of Spanish national identity in the literature of the first decades of the twentieth century. This symmetrical arrangement anticipates the sort of dichotomy that the reader will encounter in the text. The illustration as a whole can be said to stand for the opposition between 'Us' — Spain, Europe, the Old Continent — and 'Them'– New York, the United States, a new civilization.

Moreno Villa's account of New York places strong emphasis on the innovative architecture of the city, as opposed to the historical value of the Castilian ruins. Such an analytical approach to New York's urban landscape is not accidental. In the year of his visit to the city, Moreno Villa was appointed *secretario de redacción* [editorial co-ordinator] of the magazine *Arquitectura*, to which he also contributed a series of articles until 1933 (Huergo 2010: 19). He also wrote several essays about architecture for other publications, such as *La Gaceta Literaria* [*The Literary Gazette*] and the newspaper *El Sol* (Tomás Llavador 2010: 15).[4] José María Tomás Llavador has even argued that Moreno Villa was the first critic of modern architecture in Spain (2010: 12). Moreover, architecture was of great interest to the *Institución Libre de Enseñanza*, which not only invited some of the most prestigious architects of the time to the *Residencia de Estudiantes*, where Moreno Villa lived and worked, but also encouraged the study of Spanish popular architecture (Guerrero 1999: 14–16). Reflecting contemporary debates around national identity, architectural tendencies in 1920s Spain were represented by two opposing views. On the one hand, a cosmopolitan and innovative vocation willing to integrate modern European influences into the national 'artistic personality'; on the other, a defence of a 'natural' evolution of the Spanish style that aimed for a national *casticista* architecture, the so-called *estilo español* (Sambricio 2000: 22–23). Spanish advocates of modern architecture such as Leopoldo Torres Balbás, a former student in the department of archaeology in the *Centro de Estudios Históricos*, did not reject Spanish tradition, but rather the idea of a national architecture based on a nostalgic recreation of the past. Instead, they searched for ways of accommodating Spanish popular architecture to functionalist tendencies in vogue in Europe, in order to build houses that were both clean and affordable (Sambricio 2000: 44). Torres Balbás's article 'Mientras labran los sillares. Las nuevas formas de la arquitectura' ('While the Ashlars are Cut. New Architectural Forms') (1918), in which the architect criticizes the so-called *estilo español*, is reminiscent of the ideas expressed by Miguel de Unamuno in *En torno al casticismo* (1895): Torres Balbás suggests a combination of Spanish tradition with European modernity, in order to convey the traditional spirit of Spanish architecture through a modern style (1918: 31–34). A similar attitude was shown by Moreno Villa in his articles about architecture, where he promoted the modernizing tendencies developed by a group of young architects based in Madrid, which he labelled as 'Escuela Madrileña'(Huergo 2010: 21).

Moreno Villa's depiction of New York's buildings and urban planning stems from the debate between modern and traditionalist architectural tendencies developing in Spain at the time. Drawing on the widespread view of the United States as a young country without history, Moreno Villa argues that the lack of architectural tradition allows the continuous demolition of old buildings:

> en los pueblos nuevos [...] como Nueva York [...] no existe la venerable ruina. Y si algún edificio pretende alcanzar el rasgo de la veneración, lo derriban inmediatamente para levantar sobre su base uno más a tono con el tiempo y más

eficaz en todos los sentidos. La construcción que tenga veinticinco años se mira con recelo y se la señala enarbolando imaginaria piqueta. (20)

[in new towns like New York, the venerable ruin does not exist, and if some building aspires to attain features of reverence, they immediately knock it down in order to raise up another upon its base, more attuned to its times and more efficient in all senses. The building that is twenty-five years old is regarded with suspicion and they wield imaginary pickaxes when pointing it out.]

On the contrary, for 'old civilizations' such as Spain, 'venerable ruins' represent the memory of the nation, which must be preserved and respected:

hoy existe ya una responsabilidad histórica en los países viejos. Si éstos planearan a lo yanqui, no quedaría memoria del pasado arquitectónico ni urbano. Por fortuna para los yanquis, aquí no hay paredes respetables, y con su procedimiento no las habrá nunca. (22)

[today there already exists a historical responsibility in the old countries. If they planned in Yankee fashion, no memory of the architectural or urban past would remain. Fortunately for the Yankees, here there are no respectable walls, and with their methods there never will be.]

Behind these two divergent concepts of urban planning lies an opposition between a modernizing will of change and the stagnating weight of history. In contrast to the Spanish dependence on its past, New York represents a society in constant flux. The flats inside the skyscrapers are compared to a ship's cabin, owing to their small dimensions. Moreno Villa extends this comparison by arguing that the whole of Manhattan is a vessel, since its founders were sailors (23). The image of Manhattan as a ship not only recalls the elongated shape of the island, but also suggests the idea of New York as a city in permanent motion. Its founders were 'marinos', and like sailors New Yorkers continue to navigate, not in space any more, but in time, embarked on an unstoppable voyage towards the future, fearless of roots and conventions, constant and destructive. On the other side of the Atlantic Ocean, Spain remains static, paralysed by the burden of derelict yet steady ancient buildings, remnants of a shipwrecked past conditioning the present in its significance as national heritage.

The view of US architecture given in the text straddles self-distance and pragmatic appreciation. On the one hand, urban cleanliness is seen by the writer as an expression of innovation and progress. On the other, he argues that in Spain old edifices have a historical value that prevails over urban improvements:

cuando van a España, estos norteamericanos genuinos fruncen el ceño ante la suciedad y no les quedan ojos para comprender lo otro. Nosotros amamos Toledo, a pesar de sus cosas, porque lo miramos con sentido histórico; pero el hombre que lo mire con sentido higienista, o un principio imperativo de limpieza no puede hacer la vista gorda como nosotros. (21)

[when they go to Spain, these genuine North Americans furrow their brow at the filth and are incapable of understanding the Other. We love Toledo, in spite of its issues, because we look at it with a sense of history; but the man who looks at it with a sense of hygiene, or with an imperative principle of cleanliness, cannot turn a blind eye as we do.]

Moreno Villa's allusion to Toledo as archetype of the historical Spanish city echoes the image of the Castilian landscape as expression of national identity in writers such as Unamuno, Azorín, and Baroja. Carlos Larrínaga points out how these writers conceived the landscape as the spiritual expression of Spanish collective identity that should not be altered (2002: 186). Consequently, their literary interpretation of cities such as Toledo, which remained untouched by industrial progress, dwelled on their immobility as expression of an eternal national character. As Miguel Ángel Lozano argues, such literary rendition resorted to the French literary trope of the 'dead town' that gained popularity in *fin de siècle* European literature and represented a reaction towards industrialization (2000: 23–24).

In spite of his defence of Toledo as representative of Spanish history, Moreno Villa's position remains ambiguous. Expressions such as 'a pesar de sus cosas' and 'hacer la vista gorda' also convey a certain criticism of the immobility — even death — caused by the will to preserve essentialist notions of national identity purely based on a mythicized past. The following lines confirm and strengthen such disparagement:

> muchos de nuestros hombres inteligentes — no digo ya el vulgo — consideran risible tener por ideal la limpieza. A lo sumo, conceden que sea un ideal femenino. Discrepo y discrepo. Puede ser un ideal tan grande y complejo como cualquier otro. Aunque parta de la limpieza material simplemente. (21)
>
> [many of our intelligent men — not to say the common rabble — consider it risible to consider cleanliness an ideal. At most, they concede that it is a feminine ideal. I disagree and disagree. It might be as great and complex an ideal as any other. Although quite simply it starts with material cleanliness.]

In contrast with the interest in desolate moors and ruins expressed by Spanish authors such as Baroja and Azorín ('nuestros hombres inteligentes'), descriptions of New York's urban landscape as the continuous rebirth of the skyscraper, representative of innovation as a destructive force, echo the language of the avant-garde. As José María del Pino points out:

> los vanguardistas tienen prisa en destruir, y más que planes de construcción cuentan inicialmente con propósitos demoledores. Prueba de este impulso son las declaraciones manifestarias, donde se acude con placer a imágenes de voladuras y derribos: piquetas, bombas, incendios. (1995: 2)
>
> [avante-garde artists are in a hurry to destroy and, rather than construction plans, they rely initially upon destructive objectives. Proof of this impulse lies in manifesto statements, in which recourse is happily made to images of explosions and demolitions: pickaxes, bombs and fires.]

At the same time, Moreno Villa's disdain towards the 'vulgo' also connects his remarks to the dehumanized elitism of the 'new art'. In his article 'Casa "honesta" en Madrid' ["Honest" House in Madrid], published in *El Sol* in 1928, the author develops a similar idea when describing a house designed by Rafael Bergamín, as he argues that avant-garde art cannot be understood by the 'masses' (Moreno Villa 2010: 128). The similarities between Moreno Villa's words and Ortega y Gasset's treatise *La deshumanización del arte* (1987 [1925]) are evident.

In contrast with the essentialist search for an eternal tradition in the motionless Castilian landscape, New York seems to embody the modern metropolis which became the spatial location par excellence of Spanish avant-garde narrative: a city that embodies a 'pure present', representation of an unstoppable movement (Fernández Cifuentes 1993: 52–53). In fact, the encounter with New York's modern architecture leads Moreno Villa to question the symbolic value of ancient Spanish monuments and dilapidated buildings:

> en los pueblos antiguos, como son los nuestros de España, la casona, el palacio, el hospital ruinosos claman al cielo y a los Poderes, y si no consiguen que los hombres restañen las heridas que el tiempo les infirió, consiguen ir tirando, ir arrastrando su penosa vida, siendo refugio incómodo de militares, hospicianos y familias en declive. No falta la piedad; falta el dinero. Si no fueran más que cuatro docenas de monumentos... Pero son centenares. (19–20)

> [in ancient towns, as with our own in Spain, the ruined big house, palace and hospital clamour at the heavens and powers that be, and if they do not succeed in getting men to staunch the wounds that time inflicted upon them, then they do succeed in getting by, in dragging their pathetic life along, as an uncomfortable refuge for soldiers, orphans and families in decline. Pity is not needed, but money. If there were no more than four dozen monuments, then... But there are hundreds...]

Images of Castilian ruins as endowed with the essence of the national soul are here rendered as the consequence of economic scarcity, in opposition to the financial wealth and progress embodied by the skyscrapers. In line with architects such as Torres Balbás, Moreno Villa is at pains to acknowledge the benefits of more 'hygienic' urban planning. However, a few pages later, the writer reacts against the impact that such an ideal of cleanliness has in US society:

> el corazón podrá estar o no en desacuerdo con la demolición y la limpieza; pero la razón se pone de su lado sin vacilar. Este fenómeno me ocurre con muchas cosas de América; las comprendo y las alabo; pero me despido de ellas. Y es que todos los arquetipos de vida son humanos, es decir, falibles. No hay uno solo que sirva para las fuerzas contradictorias que integran la vida. Yo puedo admirar el procedimiento que usan los yanquis para limpiar las fachadas ennegrecidas por el hollín de las fábricas y de la humedad; su pulverizador de arena me parece más eficaz y rápido que el nuestro de la piqueta; yo puedo admirar la limpieza de conducta, la limpieza moral que este hombre de faz abierta y limpia observa en sus relaciones conmigo; pero no puedo sentir entusiasmo en lo [*sic*] "cabarets" "pasteurizados" de Nueva York, donde se bebe agua y se paga muy caro para evitar gente bohemia, ni con esa franquicia de que goza la mujer desde que apuntan sus instintos. En estos dos casos falla el ideal de limpieza; no sirve. Estropea o desvirtúa. El 'cabaret' requiere más franquicia, y la niña, menos. Y si al decir esto resulta demasiado español, mejor. (23–24)

> [the heart might or might not be in disagreement with demolition and cleanliness, but reason is placed by its side without hesitation. This phenomenon comes to mind regarding many things in America: I understand them and I praise them; but I dismiss them. And the thing is that all life's archetypes are human; that is to say, fallible. There is not a single one that is of use to the contradictory forces that make up life. I can admire the procedure used by Yankees to clean

the facades blackened by the soot of factories and humidity; their sand grinder seems more efficient and quicker than our own way with the pickaxe. I can admire the spotless behaviour, moral cleanliness that this open and clean-faced man observes in his relationship with me; but I cannot be enthusiastic about New York's 'pasteurized cabarets', where water is drunk and a very expensive price paid in order to avoid bohemian people, or with this exemption enjoyed by women ever since their instincts take shape. In these two cases the ideal of cleanliness fails; it is of no use. It damages and distorts. 'Cabaret' requires more exemption, and the girl, less. And if by saying this it proves to be too Spanish, then all the better.]

Whereas New York's industrial modernization is understood by Moreno Villa as a sign of progress, the writer regards excessive 'hygiene' in social life as dehumanizing. The reference to 'gente bohemia' can be read as an allusion to the intellectual class, whose distinctive individuality and unconventional views distinguish them from the 'masses'. Contradicting his previous disagreement with views of cleanliness as 'feminine', Moreno Villa seems to imply here that Prohibition has turned the masculinized public space of bars into not only a standardized location, but also a feminized place, from where the intellectual elite represented by bohemians has been expelled. In this view, capitalism has undermined the distinguished status of the intelligentsia, since social acceptance depends not on intellectual prestige, but solely on money. Moreover, the allusion to the excessive freedom of women ('franquicia') can be related to women's emancipation, an aspect that I will analyse in detail in Chapter 3. Both aspects are seen as damaging ('estropea o desvirtúa') for the national character, an idea which is also confirmed in the closing sentence: 'y si al decir esto resulta demasiado español, mejor'. Moreno Villa does in fact establish a direct connection between the skyscrapers and the transformation of social structures, especially the family, in New York. The house is seen by Moreno Villa as the centre of family life, which is in turn identified with the role of women as 'casada' (married), as he explains in a subsequent article entitled 'Casa y casada' [The House and the Married Woman] (1928). In this text, the writer establishes a contrast between Fray Luis de León's *La perfecta casada* [*The Perfect Wife*] (1583) and Le Corbusier's architectural ideal of a 'perfect house'. According to Moreno Villa:

> en ningún lenguaje se funden como en el español los conceptos de mujer y de casa para crear ese término tan sustancioso y concreto y elocuente que se dice 'casada'. Mujer casada es mujer que se casa, que se encasa, que la comparte con el varón y que se hace casa ella misma. (2010b: 120)

> [in no language other than Spanish are the concepts of woman and house fused in order to create this so solid and specific and eloquent a term that is 'married'. A married woman is a woman who gets married, who sets up house, who shares it with the male and who herself becomes the home.]

The gender issues raised by this quotation will be examined in the next chapter. Nevertheless, it is worth noting how the writer relates the perfect wife described by Fray Luis to the house itself, not only implying that the family home is the space 'naturally' designated for women, but also that the success of the family depends on the symbolic merger between 'la casa' and 'la casada'. In the United States, however, the role of the house as the sanctuary of family values is threatened by social change:

> el vivir fuera — incluso para comer — trae consigo muchas cosas importantes: independencia entre los miembros familiares, administración particular y ajuste previo de las horas en los días venideros [...] cada individuo — hombre o mujer — anda por su cuenta, hace su vida, se paga sus gastos, elige sus amistades y lleva un calendario donde apuntar las citas y quehaceres de la semana. Por todo esto, el hogar no existe; la casa es un refugio donde, si se encuentran los familiares a una hora del día, se dicen las cosas de sopetón, sin calma ni recreo. (15–16)
>
> [life outside the home, even eating, brings with it many important things: independence between family members, personal responsibility and timetabling for forthcoming days [...]; each individual (man or woman) does their own thing, lives their life, pays their bills, chooses their friendships and carries a calendar around in which to note down appointments and errands for the week. For this reason, the home does not exist; the house is a refuge where, if family members find themselves together at a given time of day, they say things unexpectedly, without calm or leisure.]

A similar remark can be found in Paul Morand's travelogue *New York* (1929), a fact that highlights the analogous reactions to American society expressed by European authors at the time: 'family life no longer exists. [...] People are always moving. [...] People eat all the time, and never. The midday meal, that Latin relaxation half-way through the day, is unknown' (Morand 1931: 304–05). The loss of the house as family home implies the dismantlement of the family and therefore of the national community in a society dominated by the frantic rhythm of life, and by the machine. In 'Casa y casada', Moreno Villa argues that women will cease to be 'la casada' (a play on words between 'house' and 'married'), and that the house might become Le Corbusier's 'machine for living' (2010b: 121). Similarly, in *Pruebas de Nueva York* the writer states that the house is a mass-produced machine (55). The reference to Le Corbusier's concept of the house as *la machine à habiter* suggests that the disappearance of the house as a family home not only leads to a change in women's role as wife but also to dehumanization:

> yo creo firmemente que la falta de intimidad es una desgracia para el hombre. Sin ella no profundiza en nada. Hay que entregarse con fuerza, regularidad y abstracción para penetrar en cualquier cosa. Y si el neoyorquino o la neoyorquina siguen muchos años en el plan de hoy acabarán siendo gentes superficiales, mecánicas y desnaturalizadoras. (27)
>
> [I firmly believe that the lack of privacy is a disgrace for man. Without it he cannot think deeply about anything. One has to commit oneself with strength, frequency and abstraction in order to fathom anything. And if the male or female New Yorker spends many years in the way they do today then they will end up being superficial, mechanical and unnatural people.]

Mechanization is explained by the accelerated pace of modern urban life in New York, where time is scarce because the distances are enormous (16). The solution to this problem is the use of 'la mecánica', and for that reason, New York is devoted to 'mecanicismo' (16). The writer refers to the underground and elevated railways, lifts, ticket machines, and self-service restaurants, which are dominated by the presence of a variety of mechanical artefacts. New York is described as 'mecanismo' (8) and 'engranaje' [gear wheel] (32), where everything (and everyone) is mass-produced. As a consequence, the 'human mass' is uniform, and is hard to distinguish individuals from each other (53). Moreno Villa states that:

> quiere tener el yanqui más gruesas los [*sic*] extremidades de los pies, los dedos, que todas las razas del mundo. Para facilitar el desarrollo del pie en tal sentido confecciona calzados de punta muy ancha [...] que imprimen a las extremidades inferiores del hombre un sello de rudeza [...] No hay que buscar lo típico yanqui en la cara. No existe la cara yanqui. Conviven allá en América las caras judías, alemanas, rusas, inglesas, noruegas, italianas, etc. Nueva York es un índice de caras, como casi todo lo americano; pero el molde al que aspiran sus hombres acaba por imprimirles cierta uniformidad en la expresión. (56–58)

> [the Yankee wants the tips of his feet and fingers to be fatter than those of all the other races of the world. In order to facilitate the development of the foot in this way he makes very wide, pointed shoes which impress a stamp of simplicity upon man's inferior points. The typical Yankee does not have to be sought by his face. The Yankee face does not exist. There in America, Jewish, German, Russian, English, Norwegian and Italian, etc., faces co-exist. New York is an index of faces as are almost all things American; but the mould to which its men aspire ends up imposing upon them a certain uniformity in their expression.]

The writer suggests that US men are becoming increasingly standardized. He also alludes to their lack of intelligence and spirituality (45). The United States are described in fact as a 'primitive' society (42, 63). In the writer's view, such primitiveness stems from the dehumanization caused by the machine, and by the consequent acceleration of urban life in a society dominated by capitalism that denigrates the intellectual class. According to Moreno Villa, intellectual activity requires a 'slow tempo', and New York's frantic rhythm does not allow intellectuals to leave an imprint in this society (32). The image of a mechanized mass that works according to the rhythm established by the machine-city, where the intellectual class has been dispossessed of any influence in social life, reflects fears of the 'masses' out of control in Europe and Spain. Without the leadership of the intellectuals — the leading minority — US society becomes an amorphous group in which individuality is lost in favour of standardization and capitalism. In addition, Moreno Villa argues that the 'capitalist greed', that drives US citizens to devote all their time to work, has a negative impact on their health:

> montado en un concepto viejo, si se quiere; montado en una ilusión vana, yo soy más señor que ese hortera de hoy, millonario de mañana. Ese hortera que monta [...] dos veces o cuatro al día en el tiznado "subway", con cara de hombre reventado, destripado, "desnervizado", aniquilado. ¿Para qué los dólares, si a los cuarenta años estoy en la ruina que veo? [...] Prefiero paladear la vida y comunicar su grandeza y complejidad a los otros, aunque me falten dólares [...] prefiero ser hidalgo de migajas, y mucho tiempo, a ser ganapán desriñonado y con oro. (33)

> [based upon an old concept, if you wish; based upon a vain illusion, I am more a gentleman than this shop assistant today, this millionaire tomorrow. This shop

assistant who rides [...] two or four times a day on the grubby subway, with the face of a broken, gutted, unnerved and annihilated man. Why the dollars, if at forty years of age I find myself in the ruin I see around me? [...] I prefer to relish life and communicate its greatness and complexity to others, although I do not have enough dollars [...] I prefer to be an hidalgo living off scraps and for a long time, to being a worn-out errand boy with gold.]

'Hortera' was the name given to shop assistants in certain shops in Madrid, and 'ganapán' refers to errand boys. Both terms are pejorative adjectives that denigrate the labour of the working class, in opposition to the decadent 'hidalgo', a poor nobleman with no occupation. The rise of the 'hortera de hoy, millonario de mañana' is opposed to the elitism of the 'hidalgo', whose social position derives not from work but from inherited privileges. At the same time, the writer also criticizes the advent of a materialistic society controlled by money, in which the individual sacrifices his life to accumulate wealth. The 'hidalgo', reminiscent of Cervantes's Don Quixote, serves as a strong symbol of national identity, based on the alleged idealism and spiritualism of the Spanish nation. As Christopher Britt indicates, intellectuals such as Costa, Ganivet, Unamuno, Maetzu, and Ortega y Gasset

> did not only seek to make sense of modern Spain's decline from Empire but to also offer to their compatriots an imaginative program for national and imperial regeneration. They identified Spain's new role in the modern world with the idealistic mission undertaken by Don Quixote [...] Inspired by the example of Don Quixote's quest to recuperate the Golden Age of chivalry, they suggested that modern Spain also needed to revive its chivalric values and seek to recuperate its Golden Age. (2005: 6)

Moreover, the war with the United States was interpreted by these intellectuals as 'a conflict between the archaic spiritual, moral, and civilizing ideals of the Spanish Empire and the progressive technological and economic ideals of an increasingly secularized Anglo-American Empire' (Britt 2005: 2).

Moreno Villa's account of New York does, however, strive to overcome discourses of 'Otherness' that shaped European and Spanish perceptions of the United States. Throughout his travelogue, one can perceive the struggle between the preconceived system of representation that initially influences his view of US society, and the acceptance of the fact that technological progress makes the United States a more advanced and richer country in comparison to Spain's stagnation. Breaking with the archetype of US citizens as primitive and mechanized people that he follows in some parts of the text, he also states that

> cuantas veces hablo ahora con paisanos míos sobre el carácter norteamericano encuentro cierta disconformidad. Las ideas que manejan unos y otros son en muchos casos certeras; pero desde un punto de vista. Si me dicen que el americano es un hombre primitivo, no puedo aceptarlo del todo; si me dicen que es duro, insensible, mecanizado, etc., me inclino a distinguir, a paliar conceptos tan recortados [...] Y yo creo que en el yanqui no debo considerar si le falta ternura, sentimiento u otras virtudes nuestras, sino atender a las virtudes que ellos han desarrollado por encima de nosotros. (41–42)

> [on every occasion that I speak now with fellow countrymen about the North American character, I come across a certain disagreement. The ideas expressed

by one or the other are in many cases accurate, but from their point of view. If they tell me that the American is a primitive man, I cannot fully accept this; if they tell me that he is tough, insensitive, mechanized, etc., then I tend to distinguish, to mitigate such uneven concepts. I believe that with the Yankee I must not wonder as to whether he lacks in tenderness, feelings or other virtues of ours, but look to the virtues that they have developed more than we have.]

The expression 'las ideas que manejan unos y otros' seems to point to the existence of a preconceived discourse of the United States as a country dominated by the machine and the 'masses'. Nevertheless, Moreno Villa tries to go beyond this image in order to undertake a multilayered analysis. Although this task is flawed from the start — since he does not deny the idea of Americans as rough and primitive — the writer attempts to find a positive interpretation of such alleged primitivism. With the intention of reconciling opposite views, he interprets US 'primitivism' as a consequence of the eagerness and capacity for transforming their European heritage, similar to the desire for constant progress and change that characterizes New York's architecture (48). Therefore, according to Moreno Villa, the United States departed from the civilized delicacy of its European roots in order to create a more efficient, stronger, and happier civilization (48). As a matter of fact, when he returns to Spain, Moreno Villa perceives his own country as weak and poor:

> toca el barco en Vigo. La belleza de este hombro de España no impide que al desembarcar me parezca endeble la casa, el tren, el servicio de comedor y algunos otros detalles. Mi visión de España en América no era ésta; puede ser que cambie a su vez ahora mi visión de Nueva York desde aquí. ¿Cuántas caras tiene la verdad? (49)

> [the boat puts into Vigo. The beauty of this shoulder of Spain does not prevent the house, train, dining-room service and some other features from seeming feeble to me as I disembark. My vision of Spain in America was not this; perhaps now in turn my vision of New York will change from here. How many faces does the truth possess?]

The author notes that the 'truth' is a constructed artefact, and that reality is multifaceted. When he compares Americans to Spaniards, he argues that 'en este "pueblo bárbaro" que yo dejo hay un nivel de formas o formalidades sociales, indudablemente más elevado [...] Nadie es entrometido; a nadie le importa la vida ajena; nadie se lanza a consideraciones y juicios sobre lo que no conoce' [in this "barbaric people" that I leave behind there is an undoubtedly more elevated degree of social habits and manners [...] Nobody is obtrusive; nobody is bothered by other people's lives; nobody takes to casting opinions or judgements about things they do not know] (51). The inverted commas for 'pueblo bárbaro' imply that the writer is questioning the construction of Americans as primitives that he had developed in previous chapters. It is the Spaniards who now take on the appearance of barbarians: the binary opposition between Spain and the United States which had been constructed throughout the book has been reversed. On the train to Madrid, the writer has a conversation with a traveller who had never been to the United States but nevertheless 'soltó por la espita indiscreta de su boca lo que "pensaba" de Nueva York. No llegaban a majaderías, se quedaban en lugares comunes, en noticias mancas recogidas de otros viajeros y contertulios' [what he "thought" about New York gushed out of the indiscreet tap of his mouth. It did not extend to nonsense, but was made up of commonplaces, half-baked news gathered from other travellers and acquaintances] (50). Moreno Villa thus reacts to a depiction of New York based on preconceptions. Once more, the use of inverted commas for 'pensaba' suggests that this man's opinion about New York is not his own, but an amalgamation of preconceived clichés.

However, by the end of the travelogue, Moreno Villa is still unable to overcome prevalent stereotypes of American 'primitivism' completely, as he combines this archetype with a feminized image of New York by referring to the city as 'la niña violenta' [the violent girl]: 'escritores, viajeros y simples lectores hablan del primitivismo norteamericano. Yo lo que hago es incorporar ese concepto; llamarle "niña" y "niña violenta" para luego bautizar así a la metrópolis más inquietante y violenta del mundo actual' [writers, travellers and simple readers talk of North American primitivism. And what I do is incorporate this concept; call it "girl" and "violent girl" so as to baptise in this way the most disturbing and violent metropolis in the world today'.] (63). The use of the word 'niña' characterizes non-Europeans as childish and inferior, in contrast to the alleged superiority of the 'civilized West'. This image also applies the hierarchical opposition between man and woman to New York. As Loomba argues, images of America and Africa as feminine 'positioned these continents as available for plunder, possession, discovery and conquest' and consequently, 'from the beginning of the colonial period till its end (and beyond), female bodies symbolise the conquered land' (1998: 151–52). Furthermore, 'violence' also refers to savagery, to nature out of control, as traditionally applied to the West's 'Others'. New York consequently remains in a position of inferiority to Europe ('niña'), yet as a threat to civilization ('violenta'). Nevertheless, the persistence of such discourse in Moreno Villa's text does not stop him from developing a closer and more empathic understanding of the United States:

> soy, por moverme en terrenos del espíritu y del arte, idólatra de lo que tiene niñez, intrepidez y violencia. Estoy en alma con Nueva York, con Picasso y con Lindberg. Sus caminos llevan a los golpes, a los fracasos, pero llevan, y a veces llevan a las victorias, y siempre llevan a la emoción. (63–64)
>
> [I am, in inhabiting the sphere of spirit and art, a worshipper of what childhood represents: fearlessness and violence. I am at one with New York, Picasso and Lindberg. Their roads lead to blows, to failures, but they sometimes lead to victory, and always to emotion.]

The writer identifies now with the city and the modernization it represents. 'Niñez', 'intrepidez', and 'violencia' are positive qualities that contrast with the defence of tradition which he upholds in previous chapters. The reference to 'caminos' can be understood an allusion to a move forward, a call for change; by saying that 'sus caminos llevan a los golpes, a los fracasos, pero llevan', the writer acknowledges the need to embrace modernization as the only way to combat stagnation. Furthermore, the view of the United States as a cold and mechanized society has given way to emotion and spirituality. The frantic rhythm of the urban life that was so frightening at the beginning of the book is now accepted, even missed, as the writer is confronted with his own anxiety towards the barren Castilian landscape:

> después que la luz clara de la meseta castellana nos define lomas, árboles, bestias, senderos, nubes; después que el silencio se hace carne o cuerpo, alimento; después de sentir la tranquilidad, nos sobrecoge un sano terror a ella. Y como pelota rebotada salimos en busca de la violencia, de Nueva York, de la intrepidez, de la irresponsabilidad, de la Flapper, de la niñez. (64)

> [after the clear light of the Castilian meseta makes out knolls, trees, animals, paths and clouds for us; after the silence becomes flesh or the body, nourishment; after experiencing the calm, we are overcome by a healthy terror of it. And like a bouncing ball we go out in search of violence, New York, audacity, irresponsibility, the Flapper, childhood.]

The prologue, written almost a year after Moreno Villa's stay in New York, encapsulates this change of perspective:

> ir a Norte-América no es una *Empresa* para hombre alguno. Para el español, sí. Tendrá la culpa el dinero, tendrá la culpa otra mermedad [*sic*]⁵ de esas que a cada paso nos descubren los curanderos de la patria, cirujanos de siempre-mata y nunca-salva. Qué buen signo sería que los españoles sonrieran al presentarles como pavorosa aventura ese viaje de diez días de agua. Nuestros literatos y científicos, al recibir invitaciones de allá, se tientan las ropas y piden oro y moro para dejar su emplazamiento. Eso prueba que miran como descomunal empresa el viaje, con ánimo enteco de gordo Sancho. Yo quisiera verlos sonreír ante la oferta sencilla de los dólares suficientes para ir, vivir, ver, comprender y regresar. Vale la pena el oreo; tanto como el oro, si nó [*sic*] más. Y pelarse a bordo las greñas de los siglos, y zambullir catedrales, monumentos, historia, en las aguas atlánticas, aunque sea por seis semanas, término frecuente para ingleses y norteamericanos. (8–9)

> [going to North America is not an Enterprise for any man. For the Spaniard, it is. The blame will lie with money, the blame will lie with another one of these ailments which at each step reveal to us our country's quacks, always-lethal and never-lifesaving surgeons. What a good sign it would be if the Spaniards smiled when this journey of ten days across water is presented to them as an adventure. Our writers and scientists, when receiving invitations from over there, try out their clothes and demand the earth to leave their location. This proves that they regard the journey as an enormous undertaking, with the sickly zeal of a fat Sancho. I would like to see them smile at the simple offer of enough dollars to go, live, see, understand and return. The airing is worth it; as much as the gold, if not more. And to crop back the entanglement of the centuries, and take leave of cathedrals, monuments and history in the waters of the Atlantic, even just for six weeks, the normal duration for the English and North Americans.]

In the first lines of the excerpt, the writer refers to Spain's poverty and backwardness and criticizes *regenerationist* projects: the play on words 'los curanderos de la patria, cirujanos de siempre-mata y nunca-salva' is an obvious allusion to Joaquín Costa's idea of a 'cirujano de hierro' appropriated by Miguel Primo de Rivera, and to the elitist attitude of the Spanish intelligentsia. The immobility of Spanish intellectuals is characterized as the attachment to a sickly — 'enteco' — concept of national identity, which the author subverts by replacing the 'hidalgo' Don Quixote with his partner, the peasant Sancho Panza. Instead, Moreno Villa proposes to get rid of the weight of history and tradition and to move forward, and 'comprender y regresar', bringing some fresh air ('orear') from US modernization.

Anticípolis: a Polyphonic Account of New York's Modernization

Whereas the view of US modernization given in *Pruebas de Nueva York* evolves from initial ambivalence to final acceptance of some of its principles, *Anticípolis* offers a multilayered perspective of the city from the start. Written mostly in free indirect speech, the presence of the narrator in the novel is scarce, and the opinions about the 'Big Other' emanate from the words of the characters. Applying Bakhtin's definition of 'polyphony', the characters' voices are endowed 'with equal rights and each with its own world', and they are 'not only objects of authorial discourse but also subjects of their own directly signifying discourse' (Bakhtin 1984: 6–7). According to David Lodge (1990: 86), a polyphonic novel can therefore be defined as a 'novel in which a variety of conflicting ideological positions are given a voice and set in play both between and within individual speaking subjects, without being placed and judged by an authoritative authorial voice'. This does not imply the complete absence of the narrator, but a different function in comparison to the monologic narrator: rather than transforming others' consciousnesses into objects of the narrative discourse, the narrator of the polyphonic novel recreates other consciousnesses as fully valid and un-finalized voices engaged in dialogue (Bakhtin 1984: 65–68).

The views of modernization given in the novel can be summarized in two main positions that, to some extent, reflect hegemonic projects of national regeneration in Spain at the time. According to Barrantes:

> Luis de Oteyza utiliza una estrategia de tipo oposicional, sobre todo en la figura de doña Jesusa, de manera que Nueva York queda redefinido a lo largo de la novela en función de la ciudad de Oviedo. Nueva York es el símbolo del progreso y la modernidad, frente al tradicionalismo conservador de Oviedo [...] la totalidad de los individuos que aparecen en *Anticípolis* defienden los ideales modernos, frente a doña Jesusa, quien queda aislada en defensa de la tradición. (2006: 57)

> [Luis de Oteyza employs a strategy of the oppositional type, above all in the figure of Doña Jesusa, in such a way that New York is redefined throughout the novel based on Oviedo. New York is the symbol of progress and modernity, in contrast with the conservative traditionalism of Oviedo [...]. The totality of the individuals who appear in *Anticípolis* defend modern ideals, in contrast with doña Jesusa, who is isolated in her defence of tradition.]

As the religious symbolism of her name indicates, Jesusa embodies *casticista* notions of national identity. In the opening lines of the novel, the narrator defines this character as 'archiespañola' and deeply attached to Spanish customs (2006: 85). Furthermore, the choice of Oviedo as Jesusa's city of origin is not accidental. Oviedo, under the name of Vestusta ('ancient', 'old-fashioned'), has the iconic status of being the location of Leopoldo Alas's novel *La Regenta* (1885). Alas's text reflects the first decade of the Restoration system, when the persistence of traditionalism was disguised under the appearance of false modernity (Oleza 1995: 58–59). New York in fact represents for Jesusa the negation of the traditional values associated with Vestusta, and consequently she develops a strong hatred towards the city and its modern ways. She detests the height of the skyscrapers and means of transport such as the underground and elevated railway. Jesusa is also repulsed by the noises and by the street lighting and neon signs (104–05). Reflecting her traditionalist world view, Jesusa's abhorrence of technology and mass society responds to moral reasons:

> los consideraba [urban means of transport] una brutalidad y una indecencia. Sí, era brutal meter en los vagones a seres humanos, a seres vivos, apretándoles como si fuesen cosas insensibles e irrompibles, y era una indecencia que un hombre quedase pegado a una mujer, ¡incrustado en una mujer! Doña Jesusa, que llegó a Nueva York bastante apetecible aún, tuvo motivos para saber la indecentada que eso encierra. Y luego, cuando sus niñas fueron creciendo, las vio muchas veces ruborizarse y palidecer, palideciendo y ruborizándose ella paralelamente. (105)

> [she regarded them [urban means of transport] with brutality and nastiness. Yes, it was brutal to put human beings, living beings, into the carriage, pushing them together as if they were unfeeling and unbreakable, and it was obscene for a man to be stuck to a woman, encrusted in a woman! Doña Jesusa, who was still quite attractive when she arrived in New York, had reason to know the shamelessness that this holds. And then, when her daughters were growing up, she often saw them blush and grow pale, with her growing pale and blushing simultaneously.]

She acknowledges the material benefits of technological progress — when she needs to pay an urgent visit to one of her sons she even considers that the subway is useful (201) — but the challenge to social conventions is regarded by Jesusa as a moral regression that provokes the regression of New Yorkers to a state of primitivism:

> Los rascacielos. Las vías especiales para autos, los trenes por debajo y por encima del piso... Y los ascensores y montacargas, y la calefacción y la radio... Todo lo material será progresivo, aunque a mí no me guste. Pero lo moral, ¡de ninguna manera! En eso aquí, lejos de progresar, se retrocede. [...] Anticuada me llaman mis hijas, ridiculizándome [...] Yo, moralmente, no me quedo antigua. Los que se hacen antiguos son esos, según ustedes, anticipados. ¿Anticipados?... Es decir, ¿avanzados?... Marcharán, pero hacia atrás. Porque lo que logran es retroceder. Y retroceder hasta los orígenes, hasta el salvaje y hasta el mono [...] Lo que usted considera hombres anticipados y mujeres anticipadas, doctor — fallaba doña Jesusa –, yo no puedo considerarles ni hombres ni mujeres [...] Solamente machos y hembras. (187)

> [Skyscrapers. The special lanes for cars, trains below and above the apartment... And the elevators and forklifts, central heating and radio... All this equipment might be progressive, although I do not like it. But morality, not at all! With that here, far from progressing, it is going backwards! My daughters call me old-fashioned, poking fun at me [...] I, morally, am not old-fashioned. Those who become old are those, according to you, who are ahead of their time. Ahead of their time...? That is, advanced...? They might move, but backwards. Because what they succeed in doing is going back. To go back to their origins, to the savage and even to the monkey [...] What you regard as anticipated men and anticipated women, doctor', Doña Jesusa passed judgement, 'I cannot consider as men or women [...] Only as males and females'.]

Despite Jesusa's characterization as an ignorant and naïve woman, especially through her children's words, her reasoning does in fact respond to common stereotypes of the United States as a primitive country developed by thinkers such as Ortega y Gasset, who argued that 'yo siempre, con miedo de exagerar, he sostenido que [the United States] era un pueblo primitivo *camouflado* por los últimos inventos' [I have always held, even at the risk of exaggerating, that [the United States] was a primitive people *camouflaged* by the latest inventions'.] (2007b: 201, emphasis in the original). The agreement between Jesusa's traditionalist stand and the opinions of Ortega, the main defender of the need to Europeanize — and therefore modernize — Spain in the early twentieth century, reveals the similar influence of discourses of 'Otherness' in both *casticista* and Europeanizing projects of national regeneration. Moreover, Jesusa's views, which are interspersed with references to Darwin's theory of evolution — 'retroceder hasta los orígenes, hasta el salvaje y hasta el mono' –, mirror fears of degeneration in Europe. US materialism and moral laxity are, according to this character, the opposite of the ethical refinement achieved by civilization. Therefore, she considers her moral conventions as the result of progress, and the transformation of such values as the path to dehumanization:

> explicaba la tesis del retrogradismo, declarándose 'producto de la civilización'. Para doña Jesusa, el origen de sus escrúpulos y de sus pudores en la civilización estaba. Por la civilización, por ese verdadero avance a través de los siglos, dejaron de ser brutales los hombres y las mujeres deshonestas. En cambio, ¿de dónde procedía aquello de obtener la riqueza y el goce como se pudiese?... La conquista del oro a tiros no es sino equivalente de la lucha por la vida a mazazos, a dentelladas. El aplacamiento del deseo, sin que el amor siquiera medie, no constituye otra cosa que simple contacto sexual. Y a la horda o a la manada habría que acudir para encontrar acciones semejantes. (187)

> [she was explaining the theory of retrogression, declaring herself a 'product of civilization'. For Doña Jesusa, the origin of her scruples and shyness lay in civilization. Men stopped being brutal and women dishonest thanks to civilization, to that true advancement throughout the centuries. However, where did the matter of gaining wealth and pleasure however one could derive from...? The conquest of gold by violence is but the equivalent of the struggle for life with cudgels and biting. The appeasing of desire, without love even acting as mediator, constitutes nothing more than simple sexual contact, and to find similar actions one must look to the horde or herd.]

'Civilization' involves for Jesusa two specific principles: patriarchy and social elitism. First, her criticism of New York's moral regression is directly related to the subversion of the compliant role of woman as the 'Ángel in the House' that she represents. As I will show in detail in the next chapter, Jesusa reacts strongly against the implementation of companionate marriage and divorce laws, birth control, and above all, the freedom of women in New York to have sexual relationships without the social imperative of marriage. All these practices entail a challenge to the patriarchal family, which Jesusa — in tune with both traditionalist and modernizing standpoints in Spain — regards as a product of civilization and the basis of the Western nation. The reference to 'simple contacto sexual' reflects the fear of women as 'nature out of control', free to break with a conservative notion of love that chains them to the authority or their husband. Without such authority, the stable cornerstone that the family represents for patriarchy runs the risk of faltering and collapsing, leading to the disintegration of a civilization established on hierarchical oppositions such as man/woman. Secondly, the American ideal of egalitarianism and equal opportunities, which allows the poor to become rich and the rich to be ruined, clashes with a Spanish social system in which class is fixed and established by inheritance. The importance given by Jesusa to social status is underscored by her reaction to the suggestion made by Mariíta, her youngest daughter, that the youngest of her sons, Pepín, could earn some money by washing up in a restaurant:

> ¿Fregar platos?... Ésa no es ocupación para un hijo mío. Me consideraría deshonrada [...] Explicó a continuación por qué no podía ser [...] Sus hijos no debían olvidar que pertenecían a una de las familias más nobles de Asturias, tierra de los hidalgos. Aunque lejanos, eran parientes del marqués del Valle de Noreña. E iba a ponderar el disgusto que ese ilustre personaje tendría al saber que uno de sus familiares se dedicaba a menesteres tan bajos. (122)

> [Washing dishes...? That is no occupation for a son of mine. I would consider myself dishonoured [...] She went on to explain why this could not be. Her children must not forget that they belonged to one of the noblest families of Asturias, a land of hidalgos. Although distant, they were relatives of the Marquis of Valle de Noreña, and she was to ponder the disgust that this illustrious character would suffer upon discovering that one of his relatives was engaged in such a lowly occupation.]

Similarly to Moreno Villa's opposition between 'el hidalgo' and 'el hortera', Jesusa's attitude mirrors the view of Spain as repository of aristocratic values. The starting point of the *Reconquista*, one of the great myths of the *casticismo*, was traditionally located in the mountains of Asturias, and regarded as

> una épica que unía en una empresa común a una raza indómita de auténticos hispanos, perennes defensores de sus creencias desde que los romanos llegaron a sus dominios, especialmente cántabros y astures, con la sangre renovadora de los germanos, civilizada por su contacto con Roma, y sobre todo, por su conversión al catolicismo. (Menéndez Bueyes 2001:13)

> [an epic that united in a common enterprise an indomitable race of authentic Spaniards, perennial defenders of their beliefs ever since the Romans reached their domains; especially Cantabrians and Asturians, with the reformist blood of the Germans, civilized by their contact with Rome, and, above all, by their conversion to Catholicism.]

Social degradation from a lineage allegedly connected to an aristocratic past would, therefore, imply rupture with a hierarchical class division created by 'civilization'. Applying the same reasoning to the opposition between 'civilized' and 'primitive' societies, the former, such as Spain, supposedly remain in a position of authority thanks to the privileges granted by their long history and tradition. The United States, by contrast, is seen as a society where such moral and social principles are not respected, and hence as an 'uncivilized' country.

The reference to 'la horda' and 'la manada' also connects Jesusa's words with the widespread image of 'the threatening masses', seen as a barbarous and amorphous entity closer to animals than to human beings. In this view, without the control of the elite, civilization returns to a primitive stage, to a jungle where individuals follow their instincts rather than a set of prescribed moral conventions. Jesusa's allusion to US 'primitivism' recalls Ortega y Gasset's concerns about regression conveyed in *La rebelión de las masas*:

> la civilización no está ahí, no se sostiene a sí misma. [...] En un dos por tres se queda usted sin civilización. ¡Un descuido, y cuando mira usted en derredor, todo se ha volatilizado! Como si hubiese recogido unos tapices que tapaban la pura naturaleza, reaparece repristinada la selva primitiva. La selva siempre es primitiva. Y viceversa: todo lo primitivo es selva. (Ortega y Gasset 2007: 152)

> [civilization is not there, does not sustain itself [...] In no time at all you are left with no civilization. A moment's carelessness, and when you look around yourself, everything has vanished! As if a tapestry that covered pure Nature had been pulled back, the primitive jungle reappears, restored to its original state. The jungle is always primitive. And vice-versa: everything primitive is jungle.]

At the same time, the link made by Jesusa between violence and materialism — 'la conquista del oro a tiros' — also refers to the criminality caused by the Prohibition Law, one of the aspects of US society commented upon in the novel. Carlos, one of Jesusa's sons, does in fact become a gangster himself after Antonio's death. His view of materialism is completely opposed to the one represented by his mother. He argues that working as a washer-up does not involve any kind of dishonour, but rather, that the greatest shame comes from not being able to earn any money (123). Prohibition and organized crime are issues discussed by Jesusa and Felipe Muñiz, an Argentine journalist known as *el Milonguero* [the Liar] because of his ironic remarks about New York society. Resorting to an acid sense of humour, Muñiz unveils the contradictions of the double standards in play surrounding the consumption of bootleg alcohol and the racketeers:

> se han publicado, y con gran éxito de venta, por cierto, las *Memorias de Al Capone* [...] Mientras se lee esta obra, el protagonista inverna muy tranquilo en su paradisíaca isla finca de Miami. Si algún policía va por allá, es en funciones de vigilancia: ¡con objeto de impedir que le roben al propietario las flores del parque! (167)

> [the *Memoirs of Al Capone* have been published, and with great commercial success, by the way [...] Whilst you read this work, the protagonist winters in his paradisiacal island estate of Miami. If a policeman goes there, it is to keep watch, with the purpose of preventing the owner's flowers being stolen from the park!]

Muñiz's criticism, devoid of religious implications, adds another layer to the polyphonic character of the novel. *El Milonguero*, who refuses to learn English as an exercise of patriotism, also represents a denunciation of US imperialist policies in Central and South America (125). His statements about New York are, however, endowed with a strong sense of humour, and therefore with ambiguity. In fact, in spite of his sardonic comments about the United States, he agrees with the decision taken by Jesusa's children to stay in New York: 'sí, Oviedo debe de ser un agujero sin salida [...]. Nueva York tiene que resultar menos malo. Pero no mucho menos, ¿eh? No vayáis a creeros...' [yes, Oviedo must be a bottomless pit [...] New York can't be that bad. But only just, eh? Don't go thinking that...] (126). Muñiz's contradictory statements about the United States condense the ambivalence that permeates the novel: the opinions given by the characters are presented in conflict, offering a multifaceted perspective in which none of their voices is privileged.

Don Antonio, Jesusa's husband, embodies a more positive view of New York. He decides to abandon the comfort of his petit bourgeois life in Oviedo, guaranteed by an inherited income and a stable job, and take his entire family to the American city. In spite of his secure existence in Spain, Don Antonio did not feel fulfilled. He considers himself a great inventor, an activity that he has developed outside his professional occupations. According to the narrator, Antonio suffers from delusions, since he is only able to design harebrained creations (93). Unable to find investors in his home town, and in a state of frantic insanity, he suddenly realizes that New York is the Promised Land where his talent would finally be rewarded (97). Once in the United States, although his projects never succeed, he immediately falls in love with New York. In contrast to the negative reaction of his wife:

> no le impusieron temor aquellas recias moles [the skyscrapers] al hallárselas enfrente emergiendo del mar cual acantilados gigantes, ni se sintió abrumado por su pesadumbre sombría cuando introdújose luego en los profundos cañones que más bien que calles forman. Como no le produjo pasmo que esas calles, abismáticas bajo la altura de los edificios que las flanquean, se prolongasen sin término, y no le causó trastorno sentirse metido entre la muchedumbre que por ellas circula torrencialmente. [...] Ésa, la presentida y anhelada, fue para don Antonio la ciudad disforme. (98–100)

> [Those solid bulks [the skyscrapers] did not cause him to be afraid as they appeared before him, emerging from the sea like giant cliffs; nor did he feel overwhelmed by their dark sorrow when he later went into the deep canyons, which they form, rather than streets. He did not experience astonishment that these streets, abysmal beneath the height of the buildings that flank them, went on endlessly, and did not feel upset with being amongst the mass that passes like a torrent through them [...] This, the anticipated and desired, was for Don Antonio the monstrous city.]

This dystopic view of the city given by the narrator turns Don Antonio's admiration into a comical delirium, reminiscent of the Spanish literary figure par excellence, Don Quixote. Similarly to the effect that books of chivalry produce in Cervantes's character, New York is compared to a spell, capable of driving mad saner men than Don Antonio (101). One could in fact substitute the windmills that Don Quixote mistakes for giants in Cervantes's novel with the gigantic height of New York's buildings. As in Moreno Villa's travelogue, the parallels between these two characters — as we already know, Don Antonio is descended from a *hidalgo* — can be interpreted as a reference to the political use of Don Quixote as an expression of Spanish national identity. However, Don Antonio never renounces his traditional values (110), nor does he react against US technologism; rather, he is fascinated by the dynamism of the city:

> la admiró en todo, pues a quien se ama apasionadamente en todo se admira, incluso en las imperfecciones que tiene [...] El tránsito mareante y los ensordecedores ruidos de Nueva York [...] los consideraba cosa deleitosa. Arrollado por el gentío, que las calles vierten en alguna de las avenidas sobre las que el *elevated* pasa con estrépito, se mantenía firme junto al que le acompañase, para gritarle a la oreja:
> — Hay movimiento, ¿eh?... ¡Hay vida! (100)
>
> [he admired it in everything, for whoever one loves passionately one also admires in all respects, even with the imperfections they may have [...] He regarded the dizzying traffic and the deafening noises of New York [...] as something delightful. Overwhelmed by the crowd, which the streets tipped out onto one of the avenues over which the elevated train passes noisily, he remained firm against the person with him, shouting in his ear:
> 'There's hustle and bustle, eh...? There's life!]

In tune with the references to movement in Moreno Villa's text, Don Antonio's praise of New York's frantic rhythm can be seen in contrast to the view of Spain as a 'dead organism' promoted by *Regeneracionismo*. In this case, the figure of Don Antonio/Quixote goes beyond a nostalgic view of an immobile past and fearlessly embraces modernization as a source of progress and therefore of 'vida'. In addition, the elitist ideal represented by the *hidalgo* is replaced by Don Antonio's immersion in the American 'mass'.

Nevertheless, Don Antonio never succeeds in his business endeavours. Ironically, he ends up teaching Spanish language and literature, despite the fact that he only vaguely knows who the author of *Don Quixote* is, as the narrator points out (103). His failure as well as the constant references to his insanity, gives an impression of Don Antonio as an ambiguous character. On the one hand, he represents an absolute acceptance of modernization. On the other, such acceptance is undermined by the narrator's allusion to New York as a dystopic city as well as by Don Antonio's madness. Antonio dies of 'congestión' (104), a stroke probably provoked by his mental condition. Since the Spanish word also refers to overcrowding, one might say that his death is caused by the excessive internalization of New York's continuous movement in his brain. His death is, however, painless, and Antonio passes away with a smile that carves out his insanity in his deceased body. His manic fascination with modernization, bereft of any criticism, leaves the reader with an ambivalent impression. New York embodies life, movement, and progress, but at the same time all these aspects lead to the death of the character. Antonio's happiness relies on the illusion of a prosperity he never achieves in life, rendering the economic success promised by US capitalism as a chimera.

In contrast with Antonio's hallucinatory perception of the city, Dr Jiménez embodies a rational defence of New York's modernization. Jiménez is a Puerto Rican doctor to whom Jesusa turns for advice after Antonio's death. The dialogue between these two characters highlights the contrast between traditionalism and modernization that permeates the novel. Acting almost as a psychoanalyst — Jesusa does in fact end up dying after a mental breakdown — Jiménez tries to show to her the benefits of social change as well as the unstoppable expansion of modernization to the rest of the world, including Spain. In his view, New York represents not only technological advance, but also moral progress:

> admite usted el progreso material. Ya me concede algo. Y habrá de concederme todavía que el moral existe igualmente. Repare en que mis anticipados abandonan ciertas convenciones... Dejan con ello libres los instintos. Pues bien, progreso moral constituye el no ser hipócritas. (188)

> [you accept material progress. Now you have conceded something to me, and you have still to concede that morality exists too. Notice that my anticipators abandon certain conventions... They let their instincts go free with it... Well fine, moral progess constitutes not being hypocritical...]

Jiménez's counterdiscourse inverts the relation between civilization and tradition. Opposed to the false decency promoted by traditionalism, for which the repression and concealment of sexual desire is seen as the product of civilization, Jiménez regards progress as a movement towards individual freedom and the overcoming of atavist conventions. Accordingly, Jiménez especially dwells on aspects related to women's sexuality, as I will show in Chapter 3.

The term 'Anticípolis' for New York is in fact coined by the doctor. In his view, New York is the mirror of the future, an avant-garde city, a new civilization in which material progress goes hand in hand with social change:

> según la teoría de Jiménez, Nueva York se anticipaba. Iba delante, muy por delante de todas las demás ciudades en la marcha hacia lo futuro. Tanto materialmente, con la audacia de sus construcciones, como espiritualmente, con el frenesí de sus habitantes. Nueva York debiera llamarse Anticípolis, por ser la ciudad de la anticipación. (186)

> [according to Jiménez's theory, New York was ahead of its time. It went in front, far in front of all the other cities in their march towards the future. Materially, with the audacity of its constructions, as much as spiritually, with its inhabitants' frenzy. New York should be called Anticípolis, being the city of anticipation.]

Jiménez justifies the violence of *los anticipados* — a term used by the doctor to refer to New Yorkers — as a result of their fight against obsolete conventions. He compares New Yorkers to the pioneers who 'civilized' the Far West:

> no puede, por tanto, juzgarse aún a los anticipados. Y menos juzgarlos con arreglo a las antiguas codificaciones. Son como fueron los *pioneers*. Aquellos, en su avanzada, abrían camino. Talaban la selva para pasar y combatían contra cuanto el paso cerrábales. Si se les hubiese juzgado entonces, hubiera sido necesario condenarles por destructores de vidas vegetales, animales y hasta humanas. Hoy se les glorifica porque civilizaron el lejano Oeste. Actuales pioneros, estos anticipados luchan para imponer al mundo entero una nueva civilización. Cuando triunfen, dejarán de pelear. Entonces terminarán sus excesos. Y también entonces habrá de reconocerse lo beneficioso de que se excedieran. (224)

> [the anticipators cannot, therefore, yet be judged, and judged even less according to old codifications. They are as the pioneers were. The latter, in their advance, made a way forward. They cut down the jungle to get through and fought against everything which got in their way. If they had been judged at that time, it would have been necessary to condemn them as destroyers of plant, animal

and even human life. Today they are glorified because they civilized the Far West. The current pioneers, these anticipators, struggle in order to impose a new civilization upon the entire world. Then they triumph, they will stop fighting. That is when their excesses will cease and then the beneficial effect of them exceeding themselves will also have to be recognized.]

As one can see, the opposition between civilization and primitivism is again reversed. Following the logic of the comparison established by the doctor, the jungle that obstructs the way of the pioneers is not the result of a process of regression — as argued by Jesusa — but rather the weight of tradition, which is seen here as a set of uncivilized moral practices that hinders the achievement of individual freedom. Nevertheless, one must note the colonialist undertones behind Jiménez's praise of the violent move forward represented by modernization, in which the pioneers of European ancestry 'bring' civilization to the 'primitive' native Americans, whose life is 'destroyed' in the name of advancement. In comparison with Don Antonio's blind admiration for New York, Jiménez's modernizing ideal does not shy away from acknowledging the negative side of progress. However, he argues that the benefits exceed the disadvantages, and he believes that the path opened by this new civilization will soon inexorably reach Spain:

> le aseguró que, como Nueva York, iban siendo ya muchas ciudades. Lo serían, al cabo, todas [...] Jiménez sostuvo que hasta Oviedo. E indicó [...] que, si a Oviedo volviese, no lo encontraría como cuando salió de allí. También Oviedo había cambiado [...] rascacielos acaso no tuviese todavía, pero [...] casas nuevas se construían con más pisos que se construyeron los viejos caserones, haciendo notar que los rascacielos, con ser lo más visible, no son lo más característico de Nueva York, como lo probaba el que otras cosas producían mayores reacciones en el sentir forastero de doña Jesusa. (190–91)

> [he assured her that there were now many cities looking like New York. In the end all of them would do [...] Jiménez maintained that even Oviedo would. And he indicated [...] that if she returned to Oviedo, she would not find it like it was when she left there. Oviedo had changed too [...] perhaps it did not have skycrapers yet, but... [...] new houses were being built with more floors than the big old houses, pointing out that skyscrapers, being the most visible, are not the most characteristic feature of New York, as it proved that other things produced greater reactions in the foreign sensibility of Doña Jesusa.]

In contrast to the conflicting nature of the debates around modernization in Spain at the time, Jiménez is not suggesting Europeanization as the solution for Spanish backwardness but, taking this argument a step further, he argues that social change as well as technological advances will inevitably affect the country. Such an assertion turns the aforementioned debate into a sterile discussion. From his words we can infer that the question is not whether to incorporate Spain into modernization but, rather, that Spain must accept the unavoidable movement towards a society in which those aspects that provoked a negative reaction in Jesusa will replace moral conventions that have supported patriarchy and elitism.

The end of the novel emphasizes the ideas defended by Jiménez. Able neither to understand nor to adapt to New York's modernization, Jesusa suffers a mental breakdown. She collapses owing to her failure to keep her family within the

Spanish traditional morality she has internalized and has been instructed to perpetuate. Rosa, the eldest daughter, works as a fashion model and has an intense social and sexual life; Juan, the eldest son, marries an American woman who is pregnant by another man; Carlos gets involved in organized crime and divorces his wife; Mariíta starts a lesbian relationship with an older woman; and finally Pepín changes his religion to become a Protestant priest. Catholicism and the patriarchal family, pillars of traditionalist Spain, are thus dismantled by the new civilization. Jesusa's breakdown is aggravated by the hostile environment of the city:

> cerraba los ojos para no ver el tráfico torrencial y se tapaba los oídos para no sentir el ruido tumultuoso. Mas, aun yendo de ese modo, cegada y ensordecida, constantes estremecimientos la agitaban. Era que el hálito poderoso de la urbe daba en ella, imprimiéndole ese temblor. (248)

> [she would close her eyes so as not to see the torrential traffic and cover her ears so as not to hear the tumultuous noise. But, even in this way, blinded and deafened, constant shudders would shake her. It was what the powerful breath of the city produced in her, impressing this trembling upon her.]

Jesusa's overexcitement, caused by the excessive number of stimuli coming from the crowds, echoes George Simmel's essay 'Metropolis and Mental Life' (1903), where the German philosopher and sociologist compares the different responses of the human psyche to rural and urban environments. According to Simmel, the transient nature of urban life, and the consequent constant bombarding of violent stimuli to which the individual is exposed by the crowds, can result in mental disorders:

> if the unceasing external contact of numbers of persons in the city should be met by the same number of inner reactions as in the small town, in which one knows almost every person he meets and to each of whom he has a positive relationship, one would be completely atomized internally and would fall into an unthinkable mental condition. (2002: 15)

Jesusa's sick body becomes gradually weaker, and she dies. The diagnosis given by Jiménez goes beyond physical explanations and resorts to psychological ones — 'el estudio del alma' [the study of the soul] (249) — concluding that 'si cesó la vida de aquella mujer, fue porque no pudo acompasarse a la juntamente bárbara y civilizadora manera de vivir de quienes ocupan esa atrevida avanzada hacia el futuro que es la ciudad de la anticipación' [if the life of that woman came to an end, it was because she could not adjust to the equally barbaric and civilizing way of life of those who take part in that daring advance towards the future which is the city of anticipation.] (249). Following the interpretation of Jesusa as a symbolic character who embodies *casticista* views of Spanish national identity, her death can be seen in turn as an apocalyptic warning about Spain's degeneration. Before dying, Jesusa is secluded in a room where, protected from external influences, her condition seems to improve (248). Isolation does not, however, stop her physical decline, and her body ends up paralyzed. Her efforts to preserve tradition and her inability to adapt to modern times can be compared to an essentialist notion of Spanish national identity that was impervious to foreign influences. The implicit moral in Jesusa's death is therefore that Spain needs to open its doors both to technological and social modernization, since modernization will eventually reach that country, and if Spanish society is not renewed, the nation will perish: whether good or evil, moral or immoral, the progress embodied by New York is unstoppable, and Spain needs to free itself from 'las antiguas codificaciones' and embrace the future.

Nevertheless, the closing sentence of *Anticípolis* maintains the ambiguity towards modernization that pervades the novel. Resorting to an oxymoron, New York's 'anticipated society' is characterized by the narrator as both primitive and civilizing. Furthermore, despite their different attitudes towards New York, both Antonio and Jesusa die after a mental breakdown caused by the impact of progress on their minds. Consequently, and thanks to its polyphonic nature, the novel offers a mosaic of the views on modernization in Spain at the time. The final decision as to whether the incorporation of technological progress would bring social advances to Spain or endanger its national values is therefore left to the reader.

Mass society and Mechanization as a Threat to Social Elitism in *La ciudad automática*

Similarly to the image of New York as an 'advanced city' given in Oteyza's novel, the US metropolis is seen by Julio Camba as the embodiment of a 'pure present' that also represents the future in comparison with the rest of the world:

> visto desde Nueva York, el resto del mundo ofrece un espectáculo extemporáneo, semejante al que ofrecería una estrella que estuviese distanciada del punto de observación por muchos años luz: el espectáculo actual de una vida pretérita, quizás envidiable, pero imposible de vivir porque pertenece ya a la Historia. Es el momento presente sin más relación con el porvenir que con el pasado. El momento presente, íntegro, puro, total, aislado, desconectado. Al llegar aquí, la primera sensación no es la de haber dejado atrás otros países, sino otras épocas, épocas probablemente muy superiores a ésta, pero en todas las cuales nuestra vida constituía una ficción porque ninguna de ellas era realmente nuestra época. (1960: 10–11)

> [seen from New York, the rest of the world offers an untimely spectacle, similar to that which a star that was distanced from the point of observation by many light years would offer: the current spectacle of a past life, perhaps enviable but impossible to live because it now belongs to History. The present moment lacks just as much of a relationship with the future as it does with the past. The present, integral, pure, total, isolated and disconnected moment. On arriving here, the first sensation is not that of having left behind other countries, but other times; probably quite superior times to this one but in all of which our lives constituted a fiction, because none of them were really our time.]

In *La ciudad automática*, New York's modernity is again encapsulated by the innovative aspect of its architecture. In a statement that recalls Moreno Villa's text, Camba contrasts the new architectural style represented by the skyscraper with European buildings:

> el hecho de que el rascacielos haya adquirido un desarrollo tan rápido en América yo creo que no obedece tanto al deseo de superar las normas

arquitectónicas tradicionales como al más modesto y sencillo de destruirlas; pero el resultado es el mismo, y América empieza ya a tener una arquitectura propia. ¿Llegará esta arquitectura a ser en su día lo que han sido en los suyos la gótica o la románica? (63)

[the fact that the skyscraper has undergone such a rapid development in America leads me to believe that this is not due so much to the desire to surpass traditional architectural norms as to that of the modest and simple one to destroy them; but the result is the same, and America now begins to have its own architecture. Will this architecture one day be in its time what the Gothic and Romanesque were in theirs?]

Nevertheless, in this case the reference to destruction is not linked to innovation, but rather to regression: 'por mi parte, opino que sí, que llegará a eso y a mucho más. Para mí el porvenir de América es un porvenir de termitera, lo mismo que su pasado — civilizaciones maya, incaica, etc.–: una perfecta organización social y una arquitectura formidable' [for my part, I think that yes, that it will come to that and much more besides. For me the future of America is a future of a termites' nest, the same as its past — Mayan, Inca civilizations, etc. — perfect social organization and great architecture] (63). The view of New York given by Julio Camba juxtaposes present and past, modern and pre-Columbian eras. Paradoxically, the future of the United States — and hence of modernization — implies a return to the past. Accordingly, Camba reverses the image of New York's architecture as ground-breaking, and portrays the skyscrapers as old buildings:

¿de qué pasado remoto salen todos estos espectros? ¿A qué tumbas prehistóricas han sido arrancadas unas momias semejantes? ¿Qué diluvio universal ha conseguido evadir tales dinosaurios arquitectónicos? [...] no hay en todo el orbe estructuras que produzcan mayor impresión de arcaísmo y vetustez. (59)

[from what remote past do these spectres emerge? Out of what prehistoric tombs have such mummies been dragged? What universal flood has succeeded in sparing such architectural dinosaurs? [...] Throughout the globe there are no structures that produce a greater impression of archaism and antiquity.]

Resorting to sarcasm, the writer draws on the idea of American fickleness, of the need for constant change, to the extent that skyscrapers age rapidly because they are soon superseded by new and improved versions:

las pirámides egipcias no son viejas. Al contrario [...] constituyen todavía la última palabra en cuestión de pirámides, y quien habla de las pirámides egipcias habla de los templos mayas, o de las catedrales románicas o góticas. [...] hoy un *rascacielos* de hace diez años resulta tan anticuado por dentro como por fuera. Consideren ustedes que el *rascacielos* es una máquina, y que las máquinas envejecen en cuanto son superadas por otras. (59–60)

[the Egyptian pyramids are not old. On the contrary [...] they still embody the last word in the matter of pyramids, and whoever talks of Egyptian pyramids talks of Mayan temples, or Romanesque or Gothic cathedrals. [...] today a ten-year old skyscraper is as outdated inside as it is outside. Remember that the skyscraper is a machine, and machines grow old as soon as they are overtaken by others.]

The idea of the skyscrapers as machines, also present in *Pruebas de Nueva York*, adds yet another element to the paradox created by Camba. Whereas the 'immobility' of ancient constructions is regarded as an indication of eternal youth, the constant progress of technology implies continuous ageing. Behind Camba's sardonicism lies a fear of mechanization and modernization as a regression to primitivism. In the following description of New York's urban landscape, the impressive height of the buildings and the colourful beauty of the city lights are simultaneously identified with a futuristic scene and with the image of a primitive society:

> Nueva York [...] tan apretado entre sus dos grandes ríos, con sus enormes estructuras arquitectónicas y con la orgía de sus iluminaciones, es la ciudad más plástica del mundo, y el espectáculo que ofrece desde lo alto del Chrysler no tiene ponderación. ¡Qué maravilla, señores! Hasta que subí al Chrysler yo no había tenido nunca la emoción del mundo moderno, y estoy por decir que tampoco había tenido la del mundo antiguo, porque, en fin, la visión que se alcanza desde allí es tan extraordinaria que lo mismo puede servir como anticipación de lo futuro que como una reconstrucción de lo pasado. Uno sabe, naturalmente, que aquello es Nueva York, pero buscándole a Nueva York un término de relación, tan pronto se va al año 2200 de la Era Cristiana como al 1500 antes de Jesucristo. (67–68)

> [New York [...] so squeezed between its two great rivers, with its enormous architectural structures and with the orgy of its lighting, is the most expressive city in the world, and the spectacle that it offers from the top of the Chrysler Building has no equal. How wonderful, gentlemen! Until I went to the top of the Chrysler Building, I had never experienced the excitement of the modern world, and I should say that neither had I experienced that of the old world, because, in short, the view that is enjoyed from there is so extraordinary that it can serve as an anticipation of the future as much as a reconstruction of the past. One knows, naturally, that that is New York, but in seeking a point of comparison for New York, one must go just as much to the year 2200 of the Christian era as to 1500 before Christ.]

New York is compared to societies that pre-existed the Spanish invasion of America, and were subdued under the name of progress and civilization. At first sight, it seems that Camba praises these indigenous cultures — 'perfecta organización social', 'arquitectura formidable' (63) –, but a closer look unveils the perversity of his logic, as the writer suggests that while modernization separates the United States from Europe, it also brings it closer to American aboriginal civilizations (69). Such identification of the United States with a supposedly uneducated and primitive society reinforces the view of Europe as the cradle of progress, with the intention of strengthening the alleged superiority of the 'West', threatened by the manifest development of the 'Big Other'. The distrust of technology in European countries — as a source of dehumanization and one of the reasons for the decadence of Western civilization — influences Camba's perception of the United States as a society in which exacerbated modernization provokes the regression to a pre-civilized state.

Camba sees the gigantic stature of American architecture as an expression of massification: 'es una civilización de masas y no de individuos. Es una civilización de grandes estructuras arquitectónicas. Es una civilización de insectos' [it is a civilization of masses and not of individuals. It is a civilization of great architectural structures. It is a civilization of insects] (69–70). According to the writer, in New York, 'las hormigas, sin dejar de ser hormigas, crecen y adquieren la proporción espantosa de seres humanos' [ants, without leaving their nests, grow and take on the frightening proportions of human beings] (68). The comparison between the 'masses' and insects is not accidental. Like insects, the 'swarming masses' were seen to be acting as a group, lacking individuality and intelligence (Berman 1999: 28). And, as we have seen, Camba sees American architecture as a termite hill:

> y ya sé que los insectos gozan actualmente de gran reputación, pero a mí me parece tan sólo un resultado de la influencia que América ejerce en el mundo. Yo creo que en este asunto hay dos normas a seguir: una, la de observar a los insectos, y al ver que tienen, por ejemplo, una organización social más perfecta que la nuestra, atribuirles una inteligencia superior a la humana; otra, observar a los seres humanos y, al verles proceder como insectos, deducir que proceden de una manera estúpida. (70)

> [and I already know that today insects have a great reputation, but to me it seems to be just the result of the influence that America wields in the world. I believe that in this matter there are two norms to follow: one, that of observing the insects, and if we see that they have, for example, a more perfect social organization than ours, attribute to them a higher intelligence than that of humans; two, observe human beings and, if we see that they act like insects, deduce that they behave in a stupid manner.]

This quotation contains a reference to the studies of insects carried out by Jean-Henri Fabre [*Social Life in the Insect World*, 1911] and Maurice Maeterlinck [*The Life of the Bee*, 1901]. The writer later mentions these scientists by name:

> por mi parte, yo no acepto más que esta última norma, por mucho Fabre y por mucho Maeterlinck con que se venga, y no es que los insectos me parezcan idiotas. Me basta, sencillamente, con que sean insectos. La idiotez, en último término, es una forma, aunque negativa, de la inteligencia humana, y los insectos, por el hecho de ser insectos, no sólo quedan al margen de nuestra inteligencia, sino que quedan también al margen de nuestra idiotez. (70)

> [for my part, I can only accept the latter norm, in spite of how much Fabre and Maeterlinck I come across, and it is not because insects seem like idiots to me. It is enough for me quite simply that they are insects. Stupidity, ultimately, is a form, albeit negative, of human intelligence, and insects, in being insects, do not only remain on the edge of our intelligence, but also remain on the edge of our stupidity.]

Camba refuses to accept the idea of a society in which the individual — Ortega's 'minorías selectas' — must comply with the wishes of a multitude that allegedly acts like an indissoluble being. This idea, widespread in Europe, is also present in Georges Duhamel's *America the Menace*:

> in the United States, that far Western land which has already made us aware of the promises of the future, what strikes the European traveller is the progressive approximation of human life to what we know of the way of life of insects [...] the same submission of every one to those obscure exigencies which Maeterlinck names the genius of the hive or of the ant-hill. (1974: 194)

The characterization of the 'masses' as 'insects' creates an opposition between the multitude and the individual — 'the intellectual'–, in which the former is depicted as an unintelligent and primitive 'Other' that threatens the order established by civilization, that is, the hegemony of the minority. The fear of a society that turns into a swarm or a termite mound is also a theme developed by Ortega y Gasset in *La rebelión de las masas*. The Spanish philosopher fears that a similar type of organization would take root in Europe and lead to the end of civilization:

> la cosa es horrible, pero no creo que exagera la situación en la que van hallándose casi todos los europeos. En una prisión donde se han amontonado muchos más presos de los que caben, ninguno puede mover un brazo ni una pierna por propia iniciativa, porque chocaría con los cuerpos de los demás. En tal circunstancia, los movimientos tienen que ejecutarse en común, y hasta los músculos respiratorios tienen que funcionar a ritmo de reglamento. Esto sería Europa convertida en termitera. (2007b: 68)
>
> [the matter is horrible, but I do not believe that I am exaggerating about the situation in which almost all Europeans continue to find themselves. It is a prison where many more prisoners are piled up than for whom there is space; nobody can move an arm or a leg by choice because they would knock against the bodies of others. In such circumstances, movements have to be made in common, and even the respiratory muscles have to function to the rhythm of regulation. This would be Europe turned into a termites' nest.]

Similarly, Ortega also relates the rise of a mass society to the construction of gigantic buildings, and compares his contemporary age to the decline of ancient civilization such as the Roman Empire:

> este es el hecho formidable de nuestro tiempo, descrito sin ocultar la brutalidad de su apariencia. [...] Si hemos de hallar algo semejante, tendríamos que brincar fuera de nuestra historia y sumergirnos en un orbe, en un elemento vital, completamente distinto al nuestro, tendríamos que insinuarnos en el mundo antiguo y llegar a su hora de declinación. La historia del Imperio Romano es también la historia de la subversión, del imperio de las masas, que absorben y anulan a las minorías dirigentes y se colocan en su lugar. Entonces se produce también el fenómeno de la aglomeración, del lleno. Por eso, como ha observado muy bien Spengler, hubo que construir, al modo de ahora, enormes edificios. La época de las masas es la época de lo colosal. (2007b: 87)
>
> [this is the formidable event of our time, described without hiding the brutality of its appearance. If we have to find something similar, we would have to leap beyond our history and submerge ourselves in an orb, in a vital element, completely different to our own; we would have to work our way into the ancient world and arrive at the hour of its decline. The history of the Roman Empire is also the history of subversión, of the empire of the masses, who absorb and anull leading minorities and take their place. Then the phenomenon of agglomeration, of being full, occurs. For this reason, as has been well observed by Spengler, enormous buildings had to be built in today's fashion. The age of the masses is the age of the colossal.]

Spengler also saw in the mammoth buildings of the modern city a symptom of decadence. The Spenglerian Cosmopolis is a symptom of the final stage of civilization, in which 'the Culture-man whom the land has spiritually formed is seized and possessed by his own creation, the City, and is made into its creature, its executive organ, and finally its victim' (Spengler 1926: 99). The German philosopher argues that the destiny of such a colossal metropolis is its own annihilation and the final destruction of the civilization from which it was originated:

> this, then, is the conclusion of the city's history; growing from primitive barter-centre to Culture-city and at last to world-city, it sacrifices first the blood and soul of its creators to the needs of its majestic evolution, and then the last flower of that growth to the spirit of Civilization and so, doomed, moves on to final self-destruction. (1926: 107)

Capitalism and mechanization are regarded by Camba as the main factors for the rise of the 'masses' in the United States. Most of his criticism of 'la ciudad automática' is based on his rejection of 'la serie' and 'la producción en cadena', which in his view create a dehumanized society of enslaved individuals. The dominant principle of American industry is, according to the writer, to standardize men in order to sell standardized goods (126). One of Camba's main concerns is the erasure of individuality in favour of a standardized society, where — in an image reminiscent of Fritz Lang's *Metropolis* (1927) — machines and human beings subvert their nature and become 'robots that look like people and people that look like robots' (142). This seems to be the fate of the modern world. In his belief, there are two different civilizations — Russia and the United States — that will rule the rest of the planet on this premise, since for Camba there are no differences between capitalism and communism:

> no hay más que un obstáculo que pueda oponerse a la americanización del mundo: Rusia. Si el mundo logra liberarse de la dominación capitalista americana será para caer fatalmente bajo la dominación comunista rusa y viceversa […] Ambas representan la máquina contra el hombre, la estandardización contra la diferenciación, la masa contra el individuo, la cantidad contra la calidad, el automatismo contra la inteligencia. (87)
>
> [there is no more than one obstacle that can get in the way of the Americanization of the world: Russia. If the world succeeds in freeing itself from American capitalist domination, it will be to fall fatally under Russian communist domination and vice-versa. Both represent machine against man, standardization against differentiation, the mass against the individual, quantity against quality, automatism against intelligence.]

Camba fears the state's control over the individual:

> que se empiece por estandardizar a los hombres o que se proceda al contrario, el resultado es igual. La libertad desaparece, y no ya la libertad política de hablar o votar, sino la libertad humana de ser de un modo u de otro (89)
>
> [whether we begin to standardize men or undertake the contrary, the result is the same. Freedom disappears, and not the political freedom of talking and voting, but the human freedom of being one way or another.]

However, despite his defence of individual rights, Camba distrusts American democracy. His view of New York as a mechanical city relies on the fact that 'toda América es una gran maquinaria donde el movimiento de cada persona está siempre determinado por el movimiento de otra, donde todo funciona o se para a la vez' [all America is a great mechanism where the movement of each person is always determined by the movement of another, where everything works or stops at the same time] (141). This is his primary concern, as he states: 'al hablar, como hago tan a menudo, del carácter mecánico que tiene la vida en América, no quiero decir precisamente, que aquí haya muchas máquinas o que se haga todo a máquina. Eso sería lo de menos' [when speaking, as I do so often, of the mechanical character that life possesses in America, I do not mean exactly that here there are many machines or that everything is done by machine. This is the least important] (140–41). The United States is seen as a mechanism whose movement is determined by the combined action of the group, not by individual decisions imposed by the minority. Once again, concerns about the growing power of the 'masses' in the political sphere match Ortega y Gasset's distrust of a democratic system in which the 'masses' resist the authority of the political elite:

> al amparo del principio liberal y de la norma jurídica podían actuar y vivir las minorías. Democracia y ley, convivencia legal, eran sinónimos. Hoy asistimos al triunfo de la hiperdemocracia en que la masa actúa directamente sin ley, por medio de materiales presiones, imponiendo sus aspiraciones y sus gustos. Es falso interpretar las situaciones nuevas como si la masa se hubiese cansado de la política y encargase a personas especiales su ejercicio. Todo lo contrario. Eso era lo que antes acontecía, eso era la democracia liberal. La masa presumía que, al fin y al cabo, con todos sus defectos y lacras, las minorías de los políticos entendían un poco más de los problemas públicos que ella. Ahora, en cambio, cree la masa que tiene derecho a imponer y dar vigor de ley a sus tópicos de café. Y dudo que haya habido otras épocas de la historia en que la muchedumbre llegase a gobernar tan directamente como en nuestro tiempo. Por eso hablo de hiperdemocracia. (Ortega y Gasset 2007: 86)

> [minorities could act and live under the protection of liberal principles and legal norms. Democracy and law, legal co-existence, were synonyms. Today we take part in the triumph of hyperdemocracy in which the mass acts directly without the law, through material pressure, imposing their inspirations and tastes. It is false to interpret new situations as if the mass had grown tired of politics and entrusted its exercise to special people. The complete opposite is true. That would be what happened before; that was liberal democracy. The mass presumed that, after all is said and done, with all their spots and blemishes, the politicians' minorities understood a little more about public problems than it did. Now, however, it believes that the mass has a right to impose and give the full force of the law to their café clichés. I doubt that there have been other ages of history in which the multitude ended up ruling as directly as in our time. That is why I talk of hyperdemocracy.]

Significantly, within his examination of US society, Camba devotes an entire chapter to criticizing the education policies of the Spanish Second Republic. This chapter, entitled 'El analfabetismo, cantidad positiva' [Positive Qualities of Illiteracy], comprises a tirade against the efforts of the Republican government to reduce illiteracy in the country. By contrast, Camba regards the suppression of illiteracy as a threat to the essence of the Spanish 'race':

muy bien que en los Estados Unidos, el país de los trajes hechos y las ropas hechas, la gente utilice también pensamientos de fábrica. En este país el desarrollo de la instrucción primaria está justificado por la necesidad de destruir el pensamiento individual, pero España es el país más individualista del mundo, y no se puede ir así como así contra el genio de una raza. Ahí cada cual quiere pensar por su cuenta, y hace bien. (96)

[it is very good that in the United States, the country of tailored suits and clothes, people also use factory-made thoughts. In this country the development of primary education is justified by the need to destroy individual thought, but Spain is the most individualist country in the world, and one cannot go against a race's disposition just like that. There everyone wants to think in their own way, and good on them.]

He argues for preserving the integrity of the 'Spanish soul', which he identifies with the individual wisdom of illiterate sailors and peasants, who are not influenced by the ideas 'imposed' by education (96). Camba's point of view seems to stress the need to protect the uneducated Spaniards from the alleged pernicious influence of the liberal intellectuals of the Republic, or even of foreign ideas:

en España sólo los analfabetos conservan íntegra la inteligencia, y si algunas conversaciones españolas me han producido un placer verdaderamente intelectual, no han sido las del Ateneo o la *Revista de Occidente*, como las de esos marineros y labradores [...] Convendría dejar ya de considerar el analfabetismo español como una cantidad negativa y empezar a estimarlo en su aspecto positivo y de afirmación individual contra la estandarización del pensamiento. (96)

[In Spain only the illiterate retain complete intelligence, and if some Spanish conversations have produced true intellectual pleasure in me, they have not been those of the Ateneo or *Revista de Occidente* as much as those with sailors and labourers [...] It might now be advisable to stop regarding Spanish illiteracy as a negative quantity and begin to value it in its positive dimension and as an individual affirmation against the standardization of thought.]

The references to the *Ateneo* and to the *Revista de Occidente* point Camba's criticism at intellectuals such as Ortega y Gasset, who argued for Spain's Europeanization. Moreover, the writer associates the supposed benefits of illiteracy as repository of a 'true Spanishness' with colonial expansion in America and therefore with the imperial myth at the core of *casticista* views of national identity:

Pizarro firmó con una cruz el acta notarial en que comprometía a descubrir un imperio llamado Birú o Perú [...] Y no es que Pizarro haya descubierto el Perú a pesar de ser un analfabeto. Es que, probablemente, sólo muy lejos de la letra de molde se pueden forjar caracteres de tanto temple. (97)

[Pizarro signed the affidavit in which he undertook to discover the empire known as Biru or Peru with a cross [...] It is not that Pizarro discovered Peru in spite of being illiterate. Rather, it is probably that characters of so much mettle can be only forged very far from the printed word.]

Camba's reference to Pizarro connects his criticism of universal literacy with his previous comparison between the United States and pre-Columbian civilizations, such as the Incas. The identification between the conquistador and uneducated people reinforces the imperial rhetoric in which the mythicized peasant embodies the values of bravery, and 'racial' purity promoted by *casticista* notions of national identity. Such a construction perpetuates the Spanish alleged superiority and spirituality not only over the supposedly barbaric peoples dominated in the so-called 'discovery' of America, but also in relation to the menacing 'new primitivism' contradictorily embodied by US modernization. However, the writer is aware that Spain could not function normally if nobody knew how to read and write (97). The absurd solution given by Camba is blatantly based on pure elitism:

> mi ideal con respecto a España es éste: mientras no se descubra un procedimiento para que sean los analfabetos quienes escriban, que el arte de leer se convierta en una profesión y que sólo puedan ejercerlo algunos hombres debidamente autorizados al efecto por el Estado. (97)
>
> [my ideal with respect to Spain is this: as long as a procedure that allows the illiterate to be those who write is not discovered, the art of reading should become a profession and only a few men duly authorised for the purpose by the state should be able to practise it.]

The contradiction is obvious. Although the writer considers that a sort of 'true wisdom' resides in the poor illiterate people, only a few individuals should be granted access to education and therefore to knowledge. Eventually, although conveyed through a paradox intended to trigger a humorous effect, his ideas coincide with those of the intellectuals he despises: a leading minority must be in power.

Furthermore, limited access to education by a minority also guarantees economic and therefore class differences between the elite and the people. US capitalism and mass production facilitated the access of the working class to technological advances and its participation in the economy of the country. As Camba states in relation to the aftermath of the Wall Street Crash of 1929:

> todos estos pequeños menestrales — los limpiabotas, las criadas, los chicos de recados, etc. — se sacaban por aquel entonces sus buenos cien o doscientos dólares una semana con otra, y la vida no tenía limitaciones para ellos. [...] si las gentes no pudieran arruinarse aquí de la noche a la mañana, tampoco podrían enriquecerse de la mañana a la noche. (15)
>
> [all of these small artisans (shoeshines, maids, messenger boys, etc.), would earn at that time their good one hundred or two hundred dollars from one week to another, and life had no limitations for them. If people could not be ruined here overnight, neither could they get rich from morning to night.]

However, such class mobility is not possible in Spain, where class division responds to a 'natural order':

> cuando se enriquece un pobre en España o cuando se arruina un rico parece que se hubiera subvertido, no ya el orden social, sino el propio orden de la Naturaleza. [...] En España uno es rico o pobre como es alto o bajo, chato o narigón y de ojos negros o de ojos azules. Es rico o pobre, generalmente por herencia y por una herencia que tiene todos los caracteres de la herencia fisiológica. (16)

> [when a poor person gets rich in Spain or when a rich man is ruined, it seems that not so much the social as the natural order has been subverted [...] In Spain one is rich or poor just like one is tall or short, flat-nosed or big-nosed and dark-eyed or blue-eyed. One is rich or poor generally through inheritance or through an inheritance that has all the characteristics of physiological inheritance.]

The reference to an inherited social position is reminiscent of Moreno Villa's diatribe against the *hortera* and the *ganapán*, as well as the aristocratic stand personified by Doña Jesusa in *Anticípolis*. In this light, the contradictions behind the view of the United States as a civilization in the process of regression to primitivism through mechanization and massification displayed in *La ciudad automática* reveal the danger that similar processes could entail for the elitism of Spanish society. Standardization would erase the remnants of Spain's imperial glory, still alive in the Spanish character embodied by the mythical figure of the wise and brave peasant, free from foreign influences, seen as a symbol of a pre-industrialized society. Consequently, Spanish people must remain attached to a fixed social position determined by inheritance and nature. Otherwise, they would turn into the primitive and dangerous 'masses', which, through their demands for social equality, would destroy the culture and the social system that supports the hegemony of the ruling elite.

In these three texts, New York — and by extension the United States — is depicted as a futuristic city both with respect to its technological advances and to the transformation of social practices, which, contradictorily, is regressing to primitivism. The initial premise from which the New York narratives of Moreno Villa, Oteyza and Camba depart is similar: US technological excess has produced a new type of society in which the accelerated pace of the metropolis, the mechanization of daily life, mass production, class mobility, and democracy have subverted the social order created by civilization in Europe. The leading minorities are threatened by the increasing power of the 'masses', which may give way to a dehumanized 'swarm' where difference and individuality are erased in favour of an allegedly blunt and grey equality. Similar concerns were expressed by European and Spanish intellectuals, notably by José Ortega y Gasset. Therefore, the views of mechanization and massification developed in these three case studies must be inscribed within the European crisis of modernity and the crisis of national identity in Spain. Such a connection, however, manifests itself differently in each text.

First of all, *Pruebas de Nueva York* offers a fluid perspective. Initially, technological innovation, as embodied by the skyscrapers, is regarded with ambivalence when compared with Spain. Moreno Villa seems to praise the developments of New York's architecture from a functionalist point of view. However, he reacts against the consequences of such advances in social life, which threaten the elitist authority of the intellectual minority and challenge the patriarchal family, seen as the basis of the national community. Furthermore, preconceptions of the United States as a primitive society lead the writer to portray New Yorkers as a violent 'mass' lacking individuality. Nonetheless, the advantages of progress become especially visible for the writer after his return to Spain, where discourses of 'Otherness' are questioned by the poverty of his own country. Although Moreno Villa never abandons such a discourse completely, by the end of the text there is certain empathy with New York, and concerns about the threat posed by mass society and mechanization to Spanish national identity are substituted by criticism of *regenerationist* projects and the view that the country could benefit from modernization.

Anticípolis presents a polyphonic view of New York, in this case through the different opinions about modernization expressed by the characters of the novel. The strongest rejection of technology and social change comes from Doña Jesusa, who represents a traditionalist notion of Spanish national identity. However, her criticism of New York as a civilization in a process of regression towards primitivism is also in tune with concerns about mass society as the cause of Western decadence expressed by liberal intellectuals such as Ortega y Gasset. This fact shows the role played by discourses of 'Otherness' in the construction of European identity, which liberal projects of national regeneration saw as the solution for Spain's backwardness. Her husband Don Antonio, on the other hand, represents a different perspective, that of an unconditional surrender to the promises of US capitalism. The role played by modernization in the death of both characters stresses the multilayered structure of the narration, in which there is no clear position for or against New York, but rather, the acceptance of the inexorable influence of modernization in the rest of the world. That is precisely the stand defended by Dr Jiménez, who offers a more rational and balanced analysis of New York. Jiménez supports the social change brought about by modernizing processes, which is not regarded as regression but, on the contrary, as inevitable progress. Although he is also aware of the negative effects — mostly temporary — that such processes can provoke, in his view Spain too will benefit from its influence. Consequently, *Anticípolis*'s multiperspectivism works as a testimony of the different positions towards modernization in Spain.

Finally, *La ciudad automática* represents a strong declaration against mechanization, mass society, and standardization. The comparison between New York and pre-Columbian civilizations is used by Julio Camba to elaborate on the widespread view of the United States as a primitive society. In tune with intellectuals such as Ortega y Gasset and Spengler, the writer sees the rise of the 'masses' and New York's colossal buildings as indications of a civilization in decline. Camba focuses his concern especially on the standardization of the individual by the means of mass production. At first sight, it seems that the writer defends freedom and individuality against the control of the citizens by the state. However, a closer analysis reveals his criticism of equality and therefore of democracy. In his opinion, mass society embodies the threat both to social elitism and to the specificity of an alleged purity of the Spanish character, representative of a traditionalist notion of national identity encapsulated by Spain's imperial past. His traditionalist attack on the education policies of the Second Republic, however, ends up converging with the ideas of the liberal intellectuals he criticizes. In the end, Camba's criticism of technology and massification is the expression of contemporary concerns about the erosion of the opposition between the elite and the 'masses' caused by capitalism, democracy, and mass production.

In tune with concerns of the subversive power of the 'masses', the views of women's emancipation given in these texts also reflect fears of regression and social destabilization. As will be seen in the next chapter, women's access to the civil sphere — epitomized by the figure of the American 'modern woman' — was seen as a threat to the patriarchal system behind both traditionalist and liberal conceptions of Spanish national identity.

Notes to Chapter 2

1. Concerns about Spain's degeneration and claims for its regeneration were not new, however. Before the military defeat by the United States, the idea of a Spanish crisis and claims for national regeneration had been reflected in texts such as, amongst others, Evaristo Ventosa's *La regeneración de la patria* [*The Regeneration of the Fatherland*] (1860), Lucas Mallada's *Los males de la patria* [*The Fatherland's Illnesses*](1890), Miguel de Unamuno's *En torno al casticismo* [*Around 'Casticismo'*] (1895), and Ángel Ganivet's *Idearium Español* [*Spanish Ideology*] (1897).
2. García Lorca's verses convey the fear of losing one's individuality amongst the drunken mass on Coney Island (1998: 143–44).
3. Moreno Villa's drawing resembles a series of views of the East River painted in the mid-1920s by the American artist Georgia O'Keefe, as well as Edward Hopper's *East River* (1923). Despite the similarities, the Spanish writer does not refer to either of these painters as an influence. The drawing also presents a mysterious word, 'Linit' superimposed on the image of the factory, which could be a misspelled form of 'Limit' or 'Lignite'.
4. Moreno Villa's articles and reviews about architecture remained overlooked by scholarship until 2010, when Humberto Huergo Cardoso collected them in the volume *Función contra forma y otros escritos sobre arquitectura madrileña 1927–1935* [*Function against Form and Other Essays about Madrid's Architecture 1927–1935*].
5. 'Mermedad' is not included in the RAE Dictionary. I have interpreted this word as a misspelling of 'enfermedad'.

CHAPTER 3

❖

Images of the Modern Woman: The Challenge to the Patriarchal Nation

> Oigo decir a la mujer americana que ella toma lo que quiere y en el momento que lo desea; que no se entrega, ni se da, sino que agarra
>
> [I hear it said to the American woman that she takes what she wants and when she wants it; that she doesn't yield, or give in, but holds on]
>
> José Moreno Villa

All four New York narratives studied in this book pay substantial attention to gender issues, represented by the rebellious image of the American 'modern woman'. In these texts, the increasing entry of women into the public sphere is opposed to the submissive role traditionally given to femininity by patriarchy in Europe. This chapter will examine how New York narratives showcase the centrality of gender in debates about Spanish national identity in the first decades of the twentieth century, when patriarchal values were at the core of both traditionalist and liberal views of the nation. On the one hand, traditionalists regarded women's emancipation as a menace to the Catholic family values, seen as an essential characteristic of Spanishness. Liberals, on the other hand, saw the entry of women into the public sphere as endangering the principles of European modernity that they aimed to introduce in the country.

The view of New York and modernization developed in José Moreno Villa's and Julio Camba's travelogues takes issue with the rise of this new type of woman, the opposite in many ways of the concept of femininity promoted by the patriarchal establishment in Spain. Significantly, the 'modern woman' is embodied by one of the main characters in both Teresa Escoriaza's and Luis de Oteyza's fictional narratives, which offer a strong contrast with traditional images of womanhood.

A Disruptive Womanhood: European Views of the American 'Modern Woman'

In Europe, traditional gender roles were violently debated at the beginning of the twentieth century, challenging the nineteenth-century ideal of womanhood embodied in the figure of the 'Angel in the House', an image popularized by Coventry Patmore's eponymous poem (1854). The 'perfect wife' described by Patmore was a self-sacrificing, docile, devout, and pure woman under the authority of her husband, 'a creature in constant need of male supervision and protection'

(Noddings 1991: 59). The trope of the 'Angel in the House' reflected a biosocial conception of gender that established fixed roles according to a series of binary oppositions. On the one hand, the social category of 'man' was identified with the public sphere, and hence with the workplace, politics, civil life, society, and rationality. On the other, the category of 'woman' was located in the private sphere and therefore was associated with the home, family, nature, and emotion. Women were portrayed as irrational beings, dominated by passion — in opposition to men's rationality — defined by their bodily natures, and incapable of contributing to civil life as individuals, a view supported by male theoreticians of Western modernity such as Rousseau, Hobbes, and Freud (Pateman 1988: 25; Yuval-Davies 1997: 2). The result of this dualistic logic is the confinement of women to the private space. For Rousseau, the family is an expression of the order of nature, where 'age naturally takes precedence over youth and males over females'; henceforth his view of the family 'is necessarily patriarchal', as are the foundations of civil life, and therefore the basis of the nation (Pateman 1988: 20). Despite claims for freedom, equality, and fraternity, the project of Western modernity limited the access to citizenship to an elite of white heterosexual bourgeois European men. Nira Yuval-Davies has shown how conventional nationalist movements regard nations as a prolongation of familial bonds, establishing a gendered division of labour in which men are responsible for protecting the *womenandchildren*, the term used by this scholar to highlight the separation between public and private spheres established by patriarchy (1997: 15). The nation is referred to as 'the fatherland', and it is also imagined as 'the brotherhood' or a fraternity: there is no space in the nation for sisterhood (Eisenstein 2000: 41). Cloistered in the family home and restricted to their roles as 'mothers' and 'wives', women carry the 'burden of representation' and become 'reproducers' of the national identity (Yuval-Davies 1997: 45). However, in spite of women's confinement to the private sphere, nationalisms also promote the representation of womanhood as a national emblem, notoriously in the image of the 'motherland'. Drawing on the same private/public dichotomy, women are in this case presented as the embodiment of both the nation-state and its cultural values. In such gendered national allegory, women — as mothers and wives — are given the task of reproducing the nation in literal and figurative terms, being therefore expected to convey the values that sustain the national identity to their children, including the patriarchal order on which nationalism rests (Peterson 2000: 66; Yuval-Davies 1997: 45; Warner 1996: 12). The image of the 'mother-nation' not only goes against 'the varied realities of women's experiences in society', but is also a mask adopted by patriarchy (Eisenstein 2000: 41). Images of womanhood are therefore deployed to embody the values of the patriarchal system, giving way to a paradoxical construction, in which a false woman's body incarnates, in a manner, I suggest, not dissimilar to processes of cross-dressing, the social order created by men. Therefore, 'the fantasmatic woman' that 'becomes the body of the nation' (Eisenstein 2000: 43) is the disguise taken by patriarchy in order to continue its position of superiority.

However, women's entry into the workforce during the First World War fostered claims for civil equality between the two sexes. This period also saw an unprecedented number of women entering higher education, a rise in the number of women remaining childless, and also an increased visibility of lesbian relationships (Kaplan 1992: 18). Women's widening access to the job market provided them with economic independence and challenged social conventions. The 'Angel in the House' trope was metaphorically killed by Virginia Woolf in her speech 'Professions for Women' (delivered in 1931 and published posthumously), where the novelist tells of her experience as a professional writer in order to demonstrate the falsehood behind traditional images of women as incapable of participating in the civil sphere (Woolf 1979). The submissive nature of the 'Angel in the House', unselfishly devoted to her husband and family, is revealed by Woolf as a hindrance to women's development as individuals, since the 'Angel' 'never had a mind or a wish of her own, but preferred to sympathize always with the minds and wishes of others' (1979: 59). Therefore, the only way of liberating women from mindless obedience to men is to revolt against the imposition of such a deceitful image of femininity invented by patriarchy:

> I turned upon her and caught her by the throat. I did my best to kill her. My excuse, if I were to be had up in a court of law, would be that I acted in self-defence. Had I not killed her she would have killed me. She would have plucked the heart out of my writing (1979: 59).

First-wave feminism replaced the 'Angel in the House' with new forms of femininity, especially the figure of the 'modern woman', which became one of the icons of social modernization and was perceived as yet another sign of the decadence of the West by male intellectuals (Showalter 1996: 10). Elaine Showalter suggests the works of writers such as Émile Zola and Maurice Barrès, amongst others, as examples of 'anti-feminist literature' in France. She also refers to 'anti-suffrage groups' organized in England and the United States. Women, responsible for engendering the members of the nation and inculcating the values of national culture, were then seen to endanger the 'natural' order from which the nation stemmed — the family — if they abandoned their duties and rebelled against their masters, namely their fathers, husbands, brothers, and sons.

As the principles of patriarchy were gradually challenged, women's increasing independence was criticized as a harbinger of degeneration. Male reactions against the modern woman were, according to Showalter, twofold. On the one hand, there was an 'intensified valorisation of male power, and expressions of anxiety about waning virility' (1996: 10). On the other hand, it also generated a series of images of womanhood as a violent threat that expressed 'an exaggerated horror of its castrating potential' (1996: 10). Referring to the representations of woman as devil, vampire, castrator, medusa, flower of evil, killer, and idol of perversity, John Jervis argues that these metaphors reflect the prevailing view in modernism, according to which those women who had abandoned their fixed role in the private sphere 'had inevitably regressed to the bestial' (1999: 114). Parallels with the depiction of non-European societies and the 'masses' are evident. As Bretz points out:

> the link between women, the lower class, and primitive peoples has a long history in Western thought and continues in Freud's description of female sexuality as the 'dark continent' of psychology [...] and in Ortega y Gasset's association of women, non-Europeans, and the lower classes. (2001: 373)

Similarly, Andreas Huyssen argues that the 'masses' were portrayed in European political, physiological, and aesthetic discourse as a hysterical 'feminine threat', condensing the fear of both women and the 'masses' as the 'fear of nature out of control, a fear of the unconscious, of sexuality, of the loss of identity and stable ego boundaries in the mass' (1988: 52). The challenge to binary oppositions — civilization/nature, public/private, and man/woman — is at the root of the crisis of the project of the Enlightenment, since it questions those structures — the patriarchal family and the nation — considered to be the foundations of Western modernity. Negative reactions towards the 'modern woman' are therefore another expression of the anxieties prompted by the crisis of modernity in Europe.

The dominant discourse on gender in early twentieth-century Spain centred on the role of women as the 'Ángel del Hogar' — the Spanish crystallization of the 'Angel in the House' trope (Kirkpatrick 2003: 30–31). Susan Kirkpatrick (2003: 32) and Rebeca Arce Pinedo (2008: 116–17) explain the confinement of women to the private sphere as an expression of the values promoted by conservative and religious sectors, which resorted to traditionalist representations of womanhood in order to define a cultural identity based on the moral hegemony of Catholicism. The idea of 'hogar' or 'familia' was essential for this position and it was women, as 'Ángel del Hogar', who were held responsible for guarding the traditional model and preserving Catholic values by conveying them to their children. The close links between Catholicism and the right became especially evident during Primo de Rivera's dictatorship, for which the 'salvation' of the country depended on the 're-Christianization' of Spanish society (Arce Pinedo 2008: 156).

Nevertheless, despite the strong patriarchal mentality permeating the views of the Spanish Catholic Church, the man/woman opposition and the gendered division of spheres did not only respond to religious influences. As Bretz argues, the dichotomy between tradition and modernity is not a valid approach for understanding the construction of gender in this period (2001: 375). For Spanish liberals too — from radical democrats to constitutional monarchists — the construction of a modern nation-state was linked to the reinforcement of a masculine moral order in which

> a female out of control was not only disorderly; she was dishonourable. And the protection of honour was in Spain, central to the quest of an appropriate marriage of liberty and order — two classic nineteenth century ideals that defined the struggle to forge a liberal state everywhere in modern Europe. (White 1999: 233)

When in 1929 the global economic crisis brought an end to Primo de Rivera's regime, which had been unable to provide solutions for the devaluation of the *peseta*, the arrival of the Second Republic and its modernizing project two years later was welcomed with great enthusiasm by the liberals. The ideologues of the Republic, heirs of Francisco Giner de los Ríos's *Institución Libre de Enseñanza*, undertook a profound transformation of the country, with special interest in the secularization of Spain. Republican modernizing policies also focused on the expansion of civil rights, and the Constitution of 1931 'gave all Spaniards over the age of 23 the right to vote and established the complete equality of all individuals before the law, regardless of sex, race and social standing' (Davies 1998: 105). However, even those liberals who emphasized that equality was a core characteristic of a progressive democracy feared that the feminine vote could result in an advantage for their right-wing rivals, an idea shared by most Spanish conservative parties, who therefore voted in favour of women's suffrage (Keene 1999: 330–31). This assumption stemmed from the idea that women, regarded as an infantile mass, 'lacked the true qualities of political citizenship [...]. Ruled by their emotions and weak in reasoning, they were generally presumed to surrender their vote to the better judgment of others' (Alexander 1999: 350). Certainly, prejudices of this kind were not exclusive to Spain but rather, as Gerard Alexander argues, can be 'found in contemporary debates over female political participation and suffrage in Britain, France, Germany and Austria' (1999: 350). For both male liberals and traditionalists, women represented a force of nature to be controlled, since their freedom could jeopardize the programmes for national regeneration proposed by these two sides. As Sarah L. White argues, 'at critical moments of political transition, the proponents of revolution — or reaction — depicted such women as irrational, diseased, promiscuous, a threat to the integrity of the nation' (1999: 233). Although liberals were more receptive to the equality of women — for example through the initiatives carried out by the *Institución Libre de Enseñanza* in order to provide them with access to higher education — they still distrusted women's participation in politics.

In Spain too, male fears of the 'modern woman' were prompted by the increasing entry of women into public spaces, challenging previous hegemonic representations of womanhood embodied by the 'Ángel del Hogar' (Kirkpatrick 2003: 9; Barrantes 2007: 85). At the end of the nineteenth century, influenced by John Stuart Mill's *The Subjection of Women* (1869), female Spanish thinkers and writers such as Concepción Arenal (*La mujer del porvenir* [*The Woman of the Future*], 1869) and Emilia Pardo Bazán (*La mujer española* [*The Spanish Woman*], 1874), had already denounced the subjugation of women to men and seen the need to incorporate women into the public sphere in order to modernize the country. Continuing the ideas of these two precursors of Spanish feminism, Spanish female writers such as Carmen de Burgos and Rosa Chacel demanded the recognition of women's rights in the 1920s and 1930s (Kirkpatrick 2003: 9). In *La mujer moderna y sus derechos* [*The Modern Woman and her Rights*] (1927), Carmen de Burgos describes the 'modern woman' as wearing short hair, a short skirt, displaying her cleavage, smoking and making herself up in public (Burgos 2007: 269). The 'modern woman' described by Burgos resists complying with the limiting conditionings of patriarchy and regains ownership of her own body. According to this writer, such a change is also reflected by modern fashion in clothing, which liberates women from the weight of nineteenth-century attire such as the crinoline, impractical for those women who led a more active life, especially in the workplace, and even played sport (Burgos 2007: 261). Burgos's portrait conveys the feeling of liberation that women experienced in the modern metropolis. As Barrantes (2007: 88) states, the transformation of the urban space triggered by technological progress and industrial modernization also fostered a transformation of womanhood, to the extent that women became an image of modernization, and what is more, an indicator of the ideological progress and modernization of Spanish society.

Spanish female intellectuals also unveiled the constructedness of biosocial thought in their writings. This is the case in 'Esquema de los problemas prácticos y actuales del amor' [Outline of the Practical and Current Problems of Love] (1931), where Rosa Chacel challenges the dominant ideas expressed by George Simmel and spread in Spain by Ortega y Gasset. Chacel attributes women's subjugation to religious and social prejudices about women's 'physical impediments' (1931: 145), in a clear allusion to the reclusion of women to the private sphere and their essentialist role as mothers and wives. Ideas such as these anticipate the work of subsequent feminists, who consider that

> gender should be understood not as a 'real' social difference between men and women, but as a mode of discourse which relates to groups of subjects whose social roles are defined by their sexual/biological difference as opposed to their economic positions on their membership in ethnic and racial collectivities. (Yuval-Davis 1997: 9)

Whereas female writers considered the role of women as essential for the modernization of the country, most male intellectuals reacted against the 'modern woman', even those who celebrated change in other areas, such as Ortega y Gasset (Bretz 2001: 205; Kirkpatrick 2003: 221; Barrantes 2007: 94). Animosity towards women was reflected in a prominent quantity of misogynist representations that expressed the anxiety provoked in men by the instability of patriarchal structures. Similarly, the view of modernity given in the avant-garde novel published in the 1920s showed a male viewpoint, since the leading role is usually played by a male character (Barrantes 2007: 106). Female characters, by contrast, often represent the conflicting and threatening effects of modernity.

European depictions of the American 'modern woman' often identify modernization with women, described as a product of mass society and mechanization. Georges Duhamel's travelogue *America, the Menace*, for example, compares the woman's body to consumer goods: 'the legs, the lovely legs with their beautiful contours, obviously mass-produced, that are sheathed in glistening, artificial silk, and that the little knickers clasp with so charming a garter — where are they grown?' (1974: 64). Significantly, the woman described by Duhamel is driving a car, a symbol of technological development: the image suggests the identification between the female body and the machine, both conceptualized here as dangerous. Moreover, the male narrator — who is in the passenger seat — is not in control but rather at the mercy of the female driver. The blatant sexism of the text reflects an effort to regain a position of power by reducing the woman to a feminine body subjugated to patriarchy. The scene therefore conveys male fears surrounding the increasing power of women in the United States, incarnated in the metaphor of the 'modern goddess', a model of femininity spread by the mass media, 'published in an edition of two or three million copies, through the services of a vigilant industry, as the prize and the pride of the American citizen' (Duhamel 1974: 66). In Paul Morand's *New York*, the American woman — 'that creature hated and admired by European women' — is described as 'the woman with the most money in her handbag' (1931: 135). The context for such assertion is again illuminating, since the woman described by Morand is walking down Fifth Avenue. She is in the heart of the city, in one of the most central spots of New York, alone, without the company of a man and hence gaining control of the public space. Moreover, the association with Fifth Avenue — a street famous for its expensive shops — relates to the power of money. As Morand declares, 'the American woman makes herself supreme on the Fifth Avenue pavements with overwhelming assurance, happiness and superiority' (1931: 135). As these two texts exemplify, in European eyes, the 'modern woman' was sometimes not only identified with 'technologism', but also with materialism and capitalism.

Following a different approach, in her travelogue *America As I Saw It; or, America Revisited* (1913), the English writer Ethel Alec-Tweedie argues that women must play a significant role in the progress of a nation. Her travel book about the United States devotes an entire chapter to 'Our American Sisters', in which she emphasizes the intellectual equality between men and women:

> It is no longer possible to shrug one's shoulders and use the word 'woman' as synonymous with weakness. Physically, women may not be men's equals; but where brains and character are concerned, they have proved again and again that, given the same opportunities, they do not lag behind. (1913: 74–75)

Consequently, Alec-Tweedie suggests that women must contribute to the civil and political spheres, traditionally restricted to men:

> All the big questions that are being probed today with their suggested reforms are the outcome of women's cooperation. All women cannot be workers any more than all men can be soldiers. Childless women must do their share in the national work. The nation is crying for their aid in civic and political life. [...] I hope to see equality of the sexes in all things that concern the work of the world. Women are marching onwards in every land. Their advancement and the progress of civilisation are synonymous terms today (1913: 74–75)

Significantly, rather than resisting the increasing number of women entering the public sphere, the writer points out that this process is not exclusive to the United States, but is already ongoing 'in every land'. Such an assertion highlights how the negative reactions towards the 'modern woman' expressed by male European travellers and writers reflect their concerns about the appearance of a new type of femininity also in their home countries. Furthermore, contrary to the views of the American woman offered by her male counterparts, Alec-Tweedie praises the suffragist movement in the United States, which she defines as 'one of the great landmarks of civilisation' (1913: 88), and the fact that women can earn money in the same way men do: 'All professions are open to American women, and their work is looked upon as honourable. Thank God for that. They are admired for their wage earning capacity, and often earn wages even when they have a husband who might earn for them'. (1913: 80).

Early twentieth-century Spanish New York narratives written by men often contain references — mostly in derogatory and sarcastic terms — to the increasing access of women to the public sphere and their refusal to comply with the patriarchal authority represented by the figures of their husbands. Eduardo Criado Requena devotes a chapter of *La ciudad de los rascacielos* to 'La mujer', in which he describes American women in the following terms:

en todo el mundo no hay mujer menos femenina que la americana; parece creada solamente para imitar y explotar al hombre; ella no gusta de los quehaceres domésticos, ni de las obligaciones del hogar [...] El padre o el marido no pueden influir ni encauzar su vida; las leyes la protegen de un modo tan exagerado que el hombre ha de dejarla hacer su voluntad para evitarse el ridículo. (2004: 79)

[throughout the world there is no woman less feminine than the American; she seems created only to imitate and exploit man; she does not enjoy domestic duties, nor the responsibilities of the home [...] Her father or husband cannot influence or channel her life; laws protect her in such an exaggerated way that the man has to let her have her way in order to avoid ridicule.]

The challenge to a gendered division between the private and public spaces is also disapproved of:

no comprendemos cómo hay hombres que acepten el matrimonio en una sociedad que sólo les impone deberes y no derechos [...] no puede impedirle que se marche de paseo con un amigo, o que acepte invitaciones para el teatro o el baile, quedando en muchos casos el esposo al cuidado del hijo. (2004: 80)

[we do not understand how there are men who accept marriage in a society that only imposes duties and not rights [...] He cannot stop her from going for a walk with a friend or accepting invitations for the theatre or a dance, and the husband often ends up looking after the child.]

Moreover, his strongest criticism is directed at the participation of women in politics, and especially towards the campaigns for women's suffrage, which he describes as absurd and pompous (2004: 81). In other texts, the growing presence of women in the workplace leads to the impression that men have been belittled by women's 'arrogance' and 'independence' (Miquelarena 1930: 157). Jacinto Miquelarena's characterization of the American flapper resembles Carmen de Burgos's description of the 'modern woman':'la *flapper* se enrolla las medias debajo de la rótula, como con un borde de salchicha; fuma hasta en la calle; se talla una cabeza de *boy*; va a los parques de atracciones con *plus-four* y marinera blanca y azul de marino de guerra... Es gimnástica más que deportiva' [the flapper rolls her stockings down below her knees, in the shape of a sausage; she smokes even in the street; she shapes a boy-like head for herself; she goes to theme parks with plus-fours and a white and navy blue sailor top. She is more gymnast than sporty] (1930: 135–37). However, Miquelarena's text reflects his uneasiness with this new type of femininity and, in a statement that blatantly shows a patriarchal view of gender, he declares that 'gracias a ella, el joven americano puede realizar su sueño de la infancia, sin salir de las ciudades: la doma de potros' [thanks to her, the young American man can fulfil his childhood dream — the taming of colts — without leaving the city] (1930: 136).

In *El peligro yanqui*, Luis Araquistáin also argues that most American women long for their independence (1921: 92). This writer devotes an entire chapter to 'El feminismo', in which he includes a section entitled, 'Un caso de mujer nueva' [An Example of New Woman]. In contrast with the previous texts I have mentioned, Araquistáin seems to praise the increasing independence of women in the United States, which he likens to liberation from slavery:

Primero descubre el hombre su individualidad por diferenciación de la naturaleza; luego como miembro de la clase dominante, individualidad del talento, del poder, de los derechos heredados; después, como miembro de la clase dominada, como esclavo, como siervo, como proletario moderno. Últimamente descubre su individualidad la mujer. (1921: 91–92)

[First man discovers his individuality through differentiation from Nature; then as a member of the ruling class, the individuality of talent, power and inherited rights; later, as a member of the ruled class, as a slave, servant and modern proletariat. Recently women are discovering their individuality.]

Nevertheless, in spite of its seemingly positive view of women's emancipation, this text also expresses a concern about the position men would hold in society if traditional gender paradigms were subverted, even suggesting that men might have to endure the 'dictatorship of women' in the near future:

¡Melancólico futuro espera a los hombres! En la antigüedad, los esclavos, al hacerse libres, solían a veces revolverse violentamente contra sus señores de otro tiempo. Ahora que tanto se habla de dictaduras, ¿no estará abocada la Humanidad a la dictadura de la mujer? El 'niño de los cabellos largos y pensamientos cortos' demuestra [...] que sus palabras son tan largas como sus cabellos, ¡Ay del hombre si sus hechos son también tan largos! (1921: 95)

[A melancholic future awaits men! In ancient times, slaves, upon becoming free, tended at times to turn violently against their masters from another time. Now that so much is said about dictatorships, is humanity not heading toward a woman's dictatorship? The 'child of long hair and small thoughts' shows [...] that her words are as long as her hair. Poor man if her deeds are also that long!]

Similarly, as we will see next, Moreno Villa's and Camba's accounts of New York's modernization react strongly against the increasing independence of women in the United States. In contrast, both Oteyza's and Escoriaza's narratives offer a counter-discourse that partially challenges the submissive role traditionally ascribed to women by patriarchy. The key role played by the American 'modern woman' in these four texts highlights the centrality that gender issues, and especially the new possibilities that modernization opened to women, had in the debates around the crisis of Western modernity as well in the reassessment of Spanish national identity at the time.

Pruebas de Nueva York: 'La Niña Violenta' and The Subversion of Marriage

In *Masculine Domination* (2001), Pierre Bourdieu argues that the opposition male/female is presented 'in the whole social world' as 'normal' and 'natural', 'inevitable', as the 'the right order of things' (2001: 8). 'Sexual difference', socially and culturally constructed as a power relation in which the category 'man' holds a position of authority over the category 'woman', is seen by Bourdieu as the expression of a symbolic order that 'naturalizes' masculine supremacy:

the strength of the masculine order is seen in the fact that it dispenses with justification: the androcentric vision imposes itself as neutral and has no need to spell itself out in discourses aimed at legitimating it. The social order functions as an immense symbolic machine tending to ratify the masculine domination on which it is founded. (2001: 9)

In *Pruebas de Nueva York*, such a 'natural order', according to which women — constructed as passive, weak, and irrational beings — must be docile to men — constructed as active, strong, and rational — is strongly challenged by the increasing independence of women in the United States. The archetypical American woman is described by José Moreno Villa as a rebellious figure who refuses to accept the 'natural' authority of men: 'oigo decir a la mujer americana que ella toma lo que quiere y en el momento que lo desea; que no se entrega, ni se da, sino que agarra' [I hear it said to the American woman that she takes what she wants and when she wants it; that she doesn't yield, or give in, but holds on] (1989: 17). According to the writer, American women refuse to give themselves submissively to men; rather, it is the man who is dominated by the woman: 'el hombre se resigna a ser tomado. Es justamente lo contrario del héroe tradicional. Quien monta el caballo y rapta al amante no es el doncel sino la doncella' [the man resigns to being taken. He is exactly the opposite of the traditional hero. The one who mounts the horse and carries off the lover is not the nobleman but the maiden] (17). In the latter statement, blatantly charged with sexual symbolism, the opposition established by patriarchy between men-active/women-passive is inverted. It is women who 'ride the horse' and 'kidnap their lover', whilst men are depicted as weak and submissive. The author's disapproving tone on this point shows the nature of sexual and sentimental relationships between men and women within the patriarchal order of Spanish society at the time: socially and sexually 'broken in' by men and therefore culturally constructed as passive beings, Spanish women are supposed to be 'taken against their will'. Indeed, sexual references are not accidental. As Bourdieu points out, masculine social control makes itself visible in the cultural construction of sexuality as the expression of a gendered hierarchy in which male authority is identified with activity and women's subjugation with passivity:

> if the sexual relation appears as a social relation of domination, this is because it is constructed through the fundamental principle of division between the active male and the passive female and because this principle creates, organizes, expresses and directs desire — male desire as the desire for possession, eroticized domination, and female desire as the desire for masculine domination, as eroticized subordination or even, in the limiting case, as the eroticized recognition of domination. (2001: 21)

As discussed earlier in this chapter, the paradigm of 'sexual difference' translates socially into the gendered division between the private and the public spheres, and the seclusion of women in the family home in their roles as wives and mothers. In the previous chapter, I have already referred to the identification between 'house' and 'wife' made by Moreno Villa in his article 'Casa y casada' (2010b [1928]), where the writer draws on traditionalist stereotypes of womanhood embodied by the 'perfecta casada' trope popularized by Fray Luis de León. In tune with the ideas articulated in this article, *Pruebas de Nueva York* expresses discontent towards the subversion of 'marital values' (1989: 17). Breaking with the 'right order of things' symbolically imposed by patriarchy, in 1920s United States — according to Moreno Villa — women are not only regarded as men's equals, they are even located in a position of superiority:

consecuencia de esto es la frase Americana de 'cincuenta y cincuenta' (*fifty, fifty*), que quiere decir: seamos partes iguales, tengamos el cincuenta por ciento en todo. Emblema igualitario que inventado por ella o por él, manifiesta el alza femenina y la baja del hombre. (17)

[a result of this is the American phrase 'fifty-fifty', which means: let us be equal parts, we will take fifty percent in everything. An egalitarian emblem, which whether invented by her or by him, demonstrates the rise of woman and the fall of man.]

In a recent study analysing current racist attitudes in the United States, Michael I. Norton and Samuel R. Sommers (2011), argue that the 'emerging belief in anti-White prejudice' by white American people in the past years is the result of the view of 'race equality' as a 'zero-sum game' (2011: 215), by which 'Whites [...] now believe that this progress is linked to a new inequality — at their expense' (2011: 217). Moreno Villa's negative response to gender equality can be similarly explained by Norton and Sommers's theory. For him, gender equality means the rise of women to the detriment of men, since it implies a diminishment of the power imposed by the latter through patriarchal domination. Once again, we can deduce that for Moreno Villa the erosion of men's social preponderance goes against the sexual hierarchy promoted by a patriarchal system masquerading as 'naturalness'. Moreno Villa regards gender parity as an invention, and therefore as an anomalous demand. This idea is reinforced by a drawing appearing two pages after the previous quotation (1989: 19). In the image we see a man and two women. The man dominates the scene, conveying a sense of protective superiority over the two women sitting next to him. A book or a newspaper rests in the man's legs, reflecting the patriarchal opposition between men's reason and women's irrationality. By complementing his argument with this image, the writer is showing the reader the difference between the Spanish 'natural' order and the American 'unnatural' one.

In contrast with the image of male dominance represented in the picture, Moreno Villa emphasizes his view that civil equality between the two sexes in the United States (fifty-fifty), leads to the superiority of women over their other halves:

podrá no cumplirse, es decir, podrá no tener más valor que de prototipo o ideal; pero si no se cumple es porque la mujer tiene el cincuenta y cinco por ciento. Notemos de paso el carácter matemático o mercantil del emblema; la diferencia que va de nuestra 'media naranja' a este tanto por ciento americano. (18)

[it might not be achieved; that is, it might not have any more value than that of a prototype or ideal; but if it is not achieved it is because women have fifty-five percent. We must note in passing the mathematic and mercantile character of the emblem; the difference between our 'other half' and this so-much-percent American.]

The supposed 'mercantilism' of gender parity reflects male anxieties towards the increasing access of women to the job market, since women's economic independence would debilitate the power relations maintained by patriarchy. Hence the difference between the American 'fifty-fifty' and the Spanish 'media naranja' to which the writer refers. The latter is a Spanish expression that alludes to the perfect sentimental match, which, however, does not imply the equality of both sexes in social and economic terms. The alleged superiority of American woman is illustrated by the writer in a subsequent section of his travelogue, when he describes a scene in a shoe shop in which men are portrayed as women's servants:

> ¡Qué franqueza de piernas! Con qué amorosa sencillez calzan y descalzan los dependientes. Qué despreocupación de piscina hay en la sala inmensa y poblada. Los horteras aportan el cenicero [...] para la fumadora; traen unos zapatos negroides, de marcadísima fantasía; sacan y meten el calzado con acompañamiento de lentas y suaves razones, sin lascivia, con natural agrado. Miles de piernas se levantan y se cruzan como un imposible charlestón, de figuras sentadas. ¿Dónde está el hermetismo? ¡Ah!, pero todas hacen lo mismo. No hay, pues, indecencia. Esas piernas son "unas piernas"; total, números de la serie. (54)

> [Such frankness with the legs! The shop assistants fit shoes with such affectionate simplicity. What swimming pool-like nonchalance there is in the immense room filled with people. The attendants offer an ashtray for the female smoker; they bring negroid shoes in extremely fancy colours; they remove and fit the footwear with accompanying slow and gentle reasoning, without lasciviousness and with natural kindness. Thousands of legs are lifted up and crossed like an impossible Charleston danced by seated figures. Where is the reserve? Ah, but they all do the same! There is, then, no impropriety. These legs are 'some legs'; in short, numbers of the series.]

In New York, the feminine body enters the forbidden space of public premises, where men are at women's feet, and act merely as servants who bring the goods and ashtray dutifully to their female masters. Significantly, in this scene it is the woman who smokes — in comparison with the man smoking a pipe in the drawing –, a practice traditionally reserved for men. However, in the writer's eyes, women remain objectified, depicted as a pair of fetishized legs; they are faceless, just a mass of legs that follow the same movement, 'números de la serie', obviously alluding to mass production, and hence unveiling the connections between modernist fears of the 'masses' and of the 'modern woman' as argued by Andreas Huyssen (1988: 52).

Whereas the American woman is depicted as a strong dominatrix, the inversion of gender roles seems to be fully accepted by men, who are in fact given 'feminine' characteristics: '¿se resiente el hombre de tal estado de cosas? No se advierte. La mujer le exige mucho y le mima luego. Con frecuencia se oye decir a una esposa hablando de su marido: "¿No es dulce él?"' [is the man resentful of such a state of affairs? He does not show it. The woman demands a lot from him and then spoils him. You often hear a wife saying of her husband: "Isn't he sweet?"] (18). Breaking with traditional stereotypes of womanhood and manhood, women are here described as strong and men as soft, docile and in need of protection. According to Bourdieu (2001: 22), from the point of view of masculine domination in which sexuality and power are directly connected, 'the worst humiliation for a man is to be turned into a woman'. In this light, a 'feminized' man is a man stripped of his authority. Elaine Showalter (1996: 8) points out that the *fin de siècle* crisis brought with it 'a crisis of identity for men', since the erosion of 'sexual difference' rendered masculinity as a culturally constructed role:

> the stresses of maintaining an external mask of confidence and strength led to

> nervous disorders, such as neurasthenia [...] What was most alarming to the *fin de siècle* was that sexuality and sex roles might no longer be contained within the neat and permanent borderlines of gender categories. Men and women were not as clearly identified and separated as they had been. (1996: 9)

In tune with Showalter's argument, Moreno Villa swiftly clarifies his own words in order to preserve the 'external mask of confidence and strength' and give reassurance that, despite the subversion of gender roles, American men have not yet lost all their masculine qualities:

> esta misma mujer que le quiere por su dulzura, le quiere por lo que guarda todavía de hombre tradicional, de protector, defensor y refugio. Es decir, que la mujer americana quiere un marido que sea fuerte entre los hombres y débil ante ella; débil ante su voluntad. La relación es, pues, compleja por lo mismo que se halla en un momento de transición. Aunque parezca un poco violenta la comparación, diría que la mujer quiere que su hombre sea para todos un rascacielo [*sic*], y para ella un *apartement* [*sic*], es decir, que sea grande al exterior y pequeñito en lo íntimo. (18)

> [that same woman who loves him for his sweetness also loves him for what he still has of a traditional man, as a protector, defender and refuge. That is, the American woman wants a husband who is strong amongst men and weak before her; weak before her will. The relationsip is, then, complex as well as being in a moment of transition. Although the comparison seems a little forced, I would say that the woman wants her man to be a skycraper for everyone, and for her an apartment; that is, to be large on the outside and tiny on the inside.]

Contradictorily, the writer states that American women love traditional masculine qualities such as men's protective instinct and, at the same time, that women wish for men to be weak and small under female authority. The contradiction in Moreno Villa's words captures male angst towards women's emancipation at the time, which led to incongruous reactions by men: on the one hand, a fear of the threat posed by rebellious femininity, and, on the other, a reaffirmation of male power (Showalter 1996: 10). Furthermore, the comparison made by the writer between men, the skyscraper, and the apartment seems to complete the subversion of gender roles taking place in the United States. Instead of the merger between wife and house in 'casada', here it is the man who is identified with the household. As we have seen in Chapter 2, Moreno Villa's ambivalent opinion of New York's architecture leads him to compare the magnificent appearance of the skyscrapers with the narrowness of the small apartments contained within: the *machine à habiter* where family life barely exists, provoking the 'denaturalization' of personal relationships. Following traditionalist views of womanhood such as 'la perfecta casada' and the 'Angel in the House', the identification between 'woman' and 'house' is essential for the stability of the family home, the basis of the national community. Women who abandon their sacred role of 'reproducers of the nation' to enter the public sphere are therefore seen as a threat to the sexualized hierarchy that supports the nation, and to the same family values that perpetuate 'sexual difference'.

The view of American women as 'uncontrolled', a symbol of chaos and disorder, is encapsulated in the image of 'la niña violenta' ('the violent girl'). This is the sobriquet given by Moreno Villa to New York and the United States. In his opinion, 'la niña violenta' is an expression of the alleged violence and 'primitivism' of American society (61). The characterization of this 'niña' corresponds to the widespread image of the flapper, a beautiful and athletic woman, independent and determined:

> Esa niña es adorable. Junto con sus encantos físicos tiene otros de carácter interior capaces de embaucar también. Alta y elástica, dura y blanda en sus puntos y según leyes de perfección, limpia, y acariciada más que guarecida en telas que son velos, sin memoria ya de camisas, corsés, fajas ni piezas de la tradicional indumentaria, va y viene, monta y baja con nervio seguro, sin retemblores de carne flácida y sin apariencia de dudas intelectuales. Con ímpetu gimnástico irrumpe en todas las [sic] órdenes de la vida. (61)

> [That girl is adorable. Together with her physical charms she has others of an inner character which can also hoodwink. Tall and flexible, tough and soft in her limbs and, according to laws of perfection, clean, and caressed more than protected in clothes which are veils, without any recollection now of shirts, corsets, girdles or pieces of traditional costume, she comes and goes, goes up and down with steady nerves, without shudders of flaccid flesh and without the appearance of intellectual doubt. With gymnastic ímpetus she breaks into all aspects of life.]

Moreno Villa's words recall Carmen de Burgos's description of the new attire wore by the 'modern woman', and the writer also acknowledges the entrance of this new woman into the public sphere ('en todas las órdenes de la vida'). Certainly, the emergence of the 'modern woman' was not a phenomenon limited to the United States. Showalter (1996: 38) points out that 'on the eve of the twentieth century [...] the image of the New Woman was widespread in Europe'. In Spanish society too, the 'modern woman' was becoming increasingly noticeable in the 1920s (Kirkpatrick 2003: 9). Nevertheless, Moreno Villa is at pains to stress that the 'modern woman' is an exception in Spain, where the norm is the 'typical' Spanish woman, described by the writer in opposition to the American girl:

> No todo español estimará su belleza, porque nosotros estamos acostumbrados a juzgar por la cara, más que por el cuerpo. Nuestra raza lo pide así. Nuestras mujeres llevan la belleza en la cara: en los ojos, en la boca, en la frente, en el dibujo de la nariz, en la expresión viva y temperamental, que no siempre es larga ni profunda. La belleza yanqui es más repartida. Fluye, como un impulso, de extremo a extremo. Tal vez no complete, con rasgos de perfección, ninguno de sus miembros, pero consigue un total más armonioso. (61–62)

> [Not all Spaniards will value her beauty, because we are accustomed to judging the face more than the body. Our race demands as such. Our women wear their beauty on their faces: in their eyes, on their mouths, on their forehead, in the portrait of their nose, in their vibrant and temperamental expression which is not always extended or deep. Yankee beauty is more distributed. It flows, like an impulse, from one end to the other. Perhaps it does not complete, with features of perfection, any of its parts, but it achieves a more harmonious whole.]

Once again, women are categorized by the writer as sexual objects, defined by the male gaze and by their sexual attributes. Furthermore, women's beauty becomes the embodiment of the (allegedly) most significant characteristics of their respective nations: the movement and dynamism of US society, and the temperament of the Spanish 'race', calm and immobile like the Castilian landscape:

> es una belleza dinámica, que arrastra nuestros ojos el recorrido entero, al viaje de circunvalación. Se aparta completamente de la belleza tradicional española que invita — no al viaje — sino a la contemplación de un punto, de una parte de la persona, solicitando reposo, estabilidad. (62)
>
> [it is a dynamic beauty, which takes our eyes along a complete route, a circular journey. It is removed completely from traditional Spanish beauty which invites us not to go on a journey, but to engage in the contemplation of a point, of a part of a person, demanding respose and stability.]

A few lines later, Moreno Villa acknowledges the appearance of a new femininity in Spanish cities. However, he insists on an essentialist, almost eternal, image of the Spanish woman as representative of the Spanish 'race' (62). And even the 'metropolitan Spanish woman' cannot be compared to her American counterpart:

> de todos modos, si pensase en ésta diría que está muy lejos de la niña neoyorquina y por una razón que no se improvisa: porque toda la soltura de movimientos, toda la energía, decisión y hasta violencia de la niña norteamericana es externa e interna a la vez. (62)
>
> [nevertheless, if I thought about her [the Spanish woman] I would say that she is quite far from the New York girl and for a reason that is not improvised: because all the ease of movement, all the energy, decision and even force of the North American girl is external and internal at the same time.]

The writer implies that despite the change of women's appearance in Spanish cities, the internal characteristics of the 'race' remain unchallenged: Spanish women are portrayed as lacking dynamism, and therefore as passive and submissive. 'Race', as an expression of the national character, is hence seen as a static entity, in which the rebelliousness of the 'modern woman' cannot leave an imprint. In contrast, similar to the lack of historical roots that allows US architecture to destroy and innovate, the American woman is free to move, with energy and decision, since she is not chained to patriarchal conventions: according to Moreno Villa, American women 'amarán al padre y al marido y al novio, pero en cuanto noten que obstaculizan el dasenvolvemiento [sic] de su voluntad — a su voluntad le llaman "su vida" — se plantarán violentamente [...] no hay entrega total, no quiere haberla' [they will love their father and husband and fiancée, but as soon as they realise that they are an obstacle to the development of their will (they call their will 'their life'), they will propose forcefully that there is no absolute submission: she does not want there to be] (62). In Moreno Villa's view — informed by Western discourses of womanhood — women must give themselves completely to their husband, to the master they must serve as wife and mother of his children.

Reflecting views of the United States as a 'primitive' society, the subversion of sexual hierarchy is explained by the triumph of 'female primitiveness', identified with irrationality, nature, and violence, over an alleged 'male rationality' that created civilization:

Cultiva el movimiento radical y primitivo del corazón, pero — aquí lo grave — odia las consecuencias del corazón. Le aterra la fidelidad, le aterra la maternidad. Como alma primitiva detesta esos conceptos elaborados por la civilización. A veces llego al extremo de creer que aborrece todas las palabras que en español terminan en 'dad': caballerosidad, generosidad, caridad, piedad, sentimentalidad. Todas son trabas para su violencia. (63)

[She cultivates the radical and primitive movement of the heart, but (and here is the serious matter) she hates the consequences of the heart. Fidelity terrifies her, maternity terrifies her. Like a primitive soul, she detests these concepts elaborated by civilization. At times I reached the extreme of believing that she despises all words in Spanish which end in '-dad': gentility, generosity, charity, piety, sentimentality. All are tethers for her violence.]

As one can see, if women refuse to comply with masculine domination — presented as a product of civilization — and to fulfil their role as wife ('fidelidad') and mother ('maternidad'), they are seen as an 'alma primitiva'. Moreover, the concepts that Moreno Villa mentions at the end of the paragraph are attributes of the traditional woman or 'Ángel del Hogar'. First, 'caballerosidad' refers to the chivalrous treatment that women must receive in the public space. Second, 'generosidad', 'caridad', and 'piedad' allude to the obligation of 'the Angel' to give herself to others: father, brothers, husband, and children, and by extension, to the whole national community she represents. Finally, 'sentimentalidad' is a reference to women's weakness and also to their irrationality. Nevertheless, in spite of her violence, the American woman remains a child. Her challenge to patriarchy is therefore undermined, and presented almost as a tantrum. Once again, masculine insecurity leads to a contradictory image in which the alleged threat to civilization posed by 'violent women' is presented as infantile behaviour.

As noted in the previous chapter, Moreno Villa does not shun a sense of open-ended ambiguity in his view of New York and of modernization. Despite his rejection of the subversion of patriarchal hierarchy, the writer also declares himself to be on the side of 'violence', which he sees as an expression of emotion and youth. He praises these features and associates them with spirituality, artistic sensitivity, and intrepidness (63). The ambiguity of his statements is acknowledged by the writer himself, who declares to be confused:

En esta hora de intrepidez y confusión, el mejor nauta no es nauta de olas, sino de nubes. Pero, atendamos a un punto: ese nauta, como esa niña violenta, irrumpen en la confusión fijos los cinco sentidos y las siete virtudes o talentos en una sola presa, como el águila. En una sola presa, sin acordarse de la de ayer, ni pensar en la de mañana. Como los buenos cristianos, después de todo, sólo buscan el pan del día. La niña violenta coge la fruta del momento, y le desagrada mañana que le recordéis la fruta de ayer. (64)

[At this hour of intrepidness and confusion, the best navigator is not that of the waves, but of the clouds. But we should pay attention to one point: that navigator, like that forceful girl, both break into confusion with their five senses and seven virtues or talents focussed on a single prey, like the eagle. On a single prey, without remembering that of yesterday, or thinking about that of tomorrow. Like good Christians, after all, they only seek their daily bread. The forceful girl takes the moment's fruit, and then dislikes it tomorrow when you remind her of yesterday's fruit.]

In this obscure and contradictory paragraph, 'la niña violenta' seems to embody the *collige, virgo, rosas* Latin trope ('gather, girl, the roses'), also reminiscent of Garcilaso de la Vega's Sonnet XXIII: 'coged de vuestra alegre primavera/el dulce fruto, antes de que'l tiempo airado/cubra de nieve la hermosa cumbre' [seize the sweet fruits of your joyous spring, / now, before angry time creates a waste, summoning snow to hide the glorious summit] (2009: 42–43). 'La niña' is endowed with Christian values (the seven virtues), and is compared to a 'nauta', a term that suggests navigation and movement, and also leadership and guidance. Bearing in mind Moreno Villa's criticism of *Regeneracionismo* in the prologue of his travelogue, the intrepidness of 'la niña' and her interest solely in the present could imply a praise of modernization as a detachment from old-fashioned values, in order to overcome the stagnation represented by the dusty past. However, she is also compared to an eagle, a free and violent bird of prey, whose target is not specified. Her aggressive behaviour could denote an excessive power in sexual relations with men, who are prey at the mercy of the eagle, and discarded after she has indulged herself in the pleasure of the moment. 'La niña' would therefore remain as an irresponsible girl and a dangerous force. The ambiguity of this image reveals the contradictory attitudes towards modernization conveyed in Moreno Villa's travelogue. On the one hand, he seems to identify with characteristics such as movement, dynamism, and therefore change, acknowledging the benefits that US modernization could bring to Spain. On the other hand, however, he is reluctant to accept the modernizing role played by the 'modern woman', whose independence is seen as a threat to male authority, and to a patriarchal conception of the Spanish nation.

El crisol de las razas: Tearing the Veil of Patriarchy

In *El crisol de las razas*, we witness the power exerted by a Russian man, Boris Zinovief, over two female characters: his wife, Helen, and a Russian singer named Sonia. Boris has increasingly neglected his wife since he has become obsessed with the 'Slavic sensuality' of the Russian woman, who suffers the sexual harassment of her admirer. These two women initially represent opposite archetypes of womanhood. On the one hand, Helen is characterized as following the stereotype of the American woman: independent, educated, and fully integrated in the civil sphere. Sonia, on the other hand, embodies a fantasized image of womanhood as object of male sexual desire. As I will show, such archetypes are, however, challenged and finally subverted. Noticeably, neither of the characters of the novella is Spanish, nor are there any references to Spain. Nevertheless, the novella engages surreptitiously with contemporary debates surrounding the role of women in the Spanish society of the time.

Boris Zinovief, characterized as a rich Russian Jew who treats women as sexual objects, represents the power of patriarchy. Although Boris has lost interest in his wife, he nevertheless wants to retain Helen in his ivory palace on Riverside Drive. While Helen must remain inside the house, Boris leaves for the darkest neighbourhoods of the city, in order to seduce Sonia, an eroticized object from which the magnate wishes only to obtain sexual satisfaction. Both women are therefore trapped in spaces dominated by men. Helen is meant to remain in a place owned by Boris, where she is his property. Sonia, on her part, is ensnared in the public space of the cabaret, at the mercy of men's authority.

In spite of her seclusion in the family home, Helen is portrayed as an intrepid, rebellious, and independent woman, who is not resigned to losing the adoration she once received from her husband: 'una nube pasó por los ojos limpios de Helen [...], sacudió su hermosa cabeza como una fierecilla indómita. Era un gesto de rebelión, de desafío, del odio experimentado por el que no se somete, por el que no se resigna' [a cloud passed across the clear eyes of Helen [...], who shook her beautiful head like an untamable shrew. It was an act of rebellion, of defiance, of hatred felt by one who does not yield, who does not resign herself] (1929: 8). As in *Pruebas de Nueva York*, the 'modern woman' incarnated by Helen is defined by her aggressiveness. I suggest that in this case the reference to 'fierecilla indómita' alludes to the Spanish title of Shakespeare's *The Taming of the Shrew*.[1] As in Shakespeare's play, the narrator imbues this character with a sense of resistance towards her husband's authority. Nevertheless, Helen remains a 'fierecilla', a small animal, irrational and under the control of her male master.

Helen's resentment towards her husband is provoked not by love, but by her wounded pride. She is portrayed as a woman accustomed to being adored by men, even to governing them, as we can see in a paragraph that is reminiscent of Moreno Villa's statements about 'la niña violenta':

> ¡Ah!, ¡pero hasta aquí habíamos llegado!... Todo tenía sus límites. ¿Verse suplantada por otra mujer..., ella, Nell..., una norteamericana..., cuando es ley en los Estados Unidos que las mujeres han de ser las reinas y ellos se rendirán a sus plantas?... (10)

> [Ah! So this is where we have got to...! Everything had its limits. To be replaced by another woman..., she, Nell..., a North American.... When is it a law in the United States that women have to be queens and men will fall at their feet...?]

Accordingly, Helen is willing to win back Boris's admiration and regain her position of dominance:

> ¿El divorcio? ¡Tampoco! Desertar era una cobardía... Ni una venganza ni una separación podrían satisfacer a su orgullo pisoteado... Una reivindicación era lo que necesitaba; reconquistar a su marido, atraérselo de nuevo, rendirle otra vez a sus pies y hacerle proferir aquellas palabras suplicantes. (10)

> [Divorce? Never! To leave would be a cowardly act... Neither revenge nor separation could remedy her pride... Vindication was what she needed; to win back her husband, attract him again, make him fall at her feet once more and speak those pleading words.]

Helen is not against divorce because of her religious beliefs or a traditional view of family. She does not wish to separate from Boris because that would imply weakness, and she is ready to show her strength and determination. Similar to the 'subversion of marital values' mentioned in Moreno Villa's travelogue, here is a woman who wants to 'kidnap the man' and subdue him to her authority.

However, although she rejects the idea of divorce, Helen's economic and emotional subjugation is the result of the conditions of her matrimony. She married Boris because she was dazzled by his wealth, as the narrator states:

> La vanidad le había empujado a casarse con aquel judío poseedor de una inmensa fortuna, que la obsequiaba con preciosos ramos de flores, con costosas cajas de dulces y la agasajaba llevándola a los restaurantes más lujosos, causando con estos éxitos el asombro y la envidia de sus compañeras de promoción en el *college*. Y ahora purgaba aquel pecado de soberbia, viéndose herida en lo más interno de su amor propio. (8)

> [Vanity had pushed her into marrying that Jew with his immense fortune, who presented her with lovely bunches of flowers, with costly boxes of sweets and regaled her by taking her to the most luxurious restaurants, and causing with these successes the astonishment and envy of her classmates in college. Now she was purging that sin of arrogance, and was seeing how wounded her most intimate self-esteem was.]

According to the narrator, Helen has committed two of the deadly sins: vanity and avarice. Boris's material possessions:

> fueron para ella, frágil Eva, lo que la manzana del árbol de la Ciencia, del Bien y del Mal para la madre de la humanidad. Y las promesas tentadoras de Boris Zinovief tuvieron el mismo resultado que las de la serpiente del Edén: hicieron caer a Helen en la tentación. (9)

> [for her, a fragile Eve, were what the apple of the Tree of Knowledge, and of Good and Evil were for the mother of humanity. Boris Zinovief's tempting promises had the same result as those of the serpent in the Garden of Eden: they caused Helen to fall into temptation.]

In contrast with the strength assigned to Helen by the narrator earlier on, here she is portrayed as weak and unable to turn down the temptations offered by the devilish Boris. However, compared to Eve, an archetype of disruptive womanhood, Helen is in this case a victim. Furthermore, the subversion of Eve's symbolism turns the 'sins' committed by Helen into a betrayal of women's emancipation in the United States and also in Spain, where the reception of the archetype of the 'modern woman' by middle- and high-class urban women fostered the emergence of a group of female intellectuals that played a prominent role in social, political, and cultural advances (Kirkpatrick 2003: 9). However, by marrying Boris and becoming reliant on his wealth, Helen has renounced the benefits of her education and her economic independence. She is a prisoner, another 'beautiful object' in her husband's hands. In comparison with the alleged gender equality of American married couples, the treatment that Helen receives from the Russian tycoon is humiliating, a vestige of a primitive patriarchal tradition, foreign and uneducated, that clashes with the civil equality achieved by women in the United States:

> aquellas compañeras que la envidiaban, ahora todas casadas con muchachos de su clase y de su país, que las consideraban como saben considerar a las mujeres los norteamericanos; aquellas sus amigas le compadecían seguramente y quién sabe si en el fondo se reían con cierta satisfacción al comparar su situación actual con sus triunfos de muchacha. (8)

[those friends who envied her, now all married to boys from their class and country, who regarded them just as North Americans know how to regard women; those friends of hers surely sympathized with her and who knows if deep down they laughed with certain satisfaction when comparing her present situation with their girlhood triumphs.]

In spite of her education and rebellious character, Helen seems to be unable to break with the domination imposed by her foreign husband, since the battle to recover her pride will not be a confrontation with the man who has abandoned her but, on the contrary, with Sonia, a woman who is also a victim of Boris's authority: 'era menester derrotar a su rival, y, para derrotarla, necesitaba antes conocerla. No sería seguramente aquella rusa ni más hermosa ni más inteligente... ¡A ver cuál podía más!' [it was necessary to defeat her rival, and, in order to defeat her, she had to know her first. That Russian woman wouldn't probably be more beautiful or more intelligent... We'll see who is the stronger!] (10). Even in Helen's words we can detect a reflection of the sexual objectification carried out by the patriarchal view represented by her husband: 'no sería seguramente aquella rusa ni más hermosa'. In contrast, she also adds 'ni más inteligente'. Helen, as we have seen in a previous quotation, had access to higher education. The reference to Helen's past as a university student recalls the entry of American women into higher education, therefore indicating the progressive collapse of the dichotomy man-culture-reason/women-nature-irrationality in the United States. Helen is simultaneously depicted as weak and strong, dependent and independent. She could break with patriarchy, divorce her husband and regain her lost freedom. Marrying a rich Jewish man such as Boris is presented in the novella as a prison, although disguised as a materialistic Eden, from which Helen seems not to want to escape.

In order to gather information about her female rival, Helen embarks on a trip to the night club located in the Bowery, where Sonia performs her show. She leaves the solitude of her imprisonment in the walls of Boris's palace, moving away from the limits denoted by the feminized private space, to be part of the hustle and bustle of the streets. She penetrates into the public space, and travels by car through New York. However, her conquest of this open space is not yet complete. Although she is travelling in her own car, she is not driving. The steering wheel is in Joe's hands. Joe is Boris's young nephew, half Russian Jewish, half Norwegian, and educated in the United States, and Helen's best friend and loyal ally in the Zinovief family. Helen not only needs Joe's protection to go to the dangerous neighbourhood, but she is also portrayed as 'too nervous' to drive (12), a fact that echoes the dichotomy men-rationality/woman-irrationality. Boris's pernicious influence seems to have provoked in her a regression to a state of 'childish femininity' that contrasts with her former strength as an American woman.

Nonetheless, when they approach the Bowery, Joe is reluctant to carry on with the journey. At this point, traditional gender roles are subverted, and while Joe is afraid to enter this area of the city, Helen shows her courage and decision:

atravesaron calles y mas calles, aminorando la velocidad en el cruce de la [*sic*] calles de mayor circulación: la 42, la 34, la 23. Al llegar a esta última, donde se halla Unión [*sic*] Square, Helen rompió el silencio para decir a Joe

que torciera hacia la izquierda. Pero éste paró en seco el automóvil y rehusó terminantemente obedecerle.
— ¡Por ahí no, Nelly!
En aquella zona estaba el barrio chino y el aún más peligroso de Bowery. [...]
— Pues bájate. Iré yo sola...
Sin insistir, pues en el acento decisivo con que su tía había pronunciado aquella frase vió [sic] que todo cuanto dijera para hacerla desistir de su propósito sería inútil, encogióse [sic] de hombros, en un gesto de resignación, y volvió a poner en marcha el automóvil. (12)

[they crossed streets and more streets, reducing speed at crossroads with the greatest traffic: 42nd, 34rd, 23rd. After passing the last of these, approaching Union Square, Helen broke the silence to ask Joe to turn left. But he stopped the car suddenly and refused expressly to obey her.
'Not that way, Nelly!'
In that area was the red-light district and the even more dangerous Bowery.
'Then get out. I'll go on my own...'
Without insisting, since in the decisive tone with which his aunt had pronounced that phrase he saw that everything he said to make her desist from her objective would be pointless, he shrugged his shoulders with a gesture of resignation and got the car going again.]

The ambiguity of Helen's character is manifest here again. She is too nervous to drive, but at the same time she dominates the situation. Moreover, Joe — a masculine presence that Helen, 'as a woman', needs in order to enter into the darkest places of the metropolis — is like a puppet in her hands. The same contradiction characterizes Helen's entrance to the 'Agit Punkt Club', the place where her rival sings and which her husband frequents. She acts intrepidly, in opposition to the fearful attitude of her young friend (15). However, she still needs to be in the company of a man to enter the night club. Such necessity derives from the fact that the club is located in an area of the city described as 'uncivilized' and 'primitive', populated mainly by Jewish immigrants coming from Eastern Europe. The structures of patriarchy seem to be still very prominent in this neighbourhood, where civilized US society is taken over by what the narrator terms the violence of Jewish culture: 'en este barrio se cobija toda la gente maleante de la gran metrópolis [...] el corazón de Nueva York, constituye la denominada Ciudad Judía, por ser el elemento hebreo el que allí predomina' [in that neighbourhood all the unsavoury people of the great metropolis [...] the heart of New York, make up the so-called Jewish Quarter, given that the Hebrew element predominates there] (14). As an American 'modern woman', Helen has already been admitted to the public sphere, and she is respected by American men and by the laws of her country. Consequently, the threat to civilization — here identified with the United States — comes from the anti-Semitic view of Judaism as a strange and 'infectious' influence.

The club is depicted as a highly masculinized space, full of cigar smoke, where the only women are Helen — an intruder — and Sonia, who sings to entertain the masculine audience. The place is entirely devoted to men's pleasure. At first, Helen feels dizzy because of the masculine atmosphere of smoke and spirits, an ambience to which, according to a patriarchal view, women only belong as an 'object' displayed for men's delight.

The show commences, and Sonia appears on stage. In her first appearance in the story, the Russian singer is portrayed as an almost supernatural being, a symbol of a mythicized view of womanhood, closer to a deity than to a real girl:

> Avanzando lentamente hacia el centro de la sala, al compás de la música, tenía, en efecto, más de aparición sobrenatural que de artista de café-concert. La tiara de esmaltes de campesina rusa que coronaba su cabello, de un negro azulado, era como un nimbo que iluminaba aquel rostro perfecto, dando a su palidez reflejos de nácar. Avanzaba como hipnotizada, la mirada profunda de sus ojos negros, inmensos, perdida en la lejanía del vacío. Con aquella actitud extática, la belleza sublime parecía sustraerse a aquel ambiente turbio y grosero. Avanzaba erguida, haciendo ondular suavemente en armoniosos movimientos su cuerpo estatuario [...] como si los brutales deseos que a su paso despertaba nada tuviesen que ver con ella. (16–18)

> [Proceeding slowly towards the centre of the room, in time with the music, she had, in effect, more of a supernatural appearance than that of a café-chantant artiste. The Russian peasant's glazed tiara that crowned her hair, blue-black in colour, was like a nimbus that illuminated that perfect face, giving her pallidity a mother-of-pearl reflection. She advanced as if hypnotised, the deep gaze of her black, immense eyes lost in the distance of the emptiness. With that ecstatic posture, her sublime beauty seemed to avoid that murky and vulgar atmosphere. She advanced proudly, making her statuesque body gently sway with harmonious movement, as if the brutal desires which were awakened as she walked had nothing to do with her.]

Her performance is illustrated in the novella's front cover, based on an illustration by Enrique Varela de Seijas. The description of Sonia's concert evokes representations of woman as a mysterious 'femme fatale', so emblematic in the work of *fin de siècle* painters of the Decadent movement, such as Alphonse Mucha and Gustav Klimt. According to María Peckler (2003: 51), femininity is represented in Klimt's paintings by a beautiful, enigmatic, seductive, and perverse 'femme fatale'. Similar images can be found in Spanish painting. Hermenegildo Anglada-Camarasa's painting 'La Sibila' (1913), for instance, is reminiscent of Klimt's female characters (Peckler 2003: 58). These paintings, as well as the literary worldview of *fin de siècle* poets such as Rubén Darío, condense the ambiguity of the images of womanhood constructed during this period, which opposed an ideal womanhood, submissive, natural, and pure, to a perverse femininity, depicted as artificial, sexually strong, and independent (Luna Sellés 2002: 168). Sonia embodies a sexual fantasy for the cabaret's audience, an object available to satisfy an exclusively male desire. This perception reflects the double moral towards sexuality promoted by patriarchy in Spain at the time, where men often satisfied their sexual desires outside marriage, while their wives had to remain, virtuous and chaste, within the walls of the family home (Luengo 2008: 209). At the same time, Sonia also represents purity in a corrupted space, therefore inverting the recurrent archetype of woman as perverse in the *fin de siècle* artistic imaginary. She is defenceless against the perverse sexual desire of the audience, which violently invades the stage when the show is over:

> En el paroxismo del entusiasmo, todas aquellas gentes precipitáronse al parquet, y Nell pudo ver que era Boris Zinovief quien, alcanzando a la artista en su huida, la cogía por la cintura, mientras que el resto de aquella muchedumbre furiosa retrocedía como fiera dominada por la mirada del domador. (19)
>
> [In the paroxism of enthusiasm, all those people swept to the parquet, and Nell could see that it was Boris Zinovief who, reaching the artist in her flight, caught her by the waist whilst the rest of that furious crowd pulled back like a beast dominated by the tamer's gaze.]

Sonia is therefore in need of protection from the animal-like mass of over-excited men. Noticeably, whereas Boris is depicted as a 'domador', the out-of-control audience is referred to as a 'fiera dominada', an image that recalls Helen's previous portrayal as 'fierecilla indómita'. This parallel illustrates the extent of Boris's power in both the private and the public spheres. The Russian tycoon considers Sonia to be another of his possessions, and in the primitive society, where he seems to be the 'alpha male', he exerts his authority in order to protect his prey from his competitors.

After the turmoil, Sonia goes back to her humble home, described as a miserable hovel, where she lives with her grandfather Iván (21). By showing the mysterious singer in her misery, outside the space of the cabaret where she is seen as a 'femme fatale' and a sexualized object, the narrator again goes beyond the dichotomy purity/perversity previously discussed. The pictorial and literary representations of women carried out in *fin de siècle* art are thus shown to be an expression of male desires and anxieties, as Jordi Luengo López (2008: 204) has also discussed with regard to the view of women portrayed by late nineteenth-century and early twentieth-century art.

Sonia tells the events of the night to Iván, and we learn that she had to be protected from Boris's sexual harassment by Joe (21). Her grandfather reacts with rage: '¡Pues no volverás a cantar más! Si te salvé de las garras del príncipe Sergio Mohilev, ¡Dios sólo sabe a costa de qué sacrificios!, no ha sido para dejarte caer en manos de ese perro judío' [You won't sing again, then! If I saved you from Prince Sergio Mohilev's claws, and only God knows the sacrifices I made!, it wasn't to leave you at the hands of that Jewish dog] (21). The narrator relates how Prince Sergio's lustful advances were the reason why they had to leave their country, and also why Iván lost his health, since he had the duty of protecting Sonia from the dangers of the Prince's desires: 'cual perro fiel, el viejo Iván, había estado siempre vigilando su más precioso tesoro: Sonia, y acechando al ladrón que quisiera arrebatárselo. Y había llegado el momento de defenderla; pero el ladrón había resultado ser un lobo fiero' [like a faithful dog, old Iván had always been watched over his most valuable treasure: Sonia, and would lay in wait for the thief who sought to carry her away from him. And the time had come to defend her, but the thief had turned out to be a savage wolf] (23). Echoing *Little Red Riding Hood*, sexual desire is identified with a 'wolf' from which Iván — 'a loyal dog' — must protect the virginal granddaughter, portrayed as a possession of the grandfather. Jack Zipes (1993: 78) argues that *Little Red Riding Hood* concerns the regulation of sex roles and sexuality, since 'where order and discipline reign [...] young girls will be safe both from their own inner sexual drives and outer natural forces. Inner and outer nature must be brought under control, otherwise chaos and destruction will reign'. Sonia's sexuality is therefore 'rightfully' owned by a patriarchal figure, which must guard her from the dangers of both other men and her own sexual drive. Iván's attitude is graphically shown in a drawing by Varela de Seijas (22), which recalls Moreno Villa's illustration discussed in the previous section of this chapter. Sonia is on her knees with her face on her grandfather's lap. He is smoking a pipe and showing a protective attitude. The drawing reflects a traditionalist conception of womanhood, according to which Sonia must remain 'immaculate' so that her virginity can be handed, untouched, from her father to her husband. Only by doing this can she fulfil 'the right order' of sexual relations: her sexual organs must remain pure in order to undertake the task of 'reproducing the nation'. In a similar manner, her morality must also be impeccable, so she can convey the values of patriarchy to her offspring; otherwise, she would be relegated from the social order and would turn from 'mother' into 'whore', and thus be barred from the decency of the family home and condemned to satisfying men's sexual needs in public spaces. This is the biggest threat posed by Boris, a Mephistophelean character to whom Sonia could sell her soul and body in order to obtain wealth, just as Helen did. The description of Boris's attitude matches Sonia's previous experience in her homeland with the Russian Prince, who also tried to get closer to the singer by giving her expensive presents. Drawing on this similarity, it seems that a correlation between wealth and slavery permeates the relationships between men and women in the novella. The reference to Prince Sergio's tyranny is complemented by a subsequent scene in which Sonia dreams of the fertile Russian countryside, in the context of a prosperous, peaceful, and free Russia (26). This allusion can only be understood in relation to the 1917 Russian Revolution, as a monologue by Iván confirms:

> — ¿Siguen los campesinos Rusos apoderándose de las tierras? [...] Sí; el príncipe Sergio se habrá visto despojado de sus inmensas propiedades [...] Todos — continuaba — Litivsky, Chaupof, Rodzianko, cultivarán ahora sus propias tierras... El príncipe Sergio Mohilev, había seguramente perecido a sus manos... (24–25)
>
> [Do Russian peasants continue to seize lands? [...] Yes; Prince Sergio will have been stripped of his immense properties' [...] 'Everyone,' he continued, 'Litivsky, Chaupof, Rodzianko, will now farm their own lands... Prince Sergio Mohilev had surely perished at their hands...]

The presence of Russian characters in the novella is not accidental, but in fact reflects the interest awakened by the Bolshevik Revolution in Spain. The interest in Russian literature has been highlighted by Víctor Fuentes and Manuel Tuñón de Lara (2006: 41), who argue that not only around one hundred Soviet novels were published in Spain between 1926 and 1936, but also that such interest reflects the similarities between Spanish and Russian society at the time. Significantly, women's emancipation was also part of the principles of the Bolshevik party, since:

> there was a general assumption that women and children were potential victims of oppression within the family, and that the family tended to inculcate bourgeois values. The Bolshevik party established special women's departments

(*zhenotdely*) to organize and educate women, protect their interests, and help them to play an independent role. (Fitzpatrick 1994: 86)

Simultaneously, *El crisol de las razas* constructs a discourse against patriarchal and class domination. In the United States, the magnate Boris perpetuates such subjugation, in the face of which Sonia has no alternative but to offer her sensuality in order to subsist. The nature of anti-Semitic connections between capitalism, patriarchy, and Judaism in the text will be subjected to closer scrutiny in the following chapter.

Since Iván cannot protect Sonia any more because of his poor health, she has accepted the protection of a dancer from the club, Fomitch.[2] The dancer is described as a simple-minded and jealous man who wishes to have the privilege of being her exclusive protector. That night, however, Sonia did not need his services, since she was protected by Joe — with whom she has fallen in love — and Fomitch feels threatened in his role as Sonia's guardian (25). The Russian singer is at the centre of a network of protection and control. Sonia is allegedly in danger because of men's intentions, but she must also comply with the authority of her male masters. Only Joe seems to respect her:

> ¡Era correspondido en su amor!... Sonia le había abierto su corazón, y le había confesado sus sentimientos respecto a él, en un lenguaje desconocido que no había oído nunca entre las mujeres que frecuentaba. Ni en boca de las jovencitas refinadas que acudían a los bailes de la Universidad, ni de los labios de las mujeres galantes de 'The Midnigert Frolies' [*sic*], ni entre las damas linajudas amigas de Nell... Esta mujer enigmática, que tenía a la vez el candor de una niña, cuando escuchaba sus palabras de amor, el apasionamiento de la hembra, cuando era ella la que las pronunciaba, y la crueldad de una fiera, cuando amenazaba defendiendo su amor, ponía en ebullición toda la sangre de sus venas. (33)[3]

> [His love was requited...! Sonia had opened her heart to him, and had confessed her sentiments regarding him in an unknown language that he had never heard amongst the women with whom he was acquainted. Not even upon the mouths of refined young ladies who attended the dances at the University, or upon the lips of the gallant women of 'The Midnigert Frolies', or between Nell's blue-blooded friends... That enigmatic woman, who at the same time possessed a young girl's innocence, when he heard her amorous words, the female's passion when it was she who uttered them; and the wild cruelty when she made threats in order to defend her love: it threw the blood in his veins into turmoil.]

In contrast to the perception of Sonia as a sexual object, Joe is not afraid of Sonia's 'unleashed' sexuality, of the 'fiera' inside her. When she is in Joe's company, Sonia subverts the passivity of her role as 'protected' to become an active individual who defends — and hence protects — her own feelings and sexual desires. One must however note the distinction made by Joe between American women and Sonia's 'mysterious' sensuality. As I will show in the next chapter, Joe's attraction to Sonia corresponds to a great extent to a 'racial' empathy between the two lovers. He finds in Sonia the passion supposedly inherent in the Russian 'race'. Joe's own Russian blood, which until that moment had been obscured by his American education, seems to be awakened by the singer's passion.

Eventually, compelled by her financial needs, Sonia accepts Boris's proposition of singing for him at the 'White Eagle', one of his luxurious residences in Long Island (36). Boris's offer is a manoeuvre seemingly directed at seducing Sonia. At the same time, Helen — who has found out about Boris's private show — also heads to the mansion with the aim of dismantling her husband's plans. When Joe learns about the situation of the two women, he realizes the danger they both are in: Sonia will be at Boris's mercy, and if Helen confronts her husband, she will suffer his revenge (36). Like the hunter in *Little Red Riding Hood*, Joe turns into the 'hero' of the story, a representation of 'male governance' that must save women from their fall (Zipes 1993: 81).

Once she arrives at the 'White Eagle', Sonia is left in a room in order to dress for the show. There, she finds another woman asleep on the bed: Helen. Recalling the Prince from *Sleeping Beauty*, Sonia admires Helen's face, and Helen wakes thanks to the singer's 'mysterious powers of attraction' (38). According to Madrilena Papachristophorou, 'the passivity of Sleeping Beauty, caused by the eternal magic sleep' leads her 'to embody perfect femininity in the form of marriage and maternity' (2008: 883). However, once Helen is awake from her dream, she has a 'diabolic idea', namely to pretend to be Sonia in front of Boris, so she can either seduce or humiliate him in front of his friends:

> — [...] si hoy no conquisto a Boris con este golpe de audacia, a lo menos me habré vengado, poniéndole en ridículo ante sus amigotes, que aplauden su conducta despreciativa hacia mí y que celebran sus éxitos con las demás mujeres... ¡Ah, cuando me acerque con el rostro cubierto le daré un abrazo, y luego la *dama velada* se descubra!...
> Y esta diabólica idea le hizo prorrumpir en una carcajada irónica.... Bien se presentaba su plan de venganza. (40)
>
> [[...] If today I do not win Boris over with this audacious gesture, at least I will have had my revenge, making him look ridiculous before his chums, who applaud his contemptuous behaviour toward me and celebrate his success with other women... Ah, when he approaches me with his face covered, I will embrace him, and then the *veiled lady* will be revealed...!'
> This diabolical idea made her burst into an ironic bout of laughter... She made her plan for revenge well.]

Sonia accepts, seeing an opportunity to run away from Boris's grasp. Immediately, Helen dresses in the singer's clothes, covering her face with a veil. She contemplates herself in the mirror, and in contrast to her usual cold American temperament, it seems that she has also acquired Sonia's Slavic passion:

> contemplábase en el espejo, transfigurado su rostro por la fiebre de la ansiedad, adquiriría aún mayor belleza con el brillo de los ojos y el rojo encendido de las mejillas. Era aquella una expresión de la que solía carecer su semblante de una fría palidez. (40)
>
> [she looked at herself in the mirror. Her face, transfigured by the fever of anxiety, would take on even greater beauty with the light of her eyes and the bright red of her cheeks. That expression was one that her countenance, with its cold pallidity, tended to lack.]

Thanks to such an unexpected encounter, their roles are inverted. Helen becomes a sensual woman and Sonia wears Helen's skirt suit, an urban piece of clothing that is the opposite of the peasant's costume that the singer wears for her show (40).

By assuming Sonia's role, Helen wants to truncate the patriarchal dream and gain control in her relationship with Boris. As she did in the night club, she covers her face with a veil. In their characteristic 'bodily' vocabulary, Hélène Cixous and Catherine Clément (1996: 145) explain patriarchy as 'a kind of vast membrane enveloping everything [...] We have to know that, to change the world, we must constantly try to scratch and tear it.' Similarly, Helen — who hides her face in order to *unveil* her true identity to her husband — wishes to tear the 'membrane' of patriarchy. However, in tune with the constant ambiguity of this character, Helen's plan also entails a submissive view of her own sexuality. Her primary goal is to seduce her husband, and although she resorts to audacity in order to achieve such an objective, she also wants to become the contrary of what she is: from the independent 'modern woman' she is transformed into the sexualized object represented by Sonia on stage.

Helen's plan will in fact end in tragedy. Before she can uncover her face, she is shot dead by Fomitch in an act of jealousy, since the dancer wrongly believes that Sonia is finally going to give herself to Boris (42). Helen dies in her husband's arms, and not even Joe, the 'hero', can save her from such a terrible ending. Joe has not only failed in his role as male protector but he also needs to be protected by Sonia, for he is initially mistaken for the murderer (42). The disorder of this last scene is representative of the transformations undergone by the two main female characters in the novella. On the one hand, Helen refused to divorce her 'primitive' husband and break with his patriarchal authority. Her rebellion was therefore flawed from the start, since she would in any case have remained economically dependent and therefore one of Boris's possessions. In the opening pages of the text the narrator suggests that Helen's mistake is to marry a foreign man, to fall for the fortune of a Jewish mogul. Her tragic death consequently warns the reader about the dangers of miscegenation: by entering a culture that is not her own, Helen lost her independence. Sonia, on the other hand, ends the novella in the arms of her perfect sentimental partner. Joe is not only half Russian — and therefore one of her own kind — but has also grown up in the United States. In comparison to his uncle Boris, Joe has been brought up in a culture in which women are respected. Furthermore, in the final scene Sonia wears Helen's clothes, and acts in a protective way towards Joe. She therefore has broken with the network of protection surrounding her and has gained control of her own fate, initiating the way to leave patriarchy behind and become a 'modern woman'.

Anticípolis: the 'Modern Woman' against the 'Angel in the House'

In Luis de Oteyza's novel, gender issues are again presented by juxtaposing two archetypical characters. Jesusa, as we saw in the previous chapter, represents the traditionalist values embodied by the 'Ángel del Hogar' trope. Her daughter Rosa, on the contrary, epitomizes the American 'modern woman'. However, the confrontation between these two women does not start until Don Antonio, the head of the family, dies. While he was alive, Antonio Nieto maintained a patriarchal hierarchy within his family (2006: 110). His admiration for New York's modernity was limited to the public sphere, and in the domestic space his authority mirrored the patriarchal social structures of Spanish society at the time. The father imposed his norms and only the men of the family were allowed to work outside the home, whereas the women replicated the role played by their mother, devoted to domestic chores and subjected to a sexual hierarchy.

The attitude of the Spanish 'patriarca' contrasts with New York's customs in family life as described in the text. Mr Sanders, the father of Carlos's girlfriend, describes Antonio as a 'troglodyte father' (16). Sanders also compares the differences in parenting between the United States and Europe, arguing that in the latter the head of the family still imitates the Roman model of the *pater familias*, acting as a tyrant to his family (115). His attack on the patriarchal structures of the Old Continent reverses the opposition between American 'primitiveness' and European civilization. As we will see shortly, a similar opinion is held by Dr Jiménez.

The situation in the Nieto home changes radically after Antonio's death, when Jesusa's children revolt against her intentions of taking her family back to Oviedo, since they identify with US lifestyle and hence want to remain in New York. The head of the rebellion is Rosa, who is described as the most intelligent person in the family (123). By assuming the leading role, she takes over her deceased father's position, even over the privileges previously given to elder sons. In fact, Rosa's first decision, despite her mother's disapproval, is to allow the women of the family to work outside the home:

> Sí mamá, trabajaremos nosotras. Ya lo debiéramos haber hecho. Sobre todo yo, que desde que salí del Colegio no hago más que aburrirme. Aquí ni los cuidados de la casa distraen a la mujer, porque siendo casas tan pequeñas, están arregladas en seguida. Por eso, todas las mujeres ejercen oficios o carreras en Nueva York. Ha sido una ridiculez que no se me haya dejado trabajar. (120)
>
> [Yes mother, we will work. We should have done it already. Above all me: since I left school I've just been bored. Here not even housework keeps a woman busy, as since they're such small houses, they're tidied straightaway. This is why all women have positions and careers in New York. It's ridiculous that I haven't been allowed to work.]

Rosa's explanation for the incorporation of women in the job market in New York still contains traces of a patriarchal world view, as she believes that the primary occupation of the female members of the family is to attend to domestic chores. However, her attitude represents the break with Spanish traditionalism undertaken by the 'modern woman'. She finds a modelling job in a boutique, a professional occupation that her mother regards as an 'abomination' (132). According to Jesusa, showing her body in a public space implies a greater danger than Carlos's involvement in New York's organized crime, since Rosa's job threatened not her life but her virtue (141). Jesusa's reasoning — which recalls Iván's attitude towards Sonia in *El crisol de las razas* — follows the logic of patriarchy, according to which the virginity of young women runs the risk of being inappropriately snatched from their body, and thus must be protected, confined in the 'secure' space of the family home and safeguarded from the dangers of public places. On the contrary, Rosa does not fear entering those masculinized spaces, which in New York have already been conquered by the 'modern woman'. She not only works by exposing her body to masculine and feminine gazes, but also frequents the company of men during the night, which she spends in bars and clubs. Again, Jesusa disapproves of her daughter's way of life. She is especially concerned about Rosa's male companions (144). Rosa is, however, categorical. There is no harm in what she does, because she is always in control; in spite of her Spanish background, Rosa considers herself an American woman:

> a las mujeres de allá hay que guardarlas entre muros para que no se vayan a acostar con el primero que les hace un guiño. A lo que parece, no están esperando más que eso, las santas benditas [...] Las mujeres de aquí somos muy diferentes. Y así vamos muy seguras a todas partes con santos, con hombres y hasta con demonios. Tan seguras estamos solas como las de allá rodeadas de madres, tías, amigas y demás chaperons. No hay el menor cuidado de que nos suceda nada. (145)

> [the women back home have to be kept behind closed doors so that they do not sleep with the first man who winks at them. Apparently, they are not looking for anything else but that, the saintly things. Women here are very different and that is how we go everywhere quite safely with saints, with men and even with devils. We are as safe alone as those back home surrounded by mothers, aunts, friends and other chaperones. There is not the least worry that something will happen to us.]

The excerpt above offers a twofold insight into the opposition between modern and traditional social structures. First, Rosa refers to the protection received by women in the Old Continent, not only by men, but also by older women, often primordial actors in the maintenance of the patriarchal system (Yuval-Davies 1997: 37). However, American women, because of their independent character and thanks to civil rights that guarantee gender equality, are free of any danger when they are in the company of men. Second, the extract highlights different views about sexuality. In Spain and Europe, women are treated as 'santas benditas', and their 'virtue' must be defended from the threats posed by men and by their own sexual drive. Resorting to sarcasm — which is her way of dismantling Jesusa's stubborn stagnation in traditionalism — Rosa argues that European women must be protected because they are willing to have sexual intercourse with any man. The mordant affirmation by which she turns the 'santas' into nymphomaniacs reveals the hypocrisy of patriarchy towards female sexuality.

Such hypocrisy is also criticized by Dr Jiménez in one of his conversations with Jesusa. Whereas the latter maintains that women are not equal to men in any way (182), Jiménez argues that both sexes are completely equal, especially with regard to their sexual needs (183). The Puerto Rican doctor maintains that the inequality suffered by women is based not on physical and psychological differences between men and women as argued by patriarchal order, but are instead the result of social conventions, 'las costumbres' (183). Moreover, he declares that 'sexual difference' is a strategy used by men in order to submit women to their will, and, given that it does not respond to nature but has been artificially constructed, it can also be overcome:

> Me va usted a hablar de una costumbre que obliga a la mujer a contener sus impulsos sexuales; a estar sometida en eso, que no admite sumisión, bajo el dominio egoísta y estúpido del hombre. Podría oponer que costumbre tal es bárbara, cruel... Podría demostrarlo con pruebas irrefutables [...] Le diré sólo que las costumbres cambian, añadiendo que tal costumbre ha cambiado. (183)
>
> [You are going to speak to me of a custom which obliges women to contain their sexual impulses; to be subjected by something that accepts no submission, under the selfish and stupid dominion of man. I could state that such a custom is barbaric, cruel... I could demonstrate this with irrefutable proof [...] I will simply say that customs change, adding that such a custom has changed.]

Jiménez regards sexual submission as a primitive practice, hence challenging the opposition between US 'primitivism' and European/Spanish 'cultural refinement'. In order to support his theories, the doctor alludes to Judge Lindsey's innovative proposals for 'companionate marriage' in the United States (190). In *The Revolt of Modern Youth* (1925) and *The Companionate Marriage* (1927), marriage revisionists Ben B. Lindsey and Wainwright Evans 'denounced the evils of unscientific, authoritarian attitudes and sexual repression, promoted the goodness and importance of sexuality, especially for women, and called for greater freedom for young couples' (Simmons 2009: 106). As might be expected, Jesusa reacts fiercely against such ideas, which she regards as the legalization of concubinage and contraception (190). Attached to a traditionalist view of womanhood, for Jesusa divorce and birth control are immoral practices, since they contradict both the unconditional submission of the wife to her husband and also the primary role of women as 'reproducers'. On the contrary, Rosa argues that thanks to economic emancipation, American women do not have to marry a man in order to become a fulfilled individual. They can even have sexual relations without the blessing of the marital union:

> por ahora no pienso casarme. Estoy muy bien como estoy y no veo por qué cambiar [...] Y aunque no me casase nunca, no tendría importancia. Gano ya mi vida y siempre la podré ganar. A lo que parece, las mujeres en España no encuentran otro medio de vivir, sino ese del casamiento [...] No lo necesito para nada. Ni para... Bueno, ya sabes... De modo que sabes que para nada me hace falta un marido. Para nada en absoluto. (179–80)
>
> [for the time being I am not going to get married. I am fine as I am and I do not see any reason to change [...] And even if I never got married, it would be of no consequence. I earn my living and I will always be able to earn it. Apparently, women in Spain find no other way to live except marriage [...] I have no need for it at all. Not even for... Well, you know... So now you know that I have no need at all for a husband. No need at all.]

Women's independence from men in New York is also alluded to in the cover of the first edition of the novel, designed by Federico Ribas. The image shows a young woman, located in the foreground, highlighting the important role female characters play in the novel. She wears modern and elegant clothes that provocatively show her legs, and walks alone in the public space, moving in the opposite direction to the man behind her, therefore suggesting a departure from masculine authority. Furthermore, her defiant look at the viewer strengthens the rebelliousness of the character, which refuses to be an object constructed by the male gaze.

The different status of women in Spain and the United States is reflected by an anecdote told by Rosa in order to mock Spanish backwardness. In a satirical manner, she refers to a Spanish married couple who have just arrived in New York, and, once settled in the city, 'siguiendo la práctica, al parecer corriente en su tierra, el esposo dio una paliza a la esposa' [following the custom which seemed to be common in his land, the husband gave his wife a beating] (157). As the story carries on, 'el ruido de los golpes, más que las quejas de la víctima, que recibía el mal trato con cierta resignación, atrajo a los vecinos' [the sound of the blows, more than the protest of the victim, who received the mistreatment with certain resignation, attracted the neighbours' attention] (157). Eventually, a policeman is called to the scene and arrests the husband, who reacts with surprise and outrage: '"pero si es mi mujer", alegaba en clase de justificante completo [...] "De modo que aquí no puede uno pegar a su mujer? [...] ¡Bonito país!"' ["but she's my wife", he pleaded as a sort of absolute justification [...] "So can no one beat his wife here? What a fine country!"] (157). The narrator refers to the story as 'the joke of the countryman who brought from Spain the custom of beating up his wife' (157). The comical tone given to this tale of abuse highlights the violent treatment received by women in Spain. The narration itself also unveils the acceptance of such a practice by women themselves ('la víctima, que recibía el mal trato con cierta resignación'), a fact confirmed by Jesusa's opinion:

> Doña Jesusa, cuando Rosa acabó el cuento, estuvo tentada de sostener que, efectivamente, si allá los maridos pudiesen pegar a sus mujeres y también los padres a sus hijas, algo más derecho andarían muchas señoras y señoritas que andaban bastante torcido. (157)
>
> [Doña Jesusa, when Rosa finished the story, was tempted to maintain that, indeed, if back home husbands could hit their wives and also fathers their daughters, many ladies and misses who walked in a somewhat twisted fashion would walk somewhat more upright.]

Jesusa is completely subdued by patriarchy, to the extent that she considers that domestic violence is the way of maintaining 'the right order of things'. Rosa, however, rejects the barbarity of her nation of origin. In reference to Jesusa, she states that, after all, she was not to blame, since she had received her education in a backward nation (179). The allusion to education is highly important, since it is related to the demands for women's education by Spanish female thinkers of the time, such as Rosa Chacel and Carmen de Burgos. According to feminist writers, Spain's modernization would only be achieved by allowing women to access education and the end of 'sexual difference'. Their ideas were not only distrusted by the establishment and by most male intellectuals from both traditionalist and liberal positions, but also by those women educated to preserve the same values that were oppressing them, represented in the novel by Jesusa. E. Ann Kaplan suggests that the identification of the mother figure with patriarchy responds to the 'master-slave psychic phenomenon' by which slaves identify with their masters once freed. In a similar way, 'mothers take out their subjection to their husbands on their children' (1992: 48). As Antonio Gramsci and Pierre Bourdieu have shown, power is not only imposed through force but also through persuasion. Gramsci's notion of 'hegemony' adequately captured how the subaltern class learns to see society through the eyes of their masters, as a consequence of their education and their place in the system (Burke 2007: 131). Gramsci developed his theory to explain relations of subalternity between social classes. However, 'hegemony' is also a productive concept in relation to other cases of subalternity, such as the West/East opposition, as Edward Said proved in *Orientalism*. Furthermore, Gramsci's notion can be applied to the acceptance of patriarchy by women, and their zeal for preserving the system to which they are subjected. Similarly, Bourdieu sees the imposition of the dominant culture on subaltern groups as a 'symbolic violence', that is, a process whereby they acknowledge the culture of the ruling class as legitimate and their own culture as illegitimate (Burke 2007: 133). In this case, Bourdieu does not limit his concept to class relations, but his views also complement his analysis of 'masculine domination' (Bourdieu 2001: 1–2).

Significantly, having failed to preserve the values of traditional morality in her daughters — in her view corrupted by the immorality of the 'evil city' — Jesusa becomes obsessed with the 'salvation' of Carlos's daughter:

> entre los hombres feroces y las mujeres impúdicas de Nueva York, dentro de la ciudad monstruosa, perversa, maldita, vivía doña Jesusa temiendo y odiando. Bien que el deber sagrado de cuidar a la nieta la sostenía contra el espanto, y la esperanza de huir con ella la alentaba para el aborrecimiento. El plan de la abuela consistía en aguardar a que la niña creciese, vigilando su educación, aislándola de malas relaciones, guardándola celosamente en cuerpo y alma. Y luego, un día, pretender que deseaba ir a despedirse de su patria, de su ciudad, y solicitar a la muchachita que la acompañase [...]. Para lograr tal resultado, feliz, glorioso, con paciencia podría aguantarse mucho. ¡A Nueva York misma, incluyendo cuanto y a cuantos contiene! Todo eso [...] aguantaba la abuela por salvar a la nietecita. (238)

> [amongst New York's ferocious men and unchaste women, within the monstrous, perverse, godforsaken city, lived Doña Jesusa, fearing and hating. The sacred duty of caring for her granddaughter bore her well against the fright, and the hope of fleeing with her sustained her in her loathing. The grandmother's plan consisted of waiting for the girl to grow up, watching over her education, isolating her from bad relations, keeping her jealously in body and soul. And then, one day, to pretend that she wished to bid farewell to her country, to her city, and to request that the young girl accompany her [...] In order to achieve this happy, glorious result, she could endure patiently for some time. Endure New York itself, including everything and everyone it contains! The grandmother endured all this for the sake of saving her little granddaughter.]

Jesusa believes that the only way of fulfilling her role of 'reproducer' ('lograr tal resultado, feliz, glorioso') is to educate her granddaughter according to the values of patriarchy, protecting her from modernizing influences ('guardándola celosamente en cuerpo y alma'), and therefore continuing the family line started by her husband Antonio. As a matter of fact, Antonio's surname Nieto [grandson] suggests the idea of continuity thanks to the persistence of family values and their communication to the descendants as a way of preserving the identity of the community. Therefore, the importance of 'rescuing' the granddaughter even goes beyond the 'salvation' of the child itself: once educated according to 'the right order', she will be able to perpetuate its values in her own offspring, and the morals of the patriarchal nation will be thus preserved.

Jesusa hopes to take her granddaughter back to Spain, where she believes the child would be safe from the malign influence of the debauched American society. Nevertheless, according to Jiménez, the threat to patriarchy posed by modernization goes beyond the borders of the United States. The doctor argues that women's emancipation will eventually spread across the entire planet, including Spain:

> Digo con absoluta claridad que la mujer en Oviedo, como en toda la superficie del globo terráqueo, conseguirá la emancipación económica, que es lo que produce su liberación total. Y escapada la mujer de la esclavitud a la que le sometió el hombre, en cualquier sitio será igual que aquí, si no es más que aquí. Créalo usted, señora. (191)
>
> [I can state with absolute clarity that the woman in Oviedo, as across all the surface of the globe, will achieve economic emancipation, which is what produces her total liberation. When the woman has escaped from the slavery to which man has subjected her, in any place she will be as equal as here, if she is not more equal than here. Believe it, madam.]

Jiménez argues that Spain's modernization, embodied by social changes that will highly affect women's role in society, is unstoppable. Those changes were in fact already being made visible in Spain by feminist Spanish intellectuals and activists and their efforts to give women the legal rights that would turn them into full citizens, equal to men. Jiménez's pro-modernizing ideas and Rosa's rebellious attitude suggest a counter-discourse against the pervasive power of patriarchy in Spanish society at the time. Echoing the view of gender roles shown in *El crisol de las razas*, *Anticípolis* seems to propose that the challenge to patriarchy must not only come from the active awakening of women to the subjugation imposed by the 'naturalness' behind which masculine domination is disguised, but also from men, who must also leave old-fashioned stereotypes of womanhood behind in order to acknowledge the falseness of the paradigm of 'sexual difference'. Moreover, the reference to marriage reformers such as Lindsay certainly situates *Anticípolis* within the debates about marriage and sexuality developed in the United States between 1910 and the Second World War, when

> a range of activists, writers, and thinkers reconceived women's sexuality and the marriage relationship in response to major social shifts. Increased female employment, higher education, and voting rights were undermining older images of women as frail and innocent. Public panic over venereal disease evoked calls for sex education for both girls and boys. And after a century of Americans' private practice of fertility control, birth control advocates were asserting publicly that contraception should be legalized. Thus began a contentious public conversation that resulted in a new vision of women's sexuality and relation to marriage in the United States, one that became the predominant, though certainly not the only, cultural ideal by the 1940s. (Simmons 2009: 4)

Efforts to change social conventions, however, unveil the persistence of patriarchal rule in the United States at the time. In the early twentieth century, conservative Victorian values still exerted a strong influence in official culture, whereas the challenge to traditional views of sexuality sprang mainly from popular culture (Simmons 2009: 11). Therefore, rather than a reality already 'in place', as presented in the texts studied in this book, the challenge to 'sexual difference' in 1920s and 1930s New York should be seen as a change in progress. In this light, the opposition between patriarchal Spain and a sexually liberalized United States depicted in the novel is too simplistic. In the United States too, jocular portraits of older women identified with conservative values such as those held by Jesusa, were commonly used in popular culture to criticize the excessive puritanism promoted by the American establishment:

> The mocking of sexual repression (something that continues today as a powerful weapon of ridicule and judgment against critics of sexualized culture) blossomed during the 1920s in popular culture. The critics used these images of repression to indicate the absence of a scientific outlook and thus a lack of modernity in their targets. [...] delineators of flapper marriage created many more female characters who dramatized excessive female power as stereotypically puritanical and controlling older women. These character types, from the laughable to the threatening, undermined the legitimacy of sexual control and the Victorian style of respectable womanhood. Images of women were most common, although men were sometimes depicted as antisexual. (Simmons 2009: 144)

Moreover, the distinction made by Rosa between the traditionalism of European women and the modernity of American ones also overlooks claims for women's emancipation, feminist activism, and the increasing visibility of new forms of womanhood in the Old Continent, including Spain. Rosa's generalization of European and Spanish women as 'traditionalist' can be interpreted as an ideological manoeuvre in order to highlight the burden that sexual prejudices impose upon the modernization of Western societies, especially that of Spain. The radical opposition between the modern Rosa and the traditionalist Jesusa established in the text mirrors Jiménez's defence of the violent move forward represented by New York's modernization, as explored in Chapter 2. In order to achieve gender equality in Spain — essential for the complete modernization of the country — the 'modern woman' embodied by Rosa must act fiercely and with no mercy against the traditional figure represented by her mother. As in Virginia Woolf's speech *Professions for Women* — delivered in 1931, the year in which *Anticípolis* was published — the Victorian 'Angel in the House' must be killed in order to stop the cycle of patriarchal submission perpetuated through old-fashioned archetypes of womanhood.

Nevertheless, the counter-discourse embodied by Rosa and Jiménez does not supersede completely the sexual hierarchy and patriarchal world view against which it seems to be directed. First, both Jesusa and Rosa are symbolic constructions representing an entire community and its national values. Whereas Jesusa is the embodiment of *casticista* views of Spanish national identity, Rosa incarnates modern America and possibly the Spain of the future. They therefore remain archetypes of womanhood that do not stand as individuals but rather as the masculine illusion of 'the motherland'. Besides, Rosa's excessive aggressiveness towards the exaggerated ignorance of her mother establishes an antagonistic relationship between both women, and therefore a conflict that remains unresolved. Consequently, although Jesusa's passing can be understood as a plea for social change in Spain, this interpretation leads to a dead end. Similarly to early feminist literature, which develops an antagonism between mother and daughter in which the former is blamed for 'women's ills' (Kaplan 1992: 46), Jesusa is seen by Rosa as an enemy, therefore obviating that the submissive attitudes of women are often a consequence of the symbolic violence exerted on them by patriarchy. Her mother is a victim who dies because of her refusal to go against her own submissiveness, and the text does not offer any solution for the subjugation suffered by these women.

Moreover, in tune with the polyphonic character of the text explored in the previous chapter, Jesusa's delirious view of New York caused by her mental breakdown also suggests a critical view of US capitalism, criminality, and sexual indecency:

> Allá todo se compraba y se vendía. Mabel vendería a su hija, y nada como comprársela, pagando lo suficiente... ¿Qué mejor destino para el dinero que Carlos ganaba de criminal modo?... Y de no bastar ese dinero, ella buscaría más. Aquel dinero que, cometiendo infamias mayores, ganaran sus otros hijos: el del conformismo de Juan y el de la abjuración de Pepín. Y también por la fuerza... Que Carlos, al frente de su banda, robase a la niña y matara a la madre y a cuantos se opusieran. Caso de que él tuviera que emplearse en distintos asesinatos, ella misma cometería ésos. Con que la [sic] diesen una pistola, un automóvil y algunos bandidos para cubrirse la retirada. O, asimismo, satisfaciendo los vicios de Mabel... Rosa podía cederla [sic] los amantes que la [sic] sobraban. Y si, cansada de hombres, quería probar con las mujeres, se le ofrecería Mariíta. Ella prestaríase a servirle de encubridora, de tercera, ¡como ya había hecho! (247–48)
>
> [There everything was bought and sold. Mabel would sell her daughter, and it would be best to buy her if the price could be met... What better destination for the money that Carlos earnt by criminal means...? If this money was not spent, she would seek more. That money which, by commiting greater infamies, her other children would earn: that of Juan's conformity and that of Pepín's abjuration. And also by force... Carlos, in charge of his gang, would rob the girl and kill the mother and whoever got in his way. In the event that he had to take part in different murders, she herself would commit these. As long as they gave her a pistol, a car and some bandits to cover her getaway. Or also, by satisfying Mabel's bad habits... Rosa could pass on to her the lovers she did not need. And if, tired of men and if she wanted to try women, then she would offer her Mariíta. She would offer to act as an accessory, as a third party, just as she had already done!]

In contrast with Jiménez's utopic view of New York as 'Anticípolis', for Jesusa the city turns into an 'Anti-polis', an unsettling dystopia ruled by greed, violence, chaos, and debauchery. Although Jesusa's hyperbolic misunderstanding of New York's society can be potentially interpreted as a mockery of sexual repression, the end of the novel can also be read as an apocalyptic warning against the pernicious effects that modernization would inflict on the Catholic and traditionalist order represented by essentialist views of Spanish national identity. In an almost diabolical manner, Jesusa — the allegedly pure and chaste 'Ángel del Hogar' — is eventually corrupted by the violent and indecent influence of modernization in order to protect her granddaughter from the same corruption in which she finally agrees to participate. Her symbolic death would therefore condense traditionalist fears of the 'malefic' impact of modernization, which would twist the 'purity' of the Spanish identity, leading to its final disappearance.

La ciudad automática: The 'American Girl' as the Goddess of Chaos

In *La ciudad automática*, Julio Camba regards gender equality in the United States as the effect of 'special laws', which have allegedly been passed in order to protect women (1960: 108). However, the writer sees such regulations as unnecessary, since the 'American girl' — as Camba calls American women — already held a position of superiority over men:

> la chica americana es, sin disputa, la más guapa del mundo [...] La cosa es mucho más seria de lo que parece, amigo lector. No estamos en presencia de unas chicas más o menos monas, sino de unas mujeres de cuerpo entero, tan extraordinariamente hermosas, que uno no se atreve casi a levantar la vista hacia ellas. Parecen seres de una especie superior, y aun cuando se ponen a mascar goma lo hacen con un aire y una majestad de diosas. (108)

> [the American girl is indisputedly the prettiest in the world [...] The matter is far more serious than what it appears, dear reader. We are not in the presence of girls who are more or less cute, but women with a full body, so extraordinarily beautiful that one almost does not dare to raise one's eyes towards them. They seem like beings of a superior species, and even when they start to chew gum, they do it with an air and majesty of goddesses.]

'[S]eres de una especie superior' and 'majestad de diosas' are both descriptions that locate American women on a superior level, different from *man*kind. Yet once more, women are here transformed into sexual objects, mythical figures whose alleged power emanates from their supernatural beauty. Moreover, Camba erases the face of this 'American girl', who turns from a singular being ('la chica americana') into a plurality of women ('unas chicas'), a generalized entity and not a real individual. This is an image that echoes views of womanhood promoted by Spanish male polymaths at the time, such as Ortega y Gasset, who in 1923 argued that 'la personalidad de la mujer es poco personal, o dicho de otra manera, la mujer es más bien un género que un individuo' [woman's personality is not very personal, or expressed in another way, woman is more a gender than an individual] (Ortega y Gasset 1947: 433). Camba's flagrant alignment with patriarchy leads him to provide a similarly generalized depiction of Spanish and French women:

> La madrileña tendrá los ojos más bonitos y la parisiense tendrá la nariz más remangada. Ésta será más graciosa, aquella más picaresca, la otra más elegante, etcétera; pero si las chicas de aquí o de allí pueden vencer en detalle a la chica Americana, sería preciso que se reuniesen todas y combinaran sus diversos encantos para vencerla en conjunto. (108)

[The Madrilenian woman will have the most beautiful eyes and the Parisian the most snub nose. The latter will be funnier, the former more of a rascal, another more elegant, etc.; but if girls from here and there can beat the American girl in terms of detail, then it is necessary for them to gather together and combine their different charms in order to beat her together.]

Here 'madrileña' stands for all women in Madrid, possibly in all Spain, and 'parisiense' represents all Parisian and French women. Furthermore, Camba fosters rivalry between women — as his repeated use of 'vencer' shows — as though they were meant to be enemies to themselves. Such rivalry is, however, only related to their beauty, and hence to their bodies, since there is not a single mention of their intellectual capacities. At first, it seems that Camba is implying that women cannot be a real danger to 'rational' and 'educated' men. However, he also declares that women's 'superiority' poses a threat to men's authority, as we can infer from expressions such as 'la cosa es mucho más seria de lo que parece' and 'uno no se atreve casi a levantar la vista hacia ellas'. The depiction of women as superior beings is a subterfuge used by Camba in order to criticize legal equality between the two sexes, as becomes evident in the following paragraph:

> Ahora bien, ¿creen ustedes que las mujeres de esta categoría necesitan unas leyes especiales que las protejan? Yo me explicaría más bien todo lo contrario, esto es, que los senadores se reuniesen en Washington para garantizar contra ellas la vida y hacienda de los hombres; pero, ¿qué defensa necesita aquí la mujer? ¿Qué peligro puede suponer para ella el pobre ciudadano que se pasa el día en la oficina y al que no queda nunca una hora libre para el deporte ni para la lectura? (108–09)

> [However, do you believe that women of this class need special laws to protect them? I would instead suggest the opposite; that is, that senators meet in Washington to guarantee the life and property of men against them; but what defence do women need here? What danger can the poor citizen who spends his day in the office and who never has a free hour for sport or reading pose for them?]

Similarly to Moreno Villa, Camba sees gender equality in 'zero-sum' terms, as the decadence of masculine power; hence his description of man as a 'pobre ciudadano' whose patrimony ('hacienda') and legal rights ('vida') are in peril. However, despite Camba's complaint of men's defencelessness in the face of the 'American girl', the way in which the writer constructs his discourse unveils the pervasive strength of the patriarchal order. The text is clearly addressed to a masculine audience, as we can infer from the allusion to the reader as 'amigo lector'. The writer is assuming that only men would be reading his text, thus questioning women's intelligence and rationality. Furthermore, the reference to 'la lectura' as a masculine activity is — as in Moreno Villa's drawing, discussed earlier in this chapter — a symbolic marker of the alleged 'natural' differences between the sexes promoted by patriarchy, and reflects the limited access that women had to education in Spain at the time. The legal system that allows the increase of rights for women is also ruled by men, 'los senadores', since laws establish social order and can only be devised and approved by 'rational' beings. Following such reasoning, women can only access the privileges of civil life with men's permission. Finally, Camba makes a clear distinction between women as 'beautiful objects' and men as citizens ('pobre ciudadano'). Excluding women from citizenship, the writer reinforces the line that separates the public from the private sphere, since only citizens are in possession of the legal rights that entitle them to participate in public affairs. Although Camba protests against women's 'superiority' in the United States, his words demonstrate the hegemony of men. The reference to the American woman as the 'American girl' is also an expression of a patriarchal world-view. The denomination of those allegedly 'powerful women' as 'girls' is a way of maintaining men's dominance, since the image of women as childish strengthens the idea of femininity as irrational and in need of parental protection. This image also unveils the constructedness of gender categories, in which the representation of women changes according to men's criteria: they are seen as goddesses when men's authority is threatened, but at the same time they are depicted as children in order to justify such authority.

The 'American girl' is a variant of the image of woman as embodiment of the United States. Not without reason, the writer states that she is America's 'greatest creation', and compares such a fine 'product' to Ford cars and Waterman's fountain pens (108). Camba sees American women as mass-produced objects: they are all the same, without any trace of individuality. This 'American girl' therefore represents the means of mass production, the dehumanization and the mechanization of the United States. Whereas in Moreno Villa's travelogue 'la niña violenta' crystallized the perception of this country as a violent civilization, Camba's 'American girl' works as a metonymy of New York as the 'automatic city' and, extensively, of the United States as a mechanical society.

The ideal solution given by the writer in order to stop women's supposed 'revolt' against 'the right order of things' is even more explicit. In Camba's view, women should be enslaved:

> En una colectividad donde los hombres se diesen verdadera cuenta del hecho que constituyen unas mujeres tan guapas, se hubiese comenzado por reducirlas al estado de esclavitud, lo que valdría la pena por sí mismo, y sería, además, una medida de precaución contra trastornos sociales; pero aquí se ha procedido al revés y el resultado es que las mujeres, no sólo parecen diosas, sino que lo son efectivamente. Son diosas y, convencidas de su condición divina, no hay nada en el mundo que las arredre. (109)

> [In a community where men truly realized the fact that they are such pretty women, they might have begun to reduce them to a state of slavery, which would be worth it in itself, and would be, moreover, a means of precaution against social upheavals; but here this has happened in reverse and the result is that women do not only seem to be goddesses, but in fact are. They are goddesses and, convinced of their divine condition, there is nothing in the world that can daunt them.]

The radical and overtly sexist solution proposed by the writer is in truth not an innovative answer but rather a defence of the slavery exerted by patriarchal order. One can note the sexually charged insinuation given by Camba when he declares that women's slavery 'valdría la pena por sí mismo'. Although he does not develop his thought, we can infer that in that state of slavery, women would be obliged to serve all men's needs. In Spain, as Jordi Luengo (2008: 208) states, the idea of femininity promoted by patriarchy implied women's sexual subjugation to men. Camba argues that in the United States 'se ha procedido al revés'. Paralleling the ideas expressed by Morero Villa, Camba considers the situation of American women as a subversion of 'the right order' that has led to an 'unnatural' situation, in which the 'beautiful objects' have turned into almighty, divine-like, subjects. Freed from the chains of masculine domination, women are seen by Camba as a potential source of 'trastornos sociales'; once more, women's emancipation is seen as the catalyst for chaos. Such concern about civil disorder is also evocative of Western fears of the 'masses' analysed in the previous chapter of this book. Without masculine control, women grab aggressively and without fear whatever it is they want: 'no hay nada en el mundo que las arredre'. One may ask, however, of what women should be afraid. The answer, I suggest, is the authority given to men by their reputed rationality, which they do not respect. Women's rebelliousness is in fact regarded by Camba as a foolish act of ignorance. This is highlighted in a subsequent comparison between women's fearlessness and the alleged naivety of the 'primitive' tribes of America:

> Toda la intrepidez y toda la audacia de la *american girl* se explican como se explica la serenidad de Atahualpa cuando los jinetes españoles, corriendo a pleno galope por la llanura de Caxamarca, se pararon en seco tan cerca de él, que uno de los caballos le manchó con su hocico el manto real. Las personas del séquito de Atahualpa, que no habían visto nunca un caballo, se hicieron instintivamente atrás; pero el inca no pestañeó siquiera. Desde su nacimiento le habían dicho que era invulnerable, y como hasta aquella fecha no lo había vulnerado nadie, estaba plenamente convencido de su invulnerabilidad ante todos los monstruos conocidos y desconocidos. Pues, como para el inca Atahualpa, para la *american girl* tampoco existen peligros. (109)

> [All the intrepidness and audacity of the American girl are explained as the serenity of Atahualpa is explained when the Spanish riders, hurtling at full gallop across the Caxamarca plain, stopped sharply and so close to it, that one of the horses dirtied the royal gown with its nose. The people of the Atahualpa entourage, who had never seen a horse, instinctively pulled back; but the Inca did not even blink. From their birth they had told them that they were invulnerable, and since until that date no-one had infringed upon them, they were fully convinced of their invulnerability before all known and unknown monsters. As with the Atahualpa Inca, no dangers exist for the American girl.]

The comparison is not accidental. As I have shown in the previous chapter of this book, Camba likens the United States to pre-Columbian cultures in order to explain his view of American regression to primitivism. Likewise, here he establishes a parallel between a symbolic embodiment of the United States, the 'American girl', and the story of an Inca king. In an irrational and superstitious manner, Atahualpa believes that he is indestructible. Similarly, women, according to Camba, think of themselves as goddesses, a pagan character associated with superstition. However, Camba's statements are once more deceitful, and those who seem to be in power are actually subjected to someone else's authority. Although Atahualpa was the king of the Incas, he was imprisoned by the conquistadors led by Francisco Pizarro, and subsequently killed.⁴ In a similar way, women remain as children, and subject to masculine domination. The sarcastic tone adopted by the writer is to be noted. The sense of mockery that permeates the whole chapter devoted to the American woman in *La ciudad automática* — from women's exaggerated power to Atahualpa's story — reinforces the idea that for Camba public life is still a man's world. In Atahualpa's tale, the Inca is not afraid of any danger, and nor is the 'American girl'. However, what kind of 'monsters' does she have to face? In the next paragraph, Camba provides the answer:

> Es una chica sana, alegre e intrépida, que puede fumar dos cajetillas diarias, bailar cien bailes y beber quince *cocktails*; una chica que exhibe sus piernas ante todos los hombres con la misma despreocupación con que podría exhibirlas ante unos animales familiares, a los que no les interesara nada el espectáculo. (109)
>
> [She is a healthy, happy and intrepid girl who can smoke two packets a day, dance a hundred dances and drink fifteen cocktails; a girl who shows her legs before all the men with the same disregard with which she might show them before household pets, who would have no interest at all in the show.]

One can deduce that the 'modern woman' is adventurous and courageous because she dares to enter a dangerous territory, for whose perils she may not be at all prepared, as the naïve and irrational being that she is supposed to be. Such a terrifying space is the public sphere, where the 'American girl' behaves like a man — smoking, drinking and dancing — and refuses masculine protection, since she owns her own body and sexuality ('exhibe sus piernas [...] con la misma despreocupación con que podría exhibirlas ante unos animales familiares'). On the contrary, women's bodies under patriarchal rule belong to men (fathers and husbands) and therefore should not be exposed in public to male rivals, as the nudity of women's legs could be perceived as a sexual innuendo, a threat to their virtue.

Camba finishes his chapter on the 'American girl' with an ambiguous and contradictory statement. He points out that 'a pesar de unas leyes que le dan toda clase de facilidades para la estafa, suele ser la mejor amiga y la mejor compañera del mundo' [in spite of some laws that provide her with all kind of facility for fraud, she tends to be the best friend and best companion in the world] (109). I argue that the use of the word 'estafa' is related to Atahualpa's story, the end of which the writer does not provide: Atahualpa was executed, accused of treason by the conquistadors (Hemming 1993: 77). Unlike the Inca, who betrayed Pizarro's trust, American women seem to be more honest and 'civilized', since they do not take advantage of the 'opportunities' given to them by the law. However, Camba does not state that the 'American girl' is always reliable, but only that she *usually* is ('suele ser'). Consequently, despite appearing to come to terms with women's emancipation, Camba's words hide a warning. The reference to Atahualpa's story mirrors the distrust aroused by the 'modern women' in Spanish male intellectuals. Like the Inca, who embodies the apparent naivety and innocence of indigenous people, women can be 'la mejor amiga y la mejor compañera', a reminiscence of the myth of the 'good savage'. However, the civilized man must be careful, since their friendship can turn into betrayal and order can become chaos, leading to disastrous consequences such as social disorder.

The representation of the American 'modern woman' in the New York narratives of José Moreno Villa, Teresa de Escoriaza, Luis de Oteyza and Julio Camba reflects contemporary anxieties about the increasing appearance of Spanish women in the public sphere and the resulting challenge to patriarchal notions of national identity. In all the case studies, whether the aim is to preserve or dismantle the subjugation of women to patriarchy, womanhood is constructed as a symbol, an image of something other than mere individuals: goddesses, mothers, daughters, purity and evil, traditionalism and modernization, the family, the nation. Women do not really have a voice of their own in these works. Despite the fear of chaos and degeneration, patriarchy is still very much in control, revealing the masculine gaze behind the construction of both Spanish national identity and gender categories.

First of all, the image of 'la niña violenta' constructed by Moreno Villa in *Pruebas de Nueva York* condenses the violence and aggressiveness with which male intellectuals associated changes in sexual and social conventions. Moreno Villa's view of women's emancipation as the subversion of the 'natural order' imposed by patriarchy unveils the pervasiveness of masculine domination, according to which women must remain in a passive role as 'reproducers' and controlled by men's authority. The focus of the writer on the alleged inversion of 'matrimonial values' taking place in the United States shows the persistence of the 'Ángel del Hogar' trope in Spanish society at the time. Women's entrance into the public sphere and their participation in civil affairs are seen by Moreno Villa as an attack on men's 'natural' authority, hence the depiction of American women as violent and of American men as docile. Furthermore, the writer resorts to images of womanhood as a 'national emblem'. 'La niña violenta' is seen as the expression of US modernization: the rupture with the past, the means of mass production, and the dynamism of life in the metropolis. Although the 'modern woman' was also becoming visible in Spain, Moreno Villa identifies the Spanish 'race' with a traditionalist view of womanhood, embodied by the archetypical 'Spanish woman', who is depicted as passive and submissive. Such identification reveals the patriarchal ethos behind views of Spanish national identity promoted by male intellectuals in this period. Moreover, in spite of Moreno Villa's eventual acknowledgement of the benefits that modernization could bring to Spain and his criticism of projects of national regeneration, he is unable to accept the active participation of women in the very same modernizing process he seems to finally praise.

Teresa de Escoriaza's *El crisol de las razas* represents an attempt to challenge patriarchal discourses by exploring the potential impact that popular narratives could have on the Spanish readership. On the one hand, Helen's voluntary submission to marriage is depicted as a threat to the independence achieved by bourgeois educated women. She renounces the benefits of higher education and becomes economically dependent on a foreign husband who wants her to remain in the family home. Instead of being an active member of civil life, equal to men, the 'modern woman' embodied by Helen goes back to the old-fashioned feminine role of the 'Angel in the House'. Her death is presented as a warning against the pernicious consequences of interracial marriage, and to the allegedly degenerative consequences that the influence of a 'primitive' Jewish patriarchal society could inflict on modern societies. On the other hand, the reaction of the audience to Sonia's performance is the expression of a male gaze that opposes the 'whores' of the lower classes to the 'pure virtue' of the middle-class 'Angel'. However, rather than an image of perversity, as epitomized by *fin de siècle* art and literature, Sonia is shown to be a deprived woman who needs to play the role of an eroticized sexual object in order to survive poverty. Her final refusal to become one of Boris's possessions suggests that lower-class women can gain control of their own sexuality in order to break with patriarchy. The role of men in this process also seems to be seen as essential. Joe symbolizes a new masculinity, sensitive to and respectful of women's individuality. The veil of patriarchy must therefore not only be torn by women but also by men themselves, who must go beyond sexualized archetypes of femininity in order to see women in their whole complexity. The traditional prototype of manhood is here represented by Boris, whose behaviour towards women reflects the hypocrisy of the patriarchal system. He loses sexual interest in Helen once she becomes his wife and she must therefore comply with the role of the chaste and pure 'Angel'. Consequently, he seeks sexual pleasure outside the house, where he treats women as sexual objects at his disposal. The symbolism of this character is highly problematic, for the oppressive patriarchal authority he represents is associated with Judaism. I will analyse the anti-Semitic character of the novella in the next chapter.

Following the polyphonic premises established by the narrative style of *Anticípolis*, Luis de Oteyza's novel presents the clash between modernization and traditionalism through the juxtaposition of two archetypes of womanhood. On the one hand, Rosa embodies the challenge to patriarchal structures undertaken by the 'modern woman' in the United States, and the possibility for a similar change in Spain. On the other hand, Jesusa represents the traditional role ascribed to women in Spain as the 'Ángel del Hogar'. Rosa's aggressive attack on the values defended by her mother suggests the need to overcome violently and actively the unnatural man/woman dichotomy and the consequent seclusion of women in the role of 'reproducers of the nation', in order to embrace the complete modernization of Spain. Such a view is also argued by a male figure, Dr Jiménez, who represents the need for male intellectuals to also challenge patriarchy. Nevertheless, the counter-discourse suggested by Rosa's and Jiménez's modernizing stance relies on an antagonistic attitude towards Jesusa, who is in fact a victim of the symbolic power exerted by patriarchy. Her death, although it seems to imply the need to accept modernization and overcome 'sexual difference', also neglects the conflictive acceptance of submission by a great part of the Spanish feminine population at the time. Furthermore, owing to the polyphonic character of the novel, her death can be interpreted conversely. The impact of modernization on the 'Ángel del Hogar' role would thus represent a threat to the Catholic and traditionalist essence of the Spanish character argued from a *casticista* standpoint. In both cases, women are set to play an essential role in the redefinition of Spanish national identity.

Finally, in *La ciudad automática* Julio Camba elaborates a sexist and misogynist approach to womanhood. His apparent opinion of American women as 'goddesses' invested with power over men in fact reflects the perception of the 'modern woman' as a threat to masculine domination by male intellectuals. In tune with Moreno Villa's ideas, women's alleged supremacy in the United States is seen as going against the 'right order of things'. Gender equality is therefore regarded by the writer as the result of a loss of power by men. Camba's view on womanhood indeed exemplifies the construction of women as irrational sexual objects who must comply with men's authority and satisfy their 'manly needs'. According to this view, women are irrational beings who must be controlled by patriarchy and who are unfit to participate in the public sphere — hence the threat to social order posed by the 'modern woman', as suggested by Camba. However, despite the alleged power of the American woman, she is depicted as a girl, thus undermining the threat posed by her violent rebellion against patriarchy. Camba's paternalistic attitude, coupled with his view of the 'American girl' as a creation of mass production, not only unveils the strength of the patriarchal order that has been supposedly subverted, but also the connections between masculine domination and elitist fears of the uncontrolled 'masses'. Moreover, the comparison established by the writer between women and pre-Columbian societies also shows the links between patriarchal views of national identity and racist discourses that justified colonial domination. This aspect will be analysed in depth in the following chapter, which looks at the challenges posed by New York's incipient multiculturalism to essentialist notions of the nation as a homogeneously 'racial' community.

Notes to Chapter 3

1. The first translation of *The Taming of the Shrew* as *La fierecilla domada* by Manuel Matoses dates from 1895 (Zaro 2007: 72). The text was first staged in Madrid in the season 1918–1919 (Dougherty and Vilches de Frutos 1990: 66). It is therefore likely that this adaptation was known to Escoriaza.
2. There are constant vacillations in the name of this character: Fomitch (25), Fomiteh (24), Tomich (42). I have chosen the first one since it is the variation used in most cases by the narrator.
3. 'The Midnigert Frolies' seems to be a misspelling of *Midnight Frolics*, a 'cabaret-type production' staged at the Broadway Theatre New Amsterdam from 1915 to 1923, as the dancer Doris Eaton Travis states in her autobiography *The Days We Danced: The Story of My Theatrical Family from Florenz Ziegfeld to Arthur Murray and Beyond* (2003: 76).
4. For a complete account of Atahualpa's story, see John Hemming's *The Conquest of the Incas* (1993: 23–70).

CHAPTER 4

❖

Racialism versus Multiculturalism: The Challenge to the Ethnic Nation

> La metrópoli gigantesca donde se encuentran todas las razas y cada una de las variantes de éstas; [...] la nueva Babel donde se hablan todos los idiomas y todos los dialectos del universo; [...] ese crisol de razas, que es Nueva York, donde son lanzados unos con otros hombres y mujeres de todas las religiones y de todas las costumbres
>
> [The gigantic metropolis where all races and each variant of these can be found; [...] the new Babel where all the languages and dialects of the universe are spoken; [...] this melting pot which is New York, where men and women of all religions and customs are thrown together]
>
> TERESA DE ESCORIAZA

Along with the rise of mass society and women's emancipation, the representation of American society in the New York narratives of José Moreno Villa, Teresa de Escoriaza, Luis de Oteyza, and Julio Camba centres visibly on the consequences of the United States' incipient multiculturalism. This chapter analyses the issue of 'race' brought up by the contrast between Spanish ethnic nationalism and US polyethnicity in these texts, and the relevance of 'race' and 'racial' hierarchies for the reassessment of Spanish national identity following the demise of the empire.

Several chapters of *Pruebas de Nueva York* and *La ciudad automática* analyse the 'contaminating' influence of African Americans in New York as well as the alleged Jewish roots of capitalism and modernization. Similarly, *El crisol de las razas* can be read as a strong declaration against miscegenation, and particularly against the supposedly damaging influence of Eastern European Jews. Finally, Luis de Oteyza's *Anticípolis* suggests a more flexible approach to national identity, and in so doing it departs from the three other narratives as a text that engages with Spanish national discourses of the period in a more fluid and forward-looking fashion.

The examination of the views on 'race' shown in these texts will showcase the centrality of 'racial' oppositions in the formation of Western identity as 'superior' to its colonial and internal 'others'. In order to provide the necessary historical and theoretical context, the chapter will begin by exploring the development and relevance of 'racial' stereotypes in Western culture, and the reactions to New York's polyethnicity in early twentieth-century European and Spanish narratives.

Racist Constructions of 'Otherness' in the Formation of Western Identity: European Views on US Multiculturalism

As James W. Ceaser (1997: 87) has argued, in early twentieth-century European representations of the United States this country epitomized two opposite images of 'race' that mirrored Western concerns with 'racial' degeneration. On the one hand, the United States was seen as the repository of the purity of Aryan blood in the modern world, as a young nation founded on the 'supremacy' of the white Anglo-Saxon 'race' over 'inferior races'. On the other hand, democracy, equality, and the practice of 'racial' intermixing were perceived as a contaminating threat for the hegemony of the white 'race', to the extent that

> by allowing the increasing homogenization of blood types that shaped its vitality, America was falling to the ranks of the mediocre among the nations of the world. America, with its foundation in the rationalist ideas of equality and unity of the human species, was slowly destroying itself. (Ceaser 1997: 88)

As opposed to the concept of community promoted by European nationalism — which was highly dependent on ethnic ties — the United States represented 'a new type of nation whose national identity was not ethnically based but constructed around political values of equality, freedom and individualism' (Guibernau 2007: 119). Eric Hobsbawm has pointed out the connections between nationalism and racism in Europe, arguing that between 1880 and 1914 'ethnicity and language became the central, increasingly the decisive or even the only criteria of potential nationhood', to the extent that 'race' and 'nation' were used as virtual synonyms (1990: 63). Since the nineteenth century, scientific ideas of 'race' had been at the core of the definition and delimitation of modern nation-states. The identification between nation and 'race' led the theorists of the so-called 'modern paradigm' to consider nationalism as a doctrine that establishes the belief in nations as 'obvious and natural divisions of the human race, by appealing to history, anthropology and linguistics' (Kedourie 1993: 74). According to this view, nations are a cultural construct, 'imagined communities', as the famous definition coined by Benedict Anderson (2006 [1983]) suggests. Nationalism not only draws on myths of common ancestry and traditions in the delimitation of national identity (Kedourie 1993: 141), but also, as Ernest Gellner (1983: 48) and Eric Hobsbawm (1990: 91) argue, invents them and even obliterates other cultures. This view is especially productive when applied to centralist nationalisms, such as the Spanish one, which create an illusion of homogeneity by denying the possibility of 'other' identities within the national territory.[1]

Furthermore, the creation of a dialectics of alterity has been essential to the formation of Western modernity. Hierarchical images of the white European 'race' as superior make for a constant and essential element in the construction of European identity, since the archive of images and 'racial' stereotypes of the 'Other' has a long and pervasive influence in the history of the West. In the era of early European imperialism started by Columbus's 'discovery' of America, the representation of the 'Other' constructed by European nations was based on a series of attributes such as laziness, violence, greed, sexual promiscuity, bestiality, primitivism, innocence, and irrationality (Loomba 1998: 106). Similarly, stereotypical depictions of blacks as extraordinarily lustful were soon related to the sexual behaviour of the apes, which were discovered in Africa around the same time as the first European encounters with black people. From a very early stage, the so-called 'primitivism' of African peoples was represented through their alleged biological proximity to these animals, justifying a 'racial' hierarchy at the service of colonialist purposes. The figure of the uncivilized native was used as the axis for the opposition between 'civilized nations' and 'savages and barbarians': whereas the Old Continent represented civilization and culture, colonized lands were depicted as the territory of primitivism, 'the "dark" side — forgotten, repressed and denied; the reverse image of enlightenment and modernity' (Hall 1992: 313–14).

The process of colonization and conquest was the essential context for the subsequent scientific theorization of 'race', justifying those myths of 'Otherness' that became 'the core component of European identity from the late nineteenth century onward' (Delanty 1995: 98). Scientific theories of 'race' or 'racialism' sprang from the evolutionary theories of Darwin, which gave the basis for new ideas of European 'racial' supremacy and a view of the colonized as biologically inferior. Tzvetan Todorov (2000: 64) establishes the difference between racism and racialism as follows: whereas racism is 'a matter of *behavior*, usually a manifestation of hatred or contempt for individuals who have well-defined physical characteristics different from our own', racialism corresponds to 'a matter of *ideology*, a doctrine concerning human races'. Ali Rattansi (1994: 54) points out that scientific theories of race have two persistent characteristics: first of all, 'a biological definition of "race", therefore, "racializing" the body and conceiving of a population as having a commonality of "stock" and phenotypical features, such as coloration, hair type, shape of nose and skull'; secondly, 'attempts to create a *hierarchy* of races which, despite representing some "white" races as racially inferior to others, have consistently consigned "non-white" populations to the lowest rungs of the racial ladder'.

As has been extensively studied, black culture became a source of inspiration for the European avant-garde in the early twentieth century, which embraced the view of Negro art as a sort of 'primitive regeneration' (Rasula 2004: 16).[2] Modernist art combined images of simultaneous rejection and acceptance of urban life and resorted to so-called primitive art in order to express its uneasiness with modern life and society. As a consequence, 'the present was affirmed (and much of it denounced) by blending primitivist regeneration with futurist longing' and 'the paradox of an urban jungle emerged, often under the sign of jazz' (Rasula 2004: 27). However, at the same time as these artistic explorations of the so-called primitive sought to subvert cultural oppositions, primitivist modernism also involved 'a revulsion against crossover, a fear of dissolution and confusion, a contrary drive precisely to shore up these boundaries' (Jervis 1999: 76).[3]

The work of early twentieth-century Spanish writers reflected similar tendencies. Modernist authors such as Juan Ramón Jiménez, Ramón Gómez de la Serna, Francisco Ayala, José Moreno Villa, and Federico García Lorca, amongst others, not only mirrored the negrophilia of the European avant-garde, but also represented black people and so-called primitive art in their writings. In his article 'Temas de arte. El arte negro, factor moderno' [Themes of Art. Negro Art, a Modern Factor], published in *El Sol* in 1925, Moreno Villa argues that the origins of modern art — of Cubism in particular — are to be found in Negro art (2001c: 273–79). Spanish avant-garde artists were also captivated by jazz music. Ballesteros and Neira (2000: 20; 52) argue that jazz was often played in the *Residencia de Estudiantes*, a fact confirmed by Isabel Pérez Villanueva Tovar (1990: 217). Ramón Gómez de la Serna devoted two chapters of *Ismos* (1931) to 'Negrismo' and 'Jazzbandismo' respectively, in which he captured the essence of the attraction that the avant-garde felt towards primitivism as a purer and primordial artistic expression, in contrast with the decadence of Western art:

> en esa obscuridad de su raza y de su ignorancia han resuelto los problemas escultóricos de un modo que yo llamaría *terrible*. Encarados en la plástica humana, sin la coquetería que se podría llamar europea y que lo prejuzga siempre todo, han hallado los rasgos espantosos del ser humano y sus descaros y sus terribles cataduras y la base simiesca de su armazón. Han llegado con una sinceridad y una verdad tan grande en el descubrimiento de los *tipos humanos*, que son verdaderos ejemplos de exaltación del *carácter* (1931: 130)

> [in this obscurity of its race and of its ignorance, they have resolved sculptural problems in a way that I would call *terrible*. Confronted in human expressiveness, without the coquettishness which could be called European and which always prejudices everything, they have found frightening features of the human being and their impudence and terrible samplings of the simian base of their frame. They have reached a discovery of *human types* with such great sincerity and truth that they are authentic examples of the exaltation of *character*.]

Gómez de la Serna's assessment of primitive art encapsulates the inherent contradiction of 'primitivist modernism': whereas black art is praised for its naturalness and raw expressivity, these qualities are explained by its ignorance and lack of civilization. Similar arguments can be found in Moreno Villa's article, where he states that:

> Ninguno daba en creer que tales fetiches bárbaros, tales productos maravillosos de la humanidad inocente, encerraban el total. Semejante creencia hubiera indicado debilidad senil. Lo que veían y lo que deben realmente a los escultores negros es la preocupación salvadora, el ansia de conseguir los principios básicos del arte (2001c: 276)

> [Nobody took to believing that such barbaric fetishes, such marvellous products of innocent humanity, encompassed the whole. Such a belief would have indicated senile weakness. What they say and what they truly owe to negro sculptors is the concern for salvation, the urge to achieve the basic principles of art.]

Likewise, the cinematic tribute that Francisco Ayala devotes to Josephine Baker in *Indagación del cinema* [*Cinema Investigation*] (1929), combines appraisal for the famous dancer with statements in which there is a certain colonial overtone clearly influenced by Western discourses of 'Otherness', such as: 'Josefina — los negros — un grito raro y violento, de selva' [Josephine — the negroes — a strange and violent cry, from the jungle] (1929: 149), 'la inimitable zalamería de los negros' [the negroes' inimitable flattery] (1929: 150) and 'una sirena con ojos almendra, con sonrisas de cuchillo, coqueta como un mono' [a mermaid with almond eyes, with smiles like knives, as flirtatious as a monkey] (1929: 151). García Lorca's representation of black people in *Poeta en Nueva York* contains similar contradictions. The 'primitive' — embodied by 'El rey del Harlem' [The King of Harlem] (1998: 125–32) and the African mask of 'Danza de la muerte' [Dance of Death] (1998: 137–41) — reacts against the dehumanization of the modern metropolis and purifies New York's mechanized society. Lorca's powerful image of New York being destroyed by the anger of nature out of control led by a dancing African mask is reminiscent of the more subtle contrast made by Juan Ramón Jiménez in 'La negra y la rosa' [The Black Woman and the Rose] (1994: 142–43) between the mechanization represented by the underground and the beauty and spirituality of the black lady and her rose, which also take over and purify the mechanical environment surrounding them, although in a more delicate manner: 'Y la rosa emana, en el silencio atento, una delicada esencia y eleva como una bella presencia inmaterial que se va adueñando de todo, hasta que el hierro, el carbón, los periódicos, todo, huele un punto a rosa blanca, a primavera mejor, a eternidad...' [And the rose emanates, in the attentive silence, a delicate essence, and rises like a beautiful, immaterial presence which proceeds to become master of all, until iron, coal, newspapers, everything, smells slightly of a white rose, and more so of spring, of eternity...' (Jiménez 1994: 143). However, as Marta López-Luaces suggests, the imaginary created by Lorca is also embedded in Western discourses of 'Otherness':

> Lorca enfatiza la correspondencia entre la comunidad negra y lo primitivo. Forma a través de su poemario un binarismo entre comunidad negra/ modernidad, primitivo/moderno y bueno/malo. Este tipo de binarismo, está en la base de un pensamiento que ha justificado tradicionalmente las jerarquías sociales, raciales y de género. (2008: 130)[4]

> [Lorca emphasizes the correspondence between the black community and the primitive. Through his poetics he establishes a binary opposition between black community/modernity, primitive/modern and good/evil. This kind of binarism is part of the basis of a system of thought which has traditionally justified social, racial and gender hierarchies.]

These discourses had been deeply rooted in Spanish society and culture since the beginning of the Empire. It has been argued that the largest black population in Renaissance Europe was located in Spain (Martín and García Barranco 2008: 107). Accordingly, black people were widely represented in Golden Age Spanish literature, in all literary genres, but especially in theatre (García Barranco 2010: 153–54).[5] Spanish literary representations of blacks characterized them as intellectually and socially inferior, as brutes closer to animals than to humans (Santos Morillo 2011: 27). The strength of this type of discourse is also evident in the political life of early twentieth-century postcolonial Spain. José Luis Venegas (2009), for example, has analysed Unamuno's failure to include black people in his project of a transatlantic Hispanism that 'could restore the international prestige of Spanish culture while overcoming the traumas of four centuries of colonial domination' (2009: 453).[6]

Unamuno's Hispanic project was based on a cultural notion of 'race' in which the Spanish language was the essential bond that united the former colonies and the mainland in an enduring cultural community. Following Domínguez Burdalo, Unamuno's understanding of Hispanism was not only based on the linguistic affinities between Spain and its former colonies, but also rejected views of 'racial' homogeneity in favour of miscegenation (2006: 330). Under this light, Native Americans and creoles were seen as Spaniards by Unamuno since they belonged to a Spanish linguistic community. However, blacks were excluded, and Unamuno sometimes defended and justified their position as slaves (Domínguez Burdalo 2006: 330). The following quote from Unamuno's review of José Mas's novel *En el país de los Bubis* [*In the Country of the Bubi People*] (1931) illustrates the persistence of racist discourses that remained unquestioned in Western thought: 'esos niños grandes, lúbricos y crueles, borrachos y embusteros, que son los negros, y capaces, sin embargo, hasta de la santidad, pero de una santidad casi vegetal, constituyen uno de los más grandes misterios de la historia' [those big children, lubricious and cruel, drunkards and liars, who are the negroes, yet who are nonetheless capable of even saintliness, an almost vegetable saintliness, constitute one of the greatest mysteries of history] (quoted in Domínguez Burdalo 2006: 335).[7] Despite the emphasis placed on the cultural affinities between Spain and its former colonies, nostalgic views of the empire also retained views of 'racial' supremacy that had justified colonial domination.

In order to highlight the strength and recurrence of similar views in the chosen case studies, my examination of the representation of African Americans in early twentieth-century Spanish New York narratives will follow the theoretical framework provided by the approach to primitivism in the arts as explained by Gill Perry (1994: 4), in which primitivism is seen as 'a complex network of sociological, ideological, aesthetic, scientific, anthropological, and legal interests [...] which feed into and determine culture'. Such an approach emphasizes how these discourses involve a relationship of power, and hence 'those within Western society who analyse, teach, paint, or reproduce a view of the "primitive" would, by this activity, be dominating, restructuring and having authority over that which they define as "primitive"' (Perry 1994: 4). As Jervis also points out, 'the sophistication of these modernist explorations, their drive to reflexive awareness, will not save them from an implicit or explicit reproduction of some of the constitutive Western assumptions about otherness' (Jervis 1999: 76).

'Racial' discourses of 'Otherness' did not only originate from colonial encounters in overseas territories. Stuart Hall points out that 'the West also had its *internal* others: Jews, in particular, though close to Western religious traditions, were frequently excluded and ostracized' (1992: 280). The figure of the 'Jew' as a cultural construct — the representation of the dangerous stranger, always settled in a land to which s/he does not belong — has played an essential role in the articulation of Western modernity, as Hannah Arendt, for example, influentially argued in *The Origins of Totalitarianism* (1979 [1951]). The demonization of the Jews must be seen as a continuous process spreading to most of Europe since Antiquity, for Jewish stereotypes had already acquired their most common forms at the beginning of

Christianity. Subsequently, the spread of Christendom in Medieval Europe after the fall of the Roman Empire favoured the consolidation of a series of anti-Jewish myths such as the myth of a degenerate Judaism at the time of Jesus, the myth of a Jewish diaspora as God's punishment of the Jews for the Crucifixion, the myth of the Jews as Christ's killers, and the myth of Israel's rejection by God (Salazar y Acha 1991: 40). With the arrival of the Early Modern Era, as Delanty argues, 'secularised remnants of the Christian world-view, having survived the transition to modernity, continued to provide substance for new forms of European identity based as much on Christian humanism as on "occidental rationalism", which included the repudiation of Judaism' (1995: 65). Furthermore, the process of nation-building, based on linguistic and 'ethnic' unification, provided the European nation-state with a sense of hostility to trans-cultural influences. The Jews, seen as 'a people without a nation', were excluded from national projects.

Owing to their successful adaptation to modernization in the nineteenth century, the Jews were also seen with suspicion and increasing hatred by urban and rural groups who had been negatively affected by economic and political changes (Beller 2007: 52). The image of the 'Jew' became a symbol of liberalism, capitalism, and modernity. Anti-Semitism drew on these prejudices in order to produce a new image of the 'Jew' who was not the traditional enemy of Christendom — although it maintained physical and physiological stereotypes, such as the 'Jewish nose' and 'the Jew as moneylender' — but a scapegoat for all the 'diseases' of modernity, and therefore blamed for the degeneration and fall of civilization. The 'Jew' was seen as foreign and infectious blood in the 'national body' and felt as threat, a 'problem', the 'Jewish question' or *Judenfrage*, to which the only solution was their expulsion or complete annihilation in order to avoid 'racial' contamination, preserve the purity of the superior 'race', and halt the decline of Western civilization.

In Spain, anti-Semitic attitudes must also be contextualized within the historical persistence of the stereotype of the 'Jew' — deeply ingrained in the Spanish social and cultural imaginary since the Middle Ages — as an 'internal Other' against which Spanish identity was constructed. Despite the historical emphasis placed on their expulsion, not all Jews abandoned Spain in 1492, since many of them decided to convert to Catholicism and became an urban minority group of artisans, merchants, scribes, and doctors, separate from the majority of the Spanish population at the time, mainly made up of farmers and shepherds. It was precisely the presence of the *conversos* in positions of power that fostered a wave of antipathy from both the Church and the *castellanos viejos*; the latter, in particular, lacked the education and economic resources possessed by the *conversos*, and therefore could not compete socially with them. Such hostility would be the backdrop against which the first *estatuto de limpieza de sangre* (laws of purity of blood) was established in 1449 (Salazar y Acha 1991: 292). Social marginalization was reinforced by the use of negative sterotypes about the 'Jew', which included that of the cowardly, arrogant. and cunning traitor (Monsalvo Antón 1985: 120). Notably, the 'Jew' was represented as materialistic and as a usurer, whose patrimony was the result of extortion from Christians (Monsalvo Antón 1985: 126). Other stereotypes stemmed from religious prejudices that had their roots in the beginning of Christianity, such as the accusations of ritual crimes, the use of magic, and their association with the devil. Physical stereotypes such as the aquiline nose, secret skin or blood diseases suffered by 'the Jew', and even the possession of a little tail, were related to their alleged diabolical nature (Álvarez Chillida 2002: 40). These negative images of the 'Jew' were promoted by popular literature, such as the *refranero popular* (a popular collection of proverbs) (Monsalvo Antón 1985: 122), and the *Romancero* (a popular collection of Spanish ballads) (Álvarez Chillida 2002: 67–68), which ingrained anti-Jewish representations in Spanish literary and social imaginary, establishing an opposition between the 'true Spanish Christian' and the 'impure' and internal Jewish 'Other' that would last until the twentieth century. The persistence of anti-Jewish constructions of 'Otherness' as an identitarian device in the Spanish social imaginary becomes evident in the depictions of the United States present in the Spanish press before the 1898 war. In these portrayals, American capitalism was regarded as contemptible materialism, opposite to the moral and spiritual values of a Spanishness deeply intertwined with Catholicism (Seregni 2007: 71). In a reductive and stereotypical fashion, Americans were above all identified with money and materialism, hence recurrently depicted as a morally degraded and greedy people. Such a stereotype is illustrated by the following example provided by Seregni, taken from the magazine *Nuevo Mundo*: 'Hijos de la torpe usura / y del negocio inhumano / sólo el cobrar les apura' [Children of clumsy usury / and inhumane business / only earning hurries them] (2007: 73). References to usury and inhumanity can be related to anti-Semitic constructions of 'Otherness', a fact that is strengthened by the characterization of Americans as 'pigs'. Significantly, this is an image that recalls the *Judensau* ('Jewish pig') that since the Middle Ages characterized Jews 'as no better than animals' (Beller 2007: 13).

The construction of Jews as 'Others' also played a significant role in the debates around modernity taking place in Spain at the turn of the century, and especially as part of political projects of national regeneration. In a special issue of the *Journal of Spanish Cultural Studies* entitled 'Revisiting Jewish Spain in the Modern Era' (2011), the editors Daniela Flesler, Tabea Alexa Linhard, and Adrián Pérez Melgosa argue that the intention of the volume is to explore 'particular instances in which Spanish/Jewish junctures provide new insights into Spain's modernity' since 'while the presence of Jews certainly was minimal until the late twentieth century, Jews, real or imaginary, were important figures in the debates that were shifting the nation's present and future' (2011: 1). As Isabelle Rohr (2011: 63–64) points out in an article included in this volume, Sephardic Jews in particular gained significant prominence in nostalgic revisions of Spanish national identity, especially after the publication of Ángel Pulido's *Españoles sin patria y la raza sefardí* [*Spaniards without a Homeland and the Sephardic Race*] (1905). Pulido lamented the persistence of negative stereotypes about the Jews in Spain, and argued for the reintegration of the Sephardic Jewish community to the Spanish nation (1905: 5). The encounter with Sephardic Jews in North Africa during the Spanish protectorate in Morocco in 1912 also encouraged philosephardic campaigns, promoted not only by Pulido but also by intellectuals such as Carmen de Burgos and Unamuno. According to Bretz (2001: 217), 'the rewriting of the past and the redefinition of modern Spain accompanies a revision of Jewish-Spanish relations and a desire to foster mutual understanding and revive the commingling of cultures that characterized early Spanish society'. Resorting to the medical jargon common in regenerationist discourse, Pulido blamed Spanish degeneration on the expulsion of the Jews, since it had provoked a 'bloody amputation' and a 'long and painful hemorrhage' in the Spanish body (Rohr 2007: 15). In Pulido's view, 'racial' mixture between Spanish and Sephardic Jews in the Middle Ages had improved both 'races'; hence, the expulsion of the Jews had triggered not only 'racial' degeneration in Spain, but also economic decline. According to Pulido, the restitution of this lost element of the national culture would prompt Spain's regeneration (Rohr 2007: 16).

Philosephardism was also strongly defended in conservative and proto-fascist circles. One of the champions of the campaign was Ernesto Giménez Caballero, an avant-garde prose writer who turned to fascist positions, especially after his visit to Mussolini's Italy in 1923. *La Gaceta Literaria* — the journal directed by Giménez Caballero — was one of the main promoters of philosephardism in the 1920s and 1930s (Rehrmann 1998: 54). Rehrmann argues that such attitudes responded to the belief that the persistence of the Spanish language in the Sephardic community reinforced the 'greatness' of the Spanish culture (1998: 51). Bernd Rother also stresses the fact that Spanish Sephardic Jews represented a nostalgic view of medieval Spain, a mythical era of Spanish grandeur (1999: 621). Giménez Caballero's philosephardism can therefore be interpreted as a concept closely linked to the project of *Hispanismo* aimed at regenerating a national culture severely questioned after the 'Disaster'. As Michal Friedman argues:

> 'Sepharad' played a central role in the efforts made by Spain's political and intellectual vanguard and Giménez Caballero in particular to elaborate a vision of a New Spain and Hispanic identity in the wake of the loss of Empire in 1898 and shortly before the outbreak of Spain's civil war in 1936. Such efforts, and the elaboration of Hispanidad in this context, are connected to the reemergence of an imperial agenda in Spain and the rise of 'scientific racism' and Orientalist discourse. (2011: 36)

Nevertheless, the sympathy towards Sephardic Jews did not stop the consolidation of anti-Semitic attitudes in Spain. The sort of Spanish philosephardism promoted by Pulido was in fact strongly criticized by Catholic sectors, as shown by the publication of anti-Semitic texts such as *La cuestion judaica en la España actual y en la universidad de Salamanca* [*The Jewish Question in Present-Day Spain and in the University of Salamanca*] (1906) by Joaquín Girón y Arcas, several anti-Semitic articles published in Catholic magazines such as *La Ciudad de Dios* [*City of God*] between 1904 and 1905 and *Arte de reconocer a nuestros judíos* [*The Art of Recognizing Our Jews*] (1916) by Peiró Menéndez as well as the creation of the *Liga Nacional Antimasónica y Antisemita* [*National Anti-Masonic and Anti-Semitic League*] in 1912 (Álvarez Chillida 2002: 274–78). Modern anti-Semitism would become entrenched in Spain especially after the arrival of the Second Republic, with the rise of the radical right. The three political groups brought together under the anti-liberal right — *Acción Nacional*, the monarchists, and the Carlists — shared the view of Spain as an essentially Catholic nation like the Fascist parties that would unite in 1934 as la *Falange Española de las*

Jons (Álvarez Chillida 2007: 182). The Jews were identified by these groups with new national threats such as Socialists, Nationalists, Freemasons, and Republicans; it is during this period that the idea of a Jewish conspiracy aligned with communism was spread by anti-liberal parties. Reflecting the myth of a Jewish conspiracy, the anti-Semitic press orchestrated several campaigns that 'denounced' an alleged Jewish invasion in Spain, that of the Sephardic Jews and also German Jews arriving since 1933 (Álvarez Chillida 2007: 184). Spanish anti-Semites resorted to historical prejudices such as the 'Christ-killer' stereotype which encouraged the image of the 'Jew' as an enemy of Christendom and therefore of Spain.

References to issues of 'race' are recurrent in some of the European travel narratives about New York and the United States written in this period. Paul Morand devotes long passages of his travelogue *New York* to describing the coexistence of different nationalities in the streets of this city, where 'there are no dividing lines between these races living within a few yards of each other, but nothing could mix them' (Morand 1931: 85). Significantly in this 'round-the-world voyage' — as Morand describes the route through the Bowery (1931: 85) — the French writer was particularly taken by the presence of blacks and Jews. For example:

> If you are walking absent-mindedly up Fifth Avenue, and suddenly raise your eyes, you are surprised to notice, in the accustomed frame of low houses with brownstone fronts and front doorsteps, a completely exotic picture. Within a few yards, within a few minutes, the New Yorkers have all turned black! Or suppose you are in the subway, reading your newspaper. The name of the station attracts your attention — One Hundred and Twenty-fifth Street. Look round — your carriage has become a carriage of Negroes! (1931: 256)

Although Morand praises the prestige acquired in the arts by artists and writers of the *Harlem Renaissance* movement such as Countee Cullen and Claude MacKey (1931: 263), his depiction of African Americans also contains colonialist and racist overtones, in which the white 'race' is identified with civilization and Africans with primitivism:

> standing erect at the street crossing, symbolic of white civilization, the policeman keeps his eye on this miniature Africa; if that policeman happened to disappear, Harlem would quickly revert to a Haiti, given over to voodoo and the rhetorical despotism of a plumed Soulouque.... (1931: 258).

Morand not only highlights the large presence of Jews in New York, but also differentiates between 'real' Europeans and those Jews who 'hide' behind such national identities:

> The ghetto. Still, I think there will always be Jewish quarters. In any case, there is not one Jewish quarter here: there are five or six. New York is the largest Jewish city in the world; it contains nearly two million Hebrews. There are German Jews, Spanish and Portuguese Jews, Levantine Jews, Jews from Holland, Galicia, Hungary, Rumania, the Ukraine; there are the multi-millionaire Jews of Fifth Avenue, the millionaire Jews of Riverside Drive, the poor Jews of Harlem and the Bronx and Brooklyn [...] There are, of course, some real Hungarians, Russians, Rumanians or Poles in America, but in general it is Jews who are hidden under these European labels. (1931: 91–93)

Georges Duhamel's *America the Menace* is replete with references to the so-called 'Negro problem', or 'Negro question', two terms that reflected the uneasiness of white Americans with the increasing visibility of blacks thanks to Abraham Lincoln's 'Emancipation Proclamation' in 1863 and the victory of the North over the South in the American Civil War in 1865. The concept appeared for the first time in Hollis Read's *The Negro Problem Solved; or, Africa as She Was, as She Is, and as She Shall Be: Her Curse and Her Cure* (1864). This text posed the question of what should be done with former black slaves freed after the Civil War; Read's impracticable solution was to send them to Africa. Indeed, despite the abolition of slavery in 1865 and the ratification of the 15th Amendment in 1870, which guaranteed suffrage to all American men regardless of their ethnicity, racism was not eradicated in the United States. Klaus P. Fischer (2006: 49) points out that in the 1890s, 'race' relations

> steadily deteriorated despite the fact that the country was passing through an age of reform associated with movements such as populism and progressivism. Jim Crow laws started raining down on helpless African Americans, beginning with separate places on railroad and cars and waiting rooms in railway stations. Next came segregation on steamboats and streetcars.

In 1916, escaping from the segregation policies of the South and attracted by the job opportunities offered by Northern industry, around two million African Americans migrated to the cities of the North, West, and Midwest (Turner-Sadler 2009: 104). This so-called 'Great Migration' resulted in substantial economic, social, and political changes for the whole country. New York, in particular, grew into the American city with the biggest black population in the United States, with 60,000 African Americans in 1910–1920 and rising to 327,706 in 1920–1930 (Grant Meyer 2001: 32). Their arrival in the North was received with increasingly violent racist displays. Although it was illegal, discrimination was perpetuated in the form of a 'de facto' segregation: whites reached informal agreements in order to reduce job and housing opportunities for blacks, who, despite having the right to vote, had little political visibility, since the majority of elected officials were white and ignored their African American counterparts. Working conditions in the factories were also radically different for white and black Americans. Joanne Turner-Sadler argues that

> although African Americans could earn more money in the factories, there was discrimination in hiring. [...] In good economic times, factories hired African Americans. However, when the economy took a downtown, they were the first to be let go. In addition, African Americans were given jobs with dangerous working conditions. Some of these jobs exposed them to intense heat and fumes in the factories. Sometimes these conditions could cause injury or death, particularly in the steel industry. Whites, however, enjoyed the higher-skilled and better-paying jobs. (2009: 104–05)

In Duhamel's view, segregation policies implemented at the time were ineffective since they 'should have been done at the start; that is, two or three centuries ago', in order to avoid miscegenation (Duhamel 1974: 142–43). Duhamel's account poses the alleged dangers of multiculturalism in 'this big, mixed America where the races, brought face to face, have not sought to understand each other, and have not succeeded in loving one another' (Duhamel 1974: 148). In a chapter entitled 'The Segregation of Races' (1974: 139–51), the French writer brings to the fore the discrimination suffered by African Americans. His attitude towards this issue is highly critical. Duhamel seems to feel unease at 'racial' segregation, as he reflects in a series of conversations with white Americans who regard black people as inferior. However, when he touches upon the anxiety generated by interracial relationships in white Americans, who show a fear of 'racial' contamination and degeneration, he seems to reject the idea of 'racial' mixture:

> more plentiful than the pure-blooded Negroes are those of mixed race, innumerable witnesses to the sin of Americans. There is a swarm of half and quarter breeds, a living remorse, a living reproach to this people that, for well-founded reasons, repudiates mixed marriages (1974: 146).

Although he praises President Roosevelt for his 'heroic act in shaking the hand' of the black leader Booker T. Washington, the solution suggested by Duhamel to the so-called 'Negro Problem' is that African Americans should leave the country in order to 'seek a true fatherland, one that will not curse them' (1974: 147). His words echo the view of nations as racially homogeneous.

In *The Future in America*, H. G. Wells shows a similar stance, and devotes an entire chapter to the racism suffered by African Americans, entitled 'The Tragedy of Colour' (1906: 185–202). Although Wells criticizes 'racial' discrimination, he falls into colonial stereotypes such as the black's childish innocence and eagerness to serve the white man:

> He [*Wells is referring to a racist American man*] forgets the genial carriage of the ordinary colored man, his beaming face, his kindly eye, his rich, jolly voice, his touching and trusted friendliness, his amiable, unprejudiced readiness to serve and follow a white man who seems to know what he is doing. He forgets perhaps he has never seen the dear humanity of these people, their slightly exaggerated vanity, their innocent and delightful love of color and song, their immense capacity for affection, the warm romantic touch in their imaginations. (1906: 87)

Wells also dwells on the issue of miscegenation. Once again, although he tries to go beyond racist attitudes, his judgement retains elements of a hierarchical view of 'race' in which the black not only remains in a subaltern position, but is also characterized as having a smaller brain than white men. Moreover, a white man with black ancestry is described as 'tainted':

> It is to the tainted whites my sympathies go out. The black or mainly black people seem to be fairly content with their inferiority; one sees them all about the States as waiters, cab-drivers, railway porters, car attendants, laborers of various sorts, a pleasant, smiling, acquiescent folk. But consider the case of a man with a broader brain than such small uses need, conscious, perhaps, of exceptional gifts, capable of wide interests and sustained attempts, who is perhaps as English as you or I, with just a touch of color in his eyes, in his lips, in his finger nails, and in his imagination. Think of the accumulating sense of injustice he must bear with him through life, the perpetual slight and insult he must undergo from all that is vulgar and brutal among the whites! (1906: 194)

The Future in America also includes a chapter on immigration (1906: 133–51). Here, Wells expresses his concerns about the constant flow of foreigners entering the United States, and the social consequences of such mobility: 'into the lower levels of the American community there pours perpetually a vast torrent of strangers, speaking alien tongues, inspired by alien traditions, for the most part illiterate peasants and working people' (1906: 134). His main criticism is directed towards the alleged difficulty of transforming the immigrants into 'intelligently co-operative citizens', since he believes that the United States does not have 'any organized means or effectual influences for raising these huge masses of humanity to the requirements of an ideal modern civilization. They are, to my mind, "biting off more than they can chaw" in this matter' (1906: 143). Behind such concern lies, as Wells declares, his disbelief that the US can assimilate all these different cultures: 'I doubt very much if America is going to assimilate all that she is taking in now; much more do I doubt that she will assimilate the still greater inflow of the coming years' (1906: 142). The writer disagrees with US policies on immigration, arguing that the influx of illiterate and 'uncivilized' peoples from Europe (especially from the East) serves the purpose of turning them into modern slaves for the US industrial sector. As a solution, Wells suggests that immigration should be subjected to a stronger control (1906: 144–47).

Similarly to European texts about New York and the United States, early twentieth-century Spanish New York narratives often dwell on issues of 'race' and polyethnicity. The city is described as the epitome of cosmopolitanism, where 'se hablaba el inglés, pero también se hablaba el italiano, el castellano, el chino, el polaco y otras lenguas más o menos enrevesadas. Y todas ellas se hablaban, no de una manera esporádica [...] sino como se hablaban en los países respectivos' [English was spoken, and also Italian, Castilian, Chinese, Polish and other more or less complex languages; and all of them were spoken, not in a sporadic fashion [...] but as they were spoken in their respective countries] (Belda 1926: 117–18). The coexistence of peoples from different cultural and ethnic backgrounds is presented in different ways. Criado's text, for example, provides an aestheticized view of the Orient in which Chinatown is depicted as a mysterious neighbourhood (2004: 126–30). Belda describes New York as the 'only real cosmopolitan city in the world', and is particularly amazed by the existence of Chinese and Jewish neighbourhoods (1926: 118). Following a completely different approach, Araquistáin denounces the inequalities still suffered by black people in the United States at the time:

> En el extremo inferior de la escala de razas cuya influencia tratan de excluir los Estados Unidos, están los negros, los esclavos de ayer, ilotas todavía hoy, porque aunque estén reconocidos sus derechos civiles en la letra de la ley, se los niega la costumbre. El problema de los negros es, a juicio de los observadores más desapasionados, el más arduo de los Estados Unidos. Se les estimaba por su utilidad, mientras eran esclavos; hombres libres, se les repudia y se les teme. A ello contribuye un tradicional prejuicio de razas, que ve en el negro un ser inferior, poco más digno que las bestias. Al mismo tiempo, se les teme por su supuesta crueldad, que de ser cierta, ha de deberse seguramente en gran parte al cúmulo de vejaciones y malos tratos, pasados y presentes, padecidos por la población negra. (1921: 12)

[In the lower part of the scale of races whose influence they try to exclude from the United States, are the negroes: yesterday's slaves, helots still today, for although their civil rights are recognized in the letter of the law, they are denied in practice. The negro problem is, in the view of the most dispassionate observers, the most arduous of the United States. They were valued for their usefulness whilst they were slaves; free men, they are disowned and feared. A traditional racial prejudice contributes to this, which sees an inferior being in the negro, little worthier than animals. At the same time, they are feared for their supposed cruelty, which were it true, must surely be owed in great part to the accumulation of vexations and mistreatment, past and present, suffered by the negro population.]

By contrast, Jacinto Miquelarena's travelogue ...*Pero ellos no tienen bananas (El viaje a Nueva York)* perpetuates colonialist stereotypes that characterize African Americans as 'primitive' and whites as 'civilized'. The text includes the description of a show in which, whereas black music is praised for its expressivity when compared to the musical ineptitude of the whites, the Westernized attire of the black singers is strongly criticized for being 'artificial':

> Un negro que canta; una negra que canta; luego cantan los dos. [...] Vestidos a la *europea*; los hombres, con sus sombreros de copa, como si fueran a enterrar a alguien; más aún, como empleados de una funeraria. Las mujeres, con sombras de *music-hall*. Colorete en las mejillas; un color vinoso sobre el negro de la piel. Y lunares de artificio. Son un poco como de trapo. Y, como todo lo de trapo, un poco como de crimen. Hay que cerrar los ojos; no ver aquella cosa patética. Y oír, oír sólo. La voz de los negros siempre es caliente, serena, evocadora, dulce; una voz más musical que ninguna; hay más madera y más cuerda en esas gargantas tostadas. El blanco tiene la voz sin cocer. (1930: 110–11)

> [A negro who sings; a negress who sings; then the two of them sing [...] Dressed in European fashion; the men, with their top hats, as if they were going to bury someone; or rather, as if they were employees in a funeral home. The women, with music-hall shadows. Rouge on their cheeks; a wine colour upon the blackness of the skin. And beauty spots. They look a little as if they were made of rags. And, like everything made of rags, a little criminal-like. One has to shut one's eyes, not see that pathetic thing. And hear, simply hear. The negroes' voice is always warm, serene, evocative and sweet; a voice more musical than any other; there is much woodwind and strings in these roasted throats. The white man has a voice that has not yet been fired.]

This extract highlights the alleged inadequacy of black people for civilization, therefore reinforcing the stereotype of primitiveness.

Interestingly, Miquelarena's references to Jewish people are also placed within another spectacle. In this case it is held at the New Amsterdam Theatre in Broadway, where a Jewish comedian tells a series of jokes about Jews based on the stereotype of Jewish greed (1930: 117–18). Although these jokes are told by a Jewish man to an audience partially made of Jewish people, and therefore represents a case of self-parody and not of racism, it is symptomatic that Belda's allusions to African Americans and Jews are mediated through his position as spectator. Instead of real people, they are depicted as false ('de trapo' in the case of African Americans) and stereotyped; in both cases they are also an object of mockery. Edgar Neville's novel,

Don Clorato de Potasa (1998 [1929]) combines such racist views in the image of an African American Jew:

> — Clorato, ¿te acuerdas de ese chico moreno que salía conmigo? Pues resulta que es judío [...] ¿Te casarías tú con un judío? [...]
> — Yo, no.
> — ¿Odias también a los judíos?
> — De ninguna manera, me divierten, y tengo muchos amigos que lo son.
> — Entonces, ¿por qué crees que no se debe casar una con un judío?
> — No tengo razones muy precisas. Tal vez el pensar que te hará niños judíos, pues cada día te darás cuenta de que son niños judíos. Además, tu marido disimulará sus características de raza mientras le quede el deseo de agradarte, cosa que en nosotros es natural. Para él eso será un esfuerzo. Cuando se canse se dejará llevar por su instinto [...] cambiará tus muebles por otros, y venderá tus trajes usados a las criadas, y tendrá una serie de amigos muy sucios, con barbilla. (Neville 1998: 234–35)
>
> [Clorato, do you remember that dark-skinned boy who used to go out with me? Well, it turns out he is Jewish [...] Would you marry a Jew? [...]'
> 'Me, no I wouldn't'.
> 'Do you also hate Jews?'
> 'Not at all, I find them amusing, and I have many Jewish friends'.
> 'Then, why do you think that one shouldn't marry a Jew?'
> 'I don't have very precise reasons. Maybe it's because it makes me think that he'll give you Jewish children, since every day you'll realize that they're Jewish children. Also, your husband will disguise the characteristics of his race while he still wants to please you, which for us is something natural. For him it'll be an effort. As soon as he gets tired he will follow his instincts [...] he'll change your furniture and will sell your old clothes to the servants, and he'll have a number of filthy friends who wear a goatee'.]

The description of Jewishness in this novel follows some of the Western stereotypes of the 'Jew' discussed earlier in this chapter: filthiness, unpleasant and characteristic physical traits, greed, and materialism. The old archetype of the Jew as materialistic and representative of urban capitalism shapes the perception of US society in the Spanish literary accounts of New York by Moreno Villa, Escoriaza, and Camba, which are not exempt from other anti-Semitic stereotypes. Comparable discourses are also voiced by one of the main characters of Oteyza's novel. As this chapter will show, these Spanish New York narratives reflect the pervasiveness of discourses of 'race' in the construction of Spanish national identity, sometimes resorting to a nostalgic longing for Spain's imperial past — based on colonialist and imperialist views of 'racial' difference –, echoing fears of 'racial' degeneration, reflecting the fascination that writers of modernity had towards black art, or opening a new space in which the racist opposition between the white Spanish master and the black subaltern is challenged.

Pruebas de Nueva York: 'Black Dots' on the 'Jewish City'

In the last chapter of *Pruebas de Nueva York*, entitled 'Puntos Negros' [Black Dots] (1989: 65–68), José Moreno Villa argues that black people and their culture have a strong influence on white Americans. He uses the metaphor 'black dots' to highlight this impact: 'con estos puntos aludo a los individuos de raza negra que motean el país cuadriculado de los Estados Unidos. Puntos negros que deberían figurar en la bandera yanqui alternando con las estrellas rojas [sic]' [with these points, I allude to individuals from the negro race that mottle the squared country of the United States. Black points that should appear on the Yankee flag alternating with the red stars] (65). As throughout his travelogue, Moreno Villa declares his intention to offer an objective approach to the subject:

> no se trata de simpatía ni antipatía en este momento, sino de apuntar lo que veo. Y lo que veo se puede resumir en esto: el negro actúa desde la cabeza hasta los pies del yanqui. Es posible que éste no se dé cabal cuenta de ello, pero en la historia futura de la civilización americana quedará patente, si el historiador no se venda los ojos por antipatía. (65)

> [it is not a matter of kindness or unkindness at this time, but of noting down what I see, and what I see can be resumed with this: the negro works from the Yankee's head to toes. It is possible that the latter is not completely aware of this, but in the future history of American civilisation it will be patently clear, if the historian does not bandage his eyes with unkindness.]

However, the writer avoids engaging in the debates about 'race' taking place in the United States at the time, as he states next: 'no se ofendan mis amigos de Nueva York. No siento debilidad por ellos, ni voy a enfocar ceñudamente el problema que aportan a la sociedad' [my friends from New York must not take offence. I feel no weakness for them, nor am I going to focus grimly upon the problem that they pose for society] (65). Moreno Villa aligns himself with Anglo-Saxon Americans, whom he calls 'mis amigos', and declares not to have any 'debilidad' towards blacks, who are referred to as 'a problem' and located in a position of subalternity which is never questioned: few paragraphs later, the writer characterizes blacks by alluding to their alleged 'submissive nature' (66). As such, they occupy the lowest positions of American society, working as servants: 'los negros, en su mayoría, se dedican al servicio doméstico. Ellos friegan los cristales de los rascacielos, suben y bajan los ascensores, sirven la mesa [...] mozos de labores secundarias, si no ínfimas' [negroes, for the majority, work in domestic service. They clean the windows of the skyscrapers, go up and down in lifts, serve at table [...] and are workers in second-class if not very poor jobs] (68). However, in spite of their social inferiority to white Americans, the writer states that black servants influence their masters: 'es evidente que el criado influye en el amo, y sobre todo, en el ama [...] hay que creer en la influencia de las cosas todas, por humildes, calladas y sumisas que sean. La mera presencia, si es sostenida o constante, acaba por influir sobre uno' [it is clear that the servant influences the master, and above all the mistress [...] One has to believe in the influence of all things, as humble, silent and submissive they may be. The mere presence of something, if it is sustained or constant, ends up influencing one] (68). The imprint left by the servant on his master is a recurrent theme in Moreno Villa's work, for example in articles such as 'Magisterio de los criados' [Lessons from the Servants], 'La enseñanza de los pobres' [Teachings from the Poor], and 'Primeras nociones del mundo' [First Notions of the World], where he highlights the role played by servants in his own education: 'las primeras nociones del mundo social o de la condición humana las recibimos de los parientes y de la servidumbre' [we receive the first notions of the social world and of the human condition from our relatives and from the servants] (Moreno Villa 2010h: 187); 'me siento impulsado por una gratitud, o por un apego sordo, a escribir de unos seres humildes que me rodearon en mi infancia y hasta pudieron influir en mi manera de ver el mundo: los criados, las criadas' [I feel driven by gratitude or by a silent attachment, to write about those humble beings who surrounded me in my childhood and might have even influenced the way I see the world: the male and female servants] (2010d: 97). Moreno Villa's appreciation of his own servants contrasts with his apparent lack of empathy towards blacks. Later on, he explains that

> nosotros no desdeñamos a nuestros servidores, o, al menos, con el desdén que los americanos a los negros; pero es porque reconocemos la hermandad. Los americanos se sienten de otra estirpe, y esto les defiende del influjo; pero ellos no saben por dónde se cuela éste (68)

> [we do not disdain our servants, or at least with the disdain that Americans show towards negroes; but this is because we recognize brotherhood. The Americans consider themselves another race, and this defends them from other influences; but they do not know where this figures]

This statement could be interpreted as an expression of 'racial' difference, in which Spanish servants are recognized as 'brothers', but blacks would be excluded from such brotherhood. This idea seems to be reinforced in the opening paragraphs of the text, where the author argues that

> sin saber por qué, le adjudicaba yo a todo negro que veía el conocimiento del español y, con ello, un cierto parentesco; pero esta falsa emoción, que sin duda tiene su raiz [sic] en que Cuba fué [sic] nuestra, y que de niño vi negros que castellanizaban y hasta influían en el cante 'jondo' con sus 'habaneras', 'rumbas' y demás, no acaba de seducirme. No me casaría con una negra. (65)

> [without knowing why, I attributed to every negro I saw the knowledge of Spanish and, with that, a certain kinship; but this false emotion, which without doubt has its root in Cuba having been ours, and in that as a child I saw negroes who spoke Castilian and even influenced flamenco singing with their 'habaneras', 'rumbas' and other music, does not ultimately convince me. I would not marry a negress.]

Following the concept of 'Hispanidad' developed by regenerationist projects, it seems at first that Moreno Villa identifies language with national identity, establishing a linguistic brotherhood between the mainland and the colonies. Such kinship is, however, soon rendered as 'false' by the writer. He is even categorical about interracial marriage. When compared to his earlier work, this reaction seems contradictory. In 1925, he had openly referred to Spaniards as an interracial people: 'a primera vista, todos somos moros en Andalucía. Después se nota cierta complejidad en el tipo. Acaso en algún momento parezca que domina el semblante romano de la aristocracia' [on first sight, we are all Moors in Andalusia. Then a certain complexity in the appearance is noticed. Perhaps at some moment it might seem that the Roman countenance of the aristocracy predominates] (2001a: 307);

similarly, in 1926 he wrote: 'España, que por su judaísmo y por su gitanería sabe de chaleco, cambalache, tira y afloja, regateo' [Spain, which through its Judaism and its gypsy ways, knows of waistcoats, bazaars, hard bargaining, haggling'.] (2001a: 315). Moreover, after his exile to Mexico, Moreno Villa avoided colonialist attitudes, as his interest in Mexican art and its hybridity (Huergo 2001: 50–56) and texts such as 'Mi españolismo y mi mexicanismo' [My Spanishness and My Mexicanism] (2010e) confirm. In the former, he defines Mexican culture as the result of a 'fusión carnal' which seems to allude to 'racial' mixing: 'nadie puede sostener que la cultura prehispánica se fundió con la española. Quien se fundió fue la persona indígena con la persona ibérica. De modo que esa fusión, constitutiva del mexicano, es puramente somática y psicológica, del cuerpo y del alma' [nobody can argue that pre-Hispanic culture mixed with that of Spain. What mixed was the indigenous person with the Iberian, and in such a way that this fusion, constitutive of the Mexican, is purely somatic and psychological, and of the body and soul] (2010e: 235). Nonetheless, in spite of his rejection of Spanish colonialism, the author seems to be influenced by prevalent Western discourses about black people that characterized them as inferior and only suitable as servants. As Miguel García-Posada has argued regarding Moreno Villa's depiction of blacks in his New York travelogue, the writer avoids taking a political stance on this issue, reflecting the views held by the European left, in most cases, about colonialism until the Second World War (1990: 47). This attitude is illustrated by his volume *Locos, enanos, negros y niños palaciegos* [*Madmen, Dwarfs, Blacks and Children from the Palace*] (1930), where Moreno Villa tells the story of Ángel, the black servant of his great-grandfather, who did not want to claim his freedom and remained faithful to the family and the house, where he died as a member of the household (1930: 21). Similarly, in his account of African Americans in *Pruebas de Nueva York*, he declares his respect and appreciation for the humility of the servants, as he states, 'no se trata de simpatía ni antipatía en este momento, sino de apuntar lo que veo' (65). However, the author never questions the position of subalternity in which African Americans are located — and in which they even remain voluntarily, as in Ángel's case — despite their influence on their masters. Moreover, such influence seems to cause a certain discomfort in the writer, since it is described as a silent and hidden process: '[the black] no se engalla, no levanta cabeza; siente que su escalafón social es ínfimo; pero allá en el fondo de su conciencia le sonreirá la satisfacción de ver que actúa sobre el pensamiento y la sensibilidad de los hombres rubios y fuertes' [he does not swagger, he does not raise his head; he feels that his social ladder is negligible; but there in the depths of his conscience the satisfaction of seeing that he acts upon the thought and sensibility of fair and strong men will smile upon him] (65). Instead of highlighting the unfairness of 'racial' inequality, Moreno Villa focuses on how blacks slip their 'primitive' influence secretly into the white man's 'civilized' physique. As can be seen in the following excerpt, the author resorts to Western stereotypes of subalternity — such as the assumed sensuality and musical skills of the colonized — in order to show the pathway through which such endangering influence purportedly enters American society:

> ninguna blanca se abraza con el negro para bailar. Pero el bailarín negro será

quien imponga la danza. Y este aspecto de la sensualidad entra en América por él. Por eso digo que actúa sobre los pies y las piernas del americano. Y como a fuerza de danza se adquieren maneras y detalles dinámicos que caben en lo que ya no es danza, sino movimiento general, ademanes de la vida cotidiana, se puede notar en que en las chicas intrépidas hay "monadas" que son negroides, piruetas gráciles que no heredaron de las paquidérmicas razas rubias. Se comprende la risa enormemente blanca del negro del "jazz". [...] No puedo imaginarme cómo serían los Estados Unidos sin "jazz". Creo que es una de las cosas que más unifican su fisonomía. Es posible que este sello que pone la raza negra a las múltiples razas de los Estados Unidos sea momentáneo, transitorio; pero nadie sabe las derivaciones que trae una influencia momentánea si es fuerte. (66)

[no white woman embraces the negro to dance. But it is the negro dancer is who leads the dance and this aspect of sensuality enters America with him. That is why I say that he acts upon the feet and legs of the American. It is through dance that dynamic details and manners are acquired, and which fit into not what is now dance, but general movement, gestures of everyday life. It can be noted that in intrepid girls there are "cuties" which are negroid, graceful pirouettes which they did not inherit from the fair, pachydermic races. It explains the enormously white laughter of the "jazz" negro. I cannot imagine how the United States would be without "jazz". I believe that it is one of the things that most unifies its physiognomy. Is it possible that this stamp that the negro race puts upon the multiple races of the United States is momentary, transitory; but nobody knows the derivations that a momentary influence brings with it if it is strong.]

In spite of the pervasive racism of early twentieth-century American society and segregation policies — which are not directly alluded to but only insinuated in the first line of the excerpt — the writer argues that blacks 'impose' their culture on white Americans thanks to jazz music. Inebriated by liquor, and enraptured by the rhythm of the music, Americans seem not to be aware of the influence of the 'black'. Like a master puppeteer acting in the shadow, the spell of his arcane music moves the legs not only of the Americans, but also of the entire world. The weakness of the subaltern is here turned into strength ('virtud'), and the white master has lost his mind, intoxicated by the obscure arts of the black dancer. Moreno Villa's description of the effects caused in Americans by the influence of jazz is not entirely original, but reflects similar concerns in American society at the time:

> jazz received a fair amount of negative press in the late 1910s and then became an object of a moral panic during the 1920s. Some whites feared jazz because it was rooted in black culture, because it played a role in facilitating interracial contact, and because it symbolized, in racially coded terms, the intrusion of popular tastes into the national culture. [...] Not only were African Americans becoming more visible members of American urban society, as a result of the Great Migration, but they were becoming more vocal in their political demands as well. (Porter 2002: 9)

Nevertheless, the writer neglects the political impact that jazz could have for the demands of social equality raised by black activists at the time, or the racist fear of cultural contact by white Americans. Significantly, he highlights the pernicious consequences that the exposure to jazz causes in the American 'modern women', here denominated 'las chicas intrépidas'. By entering the public space of the jazz club, American women not only subvert gender hierarchy, but also become 'infected' by black music, which extends its influence to their daily life, turning them into 'monadas negroides', therefore suggesting cultural 'contamination'. The choice of the word 'monada' can also be understood as a sign of 'racial' involution; although semantically it refers to positive physical qualities such as beauty and cuteness, morphologically it also echoes the word 'mono' ('monkey') and therefore the racialist association between black people and apes that justified their categorization as an inferior 'race'. Significantly, Moreno Villa places this word in inverted commas, thus suggesting a meaning that goes beyond its semantic definition. Such an allegedly degenerative effect in women would be in turn poisonous for the whole 'race', since

> the fear of cultural and racial pollution [...] suggests the instability of 'race' as a category [...] Women on both sides of the colonial divide demarcate both the innermost sanctums of race, culture and nation, as well as the porous frontiers through which these are penetrated (Loomba 1998: 159)

In tune with Loomba's argumentation, Moreno Villa's words not only suggest a cultural influence — which therefore 'damages' the values women are supposed to pass on to their children — but also sexual 'contamination'. American women under the influence of jazz are described as 'negroids', since their movements have not been inherited from the 'blond races'. This remark can be connected with the previous rejection of interracial marriage. The writer seems to suggest that miscegenation is already taking place in New York, where even women who seem to be Anglo-Saxon could in fact be black women under the 'disguise' of their pale skin and fair hair. This suggestion is indeed reminiscent of the 'one-drop rule', a colloquial term used in the United States at the time to imply that even one single drop of 'black blood' was enough 'to construct a person as black' (Yuval-Davies 1997: 50).

While he seems to imply that jazz music has a corrupting effect, Moreno Villa appreciates its musical qualities, since jazz 'hace bailar al mundo entero con una embriaguez desconocida de nuestros padres envolviendo y electrizando [...] en las síncopas, quiebros y monotonía de su música peculiar' [makes the whole world dance with a rapture unknown by our parents, wrapping and electrifying [...] in its syncopations, sidesteps and the monotony of its peculiar music'.] (66). Similarly, he admires the religiosity of Negro spirituals and the holiness they bring to American society: 'desconozco la profundidad a que alcanzan estas "espirituales" en el alma Americana. Pero me inclino a que no es pequeña, porque tal vez no hay arte más penetrante que el de la música' [I do not know the profundity that is reached by these "spirituals" in the American soul. But I am inclined to think that it is not small, because perhaps there is no more penetrating art than that of music]. Moreno Villa describes spirituals as original, mystic, and transcendental, and praises their hybridity:

> las ceremonias de estos negros recién bautizados tienen un color tan aparte que lo ritual parece recién inventado [...] hay en sus ceremonias una fusión

> de elementos. [...] Y no brotan en todo momento, sino cuando el ánimo está preparado, cuando llegó poco a poco la embriaguez mística (67)

> [the ceremonies of these recently-baptised negroes are of such a different colour that the ritual seems recently invented [...] There is a fusion of elements in their ceremonies. [...] And they do not emerge at each moment, but when the spirit is prepared, when it has attained, little by little, mystic rapture]

This admiration persists after his stay in New York, and in 1953 he recalls 'los *blues* oídos en Nueva York el año 27, cantados y bailados con un recogimiento digno de una catedral', which 'se me quedaron ahí, en la cinta de la memoria' [the blues heard in New York in 1927, sung and danced with a recollection worthy of a cathedral [...] remained there for me, on the film that is memory] (2010i: 330). In both cases, Moreno Villa admires the originality of black music; however, the class divisions sustained in American society by 'racial' hierarchy are accepted as normal:

> hay un refrán ruso que dice: "Echad la naturaleza por la puerta, que ella entrará en vuestra casa por la ventana". Y a los americanos cabría decirles: "Despreciad a vuestros inferiores, que ellos os enseñarán el canto y el baile, la sensualidad y gracia refinadas" (68)

> [there is a Russian saying that goes: 'Throw Nature out through the door, and she will climb back into the house through the window'. It would be fitting to say to the Americans: 'look down upon your inferiors, for they will teach you song and dance, refined sensuality and charm]

In this image of rebellious nature — reminiscent of Lorca's poem 'Danza de la muerte' — Moreno Villa not only praises the artistic qualities of blacks, especially their musical talents, but also seems to refer to the idea of a 'primitivist regeneration' as promoted by modernist art. However, despite their artistic value, blacks are still seen as 'inferiores'. Humberto Huergo Cardoso (2001: 79) has argued that, although Moreno Villa refers to the the situation of blacks in the United States, and spirituals will leave a strong imprint on his memory, he treats blacks as an artistic subject rather than as real individuals. Yet, while he states that 'no me casaría con una negra', his fascination with black music leads him to incorporate jazz rhythms into the poetic account of his relationship with Florence in *Jacinta la pelirroja*, as he states in its opening verses: 'Eso es, bailaré con ella / el ritmo roto y negro del jazz. Europa por América' [That's right, I'll dance with her / the broken, black rhythm of Jazz. Europe through America] (Moreno Villa 2000: 77). He even expresses his loneliness, like a blues singer, through the melancholy of black music, in the poem 'Causa de mi soledad' [The Reason for My Loneliness]: '¡Ah! y cantor negro / de un jazz que siento/ a través de diez capas del suelo' [Ah! And negro singer / of a jazz I hear / through ten layers of the floor] (Moreno Villa 2000: 112). In his autobiography *Vida en claro*, he declares how he had felt 'inebriated' by the spirit and syncopated rhythm of jazz (Moreno Villa 2006: 142). Moreno Villa's account of blacks in America mirrors the attitudes of the European avant-garde towards primitivist art that he had studied prior to his visit to New York. As in the view of Negro art as 'primitivist regeneration', black music brings a sense of spirituality and renovation to the alleged materialism and excessive puritanism of American society. However, influenced by prevalent discourses of 'Otherness' deeply ingrained in the imaginary of Western modernity, the writer remains incapable of challenging colonialist views of blacks as inferior beings only fit to serve their white masters.

Moreno Villa places a similar emphasis on 'racial' difference when he refers to the presence of Jewish people in New York, a city that he defines as 'el prototipo de la ciudad hebrea' [the prototype of a Jewish city] (1989: 33). The writer gives this name to the city because of its commercial character:

> La metrópoli de Nueva York es, por su índole, comercial hasta los tuétanos. Y para un español — que, como español, es poco viajero –, nada tan extraño como una ciudad judía y negociante. Comienzan por sorprenderle los rótulos públicos en algunos establecimientos piadosos, como Hospital del Monte Sinaí, Asilo para las Hijas de Israel. Como el español tiende todavía a creerse en su patria esté donde esté, no comprende tales rótulos al primer momento. Se restriega los ojos y se pregunta cómo ha podido salir a la superficie este poderío israelita. Poco a poco va viendo luego que el acento principal de la ciudad es eso: poderío comercial. Todo es aquí negocio. Las tiendas y los despachos es lo que hay que ver en Nueva York. (31–32)

> [The metropolis of New York is, by its very nature, commercial to the core, and for a Spaniard — who, as a Spaniard, is not given to travelling — there is nothing stranger than a Jewish and merchant city. The broken lettering on some pious establishments, like the Mount Sinai Hospital and the Daughters of Israel Home, begin to surprise him. As the Spaniard still tends to believe that his country is wherever he is, he does not understand such lettering at first. He rubs his eyes and asks himself how this Israelite power has managed to come to the surface. He then sees little by little how the principal accent of the city is this: commercial power. All of this is business. The shops and offices are what has to be seen in New York.]

Moreno Villa identifies Judaism with trade and business, following stereotypes such as those of 'Jewish avarice' and of 'the Jew as moneylender'. Moreover, it seems that the writer extends the traditional identification between Jews and usury to American capitalism ('poderío comercial', 'poderío israelita'), which he sees as an expression of Jewish 'nature' ('su índole'). He contrasts the materialism embedded in American society — due to the alleged effect of Judaism — with the (Catholic) spirituality characteristic of Spanish identity. In his view, whereas New York is controlled by businessmen and the fever of business, Spanish people instinctively react against such materialism:

> El español viajero, sin tener negocio que le preocupe, siente alrededor, bajo sus plantas, sobre su cabeza, y hasta en las entrañas, una trepidación incómoda que le va echando y empujando de todas partes, como diciéndole: Es pecado pararse a contemplar; anda, que no podrás volver si no tomas el ómnibus que pasa. (32)

> [The Spanish traveller, without any business to bother him, senses around him (beneath his feet, above his head and even in his guts), an uncomfortable trepidation which begins to pull at and push him all over, as if to say: it is a sin to stop and stare; go on, you won't be able to come back if you don't take the omnibus that's passing by.]

In this excerpt, money and business are seen by the writer as a sin to be rejected by the spiritual nature of the Spanish traveller. Significantly, Moreno Villa emphasizes the surprise ('nada tan extraño', 'se restriega los ojos') and uneasiness ('una trepidación incómoda') caused in him by the visibility of Judaism in New York, where the 'Jew' — Spain's archetypical 'internal Other' — is not a stranger. I argue that the writer's amazement also derives from another long established stereotype in Western culture: the 'wandering Jew'. As Enrique Moradiellos (2009: 157) explains, the legend of Ahasuerus or Cartaphilos, the 'wandering Jew', refers to the story of a Jewish shoemaker who is said to have insulted Christ on his way to Golgotha. As punishment for his offence, Ahasuerus was condemned to wander around the world until Judgment Day. The legend became a symbol used in a variety of artistic representations and literary works, referring to the Jewish Diaspora. In a state of exile since early times, the Jews have been stereotyped by their constant movement as a 'nation' or a 'race' without a state, always strangers in a foreign land. The Spaniard, on the other hand, is depicted by Moreno Villa as 'poco viajero'. His 'race' and national identity are an expression of his 'natural' geographical origin, to the extent that 'tiende todavía a creerse en su patria esté donde esté': his homeland travels with him and is part of his identity. The Jews, however, are seen as a 'race' of wanderers that, even when established in a given territory, are not only — and always will be — foreigners, but are also a minority. Nevertheless, in New York they seem to be a majority, a fact that disconcerts the writer, hence his allusions to the visibility of Judaism in the streets of the city.

Moreno Villa's reference to the Jewish name of those 'establecimientos piadosos' is not accidental. In fact, this allusion to religion takes the reader back to the expulsion of the Jews from Spain in 1492, regarded as a historical milestone in the Catholic formulation of Spanish identity

> because the conquest of the Moorish kingdoms achieved in the thirteenth century came to be seen both as a national war of liberation and as crusade, there was a special holiness, a special Christianness and Catholicism, in Spain's very existence. [...] That holiness and therefore national identity too seemed inherently threatened by the survival of Muslim or Jew in the kingdom and especially by secret Jews or Muslims, huge numbers of double-faced people existing in the nationalist and Catholic imagination as only pretending to be Spanish and Christian. Their expulsion appeared as the consummation of the struggle for Spanish identity. (Hastings 1997: 111)

Not all Jews were expelled by the Catholic Monarchs, since those who consented to convert to the national religion were allowed to remain in the Spanish Kingdom. However, according to Salazar y Acha (1991: 292), the majority of these converted Jews still practised their religion, although secretly. By contrast, Moreno Villa's travelogue suggests that in early twentieth-century New York, Jews did not need to hide their religion.

The connections between movement (the 'wandering Jew') and capitalism ('Jewish avarice') are fused into another stereotype that arose in the nineteenth century and characterized Jews as a 'symbol of modernization'. Moreno Villa states that New York is a city dominated by anxiety and permanent movement, which he sees as an expression of the Jewish influence in the metropolis:

tal angustia, ¿es hija de Nueva York por ser esta ciudad marcadamente judaica, o no? Siempre he creido [sic] que la inquietud es una de las más profundas virtudes y defectos de la raza judía, y por eso veo en Nueva York el prototipo de ciudad hebrea. Como español y como europeo, rechazo ese dinamismo, a pesar de lo conveniente que pueda ser para mí, para el otro y para la Humanidad. (33)

[is such anguish the fruit of New York, of this city, being so markedly Judaic, or not? I have always believed that anxiety is one of the deepest virtues and defects of the Jewish race, and that is why I see in New York the prototype of the Hebrew city. As a Spaniard and European, I reject this dynamism in spite of how convenient it may be for me, for the Other and for Humanity.]

'Angustia' and 'inquietud' are seen by the writer as distinctive features of the 'Jewish character'. However, the writer seems unable to discern whether such restlessness, and therefore movement and modernization, is a virtue or a fault. On the one hand, his association between New York's modernization and Judaism follows discursive preconceptions based on fixed oppositional features such as materialism/spirituality, insider/outsider, and Catholic/Jew, traditionally used to determine Spanish identity. Therefore, by establishing 'how the Jews are', Moreno Villa is also resorting to a specific conception of Spanish national identity, reminiscent of the opposition between Spain's Catholic spirituality and American amoral materialism demonstrated by the Spanish press before the 1898 war. However, throughout his travelogue Moreno Villa criticizes Spain's immobility and eventually acknowledges some of the benefits of modernization. This view leads him to question his own words, or rather, the system of representation that is moulding his view of New York. Ultimately, he declares that American capitalism also has some positive aspects:

cuesta mucho entender algo de los matices y pequeñas divergencias de ideales, y cuesta mucho más aún transmitirlos. Es muy fácil repetir el lugar común, despectivo en boca hispana, de que al yanqui no le interesa más que el dólar [...] Pero es muy difícil comprender que en esto del dinero hay un ideal noble [...] Quiere los dólares para vivir confortablemente y perfeccionar todo lo que le rodea. Para tener baños y jabones, tapices y butacas, libros y cuadros, buenos manjares y buenos médicos, buenos aparatos y excelentes profesores, trenes rápidos, etc [...] Los quiere para obras benéficas y para que a sus hijos no les falte nada en su formación. (34)

[it is very difficult to understand something of the tones and small divergences of ideals, and it is even more difficult to transmit them. It is very easy to repeat the commonplace, derogatory when coming from a Spaniard, that the Yankee is only interested in the dollar [...] But it is very difficult to understand that in this matter of money there lies a noble ideal [...] He wants dollars to live comfortably and to perfect everything that surrounds him. To have baths and soaps, carpets and armchairs, books and paintings, fine delicacies and good doctors, good appliances and excellent teachers, fast trains, etc. [...] He wants them for charities and so that his children want for nothing in their education.]

'Cuesta mucho entender', 'es muy difícil comprender', he says. He admits that Spanish views of the United States are limited by preconceptions ('el lugar común, despectivo en boca hispana') and tries to go beyond such discursive limitations.

Later on, he states that the use of money to create a better society, 'which [...] seems so common to the general human instinct, is not ideal for the Spaniard, not even decent' (34). The opposition between American materialism and Spanish spirituality is still in force here, but it seems that Moreno Villa is now positioning himself on the other side. Modernization — condemned a few lines earlier — becomes 'common sense', as opposed to the Spanish conception of materialism as indecent. Such ambivalence reflects the struggle between the *casticista* imperative of preserving the essence of Spanish national identity and liberal calls for Europeanization. Although Moreno Villa's text constructs the 'Jew' as the embodiment of materialism against which the alleged spirituality of Spanish identity is defined, the contrast between Spain and the United States in economic terms leads the writer to question the validity of the preconceptions about American society. Furthermore, his view of Spain is also challenged, to the extent of qualifying Spanish ideals as contrary to the 'general human instinct'. As seen in Chapter 2, Moreno Villa eventually encourages Spanish intellectuals to go beyond *regenerationist* notions of Spanish national identity, to travel to the United States, and witness the benefits that American modernization could bring to their country.

'Jewish Evilness' and the Dangers of Miscegenation in *El crisol de las razas*

As its title suggests, *El crisol de las razas* places a strong emphasis on the effects of 'racial' mixture. Importantly, issues of 'race' in the text centre upon the alleged negative influence of Eastern European Jews in American society. The novella contains abundant references to the stereotypes of the 'Jew', which are especially concentrated in the figure of Boris Zinovief, described as 'un hombre enjuto, de tez pálida y nariz aguileña. Lo más característico de aquella fisonomía era la mirada, una mirada penetrante, sombría y fría' [a lean man, with pale complexion and aquiline nose. The most characteristic feature of that physionomy was the gaze, a dark, cold and penetrating gaze] (Escoriaza 1929: 15). Boris is portrayed as a diabolical force, the 'serpent' that seduces the pure and angelical Helen, who is in turn described as 'Eve' succumbing to the temptations offered by his fortune. Apart from blatant allusions to the physical peculiarities ascribed to the 'Jew', such as the aquiline nose, Boris is also described as a selfish and greedy tycoon, the embodiment of 'Jewish avarice':

> aquellos eran los suyos, los que se reunían en los antros de la parte baja del este de la ciudad: emigrantes de los países eslavos, la mayoría pertenecientes a la raza maldita, y muchos de ellos gentes sospechosas... ¿Es que, acaso, no se hablaba también de los procedimientos misteriosos empleados para acumular aquella fabulosa fortuna? (9)

> [those were his own, those who gathered in the dives of the lowest part of the city's east side: emigrants from Slav countries, the majority of them belonging to the accursed race, and many of them suspicious people... Did they not, in fact, also talk about the mysterious proceedings undertaken to accumulate that fantastic fortune?]

Going even further, the narrator insinuates that Slavic Jews are criminals ('gentes sospechosas'), and so is Boris, since he has probably obtained his capital by illegal means. Whether by usury or otherwise, the narrator seems to imply that Boris's fortune is tainted by the sins of his 'raza maldita'. The allusion to the Jews as immigrants also refers to the trope of the 'wandering Jew'. The presence of such a stereotype becomes clearer some pages later, when the Jewish neighbourhood of the East River, 'la Ciudad Judía' [the Jewish City] (14), is described as 'la Babel de Nueva York' [the Babel of New York] (14), where 'los diversos elementos eslavos: rusos, polacos, checos [...]' gathered 'por afinidades de raza, costumbre y aficiones, ya que no por la lengua, pues en aquella zona se hablan todos los idiomas derivados del eslavón' [the different Slav elements: Russians, Poles and Czechs' gathered 'through affinities of race, custom and tastes, since it would not be through language, for in that area all the languages derived from Slavonic were spoken] (14). The reference to the Babel myth confers this area with an aura of doom, destined to end in chaos and tragedy, in tune with the characterization of Jewish people as 'la raza maldita'. This expression also perpetuates the stereotype of the Jews as 'Christ killers', damned to roam for eternity.

Boris is demonized throughout the novel because of his Jewish origins, not only by the narrator, but also by other characters. Helen alludes to Boris's cultural background in order to explain her husband's attraction towards New York's underworld: 'abandonada por su marido, ¡por un ruso... ¡por un judío!.. que llevaba el escarnio hasta arrastrarse por los tugurios más inmundos del barrio del Este y rodearse con gentes maleantes, con salvajes procedentes del oriente de Europa' [abandoned by her husband, by a Russian... by a Jew! ... who ridiculed her to the extent of grovelling throughout the filthiest dives of the Eastern neighbourhood and surrounding himself with crooks, with savages coming from Eastern Europe] (8). The contrast between the United States and Eastern Europe ('el oriente') is blatantly based on the duality 'West'/'East', where the former stands for 'civilization' and the latter for 'primitivism' ('salvajes'). Furthermore, the stereotype of 'Jewish primitivism' is endowed in this case with violence and malice ('gentes maleantes'). Such primitivism is the result of innate and irrational instincts, whose influence in American society eventually leads to chaos and death. The dangers of miscegenation are therefore embodied by Boris, who is accused by the narrator as partially responsible for Helen's murder:

> su mirada, libre de aquel punto de cinismo, era más sombría que nunca. Aunque en cierto modo era él el causante de aquella tragedia espantosa, no por ello se consideraba responsable. Todo era obra de la fatalidad que, caprichosa, se empeña en mezclar unas razas con otras, sin hacer caso de sus afinidades, produciendo así daños irreparables. (42–44)

> [his look, free of that touch of cynicism, was darker than ever. Although in a way he was the cause of that frightful tragedy, he did not consider himself responsible for it. Everything was the work of fate, which capriciously undertakes to mix races together without consideration for their affinities, and producing in this way irreparable damage.]

Boris — and by extension Jewish people — functions in this text as a scapegoat for Helen's death. As we know, the real murderer is Fomitch, Sonia's Russian bodyguard, who accidentally kills the American woman in a fit of jealousy. Fomitch is described by the narrator as an 'abnormal being' with a limited intelligence (42). It seems therefore that the narrator is using Fomitch's mental handicap to exonerate him from his crime. Even Sonia, knowing that Fomitch is responsible for the tragedy, decides not to accuse him (42). Furthermore, there is no substantial reason to blame Boris for the murder. In spite of the diabolical image given of him by the narrator, and his sexual insinuations to Sonia, the novella does not relate any factually dishonest action committed by the Russian mogul. He never manages to fulfil his sexual desires with the singer, and he even declares that his sole purpose is to promote her musical career (28). His devious intentions towards Sonia are in fact insinuated by characters such as Iván, who associates Boris with another Russian character, Prince Sergio Mohilev. Boris is here presented as the embodiment of an oppressive patriarchal hierarchy, and the novella carries a strong defence of women's emancipation. Therefore, the 'Jew' is not only falsely blamed for Helen's murder, but also for perpetuating the barbarous practice of masculine domination in American society. In addition, not even the rumours about the 'mysterious procedures' by which Boris obtained his fortune are ever confirmed. From the beginning of the novella, the narrator provides a negative image of the Jewish tycoon, and as a result, the reader can accept Boris's (false) blame without remorse: even if he were not guilty, he would deserve to be so.

The perceived disastrous effects of miscegenation are also conveyed through the 'racial' construction of the other characters. First, both Helen and Sonia are presented as the feminine embodiment of their respective 'races' and nations. On the one hand, Helen is depicted according to the stereotype of the American girl: blonde, beautiful, independent, and rebellious. On the other hand, Sonia is portrayed as the archetype of the Russian woman: dark-haired, mysterious, superstitious, and passionate. Sonia is in fact described as an exemplary representative of her 'race', especially when she sings, since her singing condenses 'the sorrowful soul of a whole race' (19). As one can note, the psychological features of these two characters are conditioned by their particular 'race' and culture. As we have seen in Chapter 3, when Helen disguises herself in Sonia's clothes, her American coldness is temporarily transformed into Slavic passion and excitement (40). However, in spite of the disguise and of her momentary awakening to sensuality, she cannot completely embrace the Russian passion incarnated by the singer, since 'she didn't know how to differentiate between those feelings acquired through education and those which are innate and characteristic of other races' (41). Helen is therefore unable to understand the nature of her husband's 'race' because she belongs to a different one, which has been moulded by education (civilization), in opposition to the 'natural' attributes inherited by the Russian 'race'.

Second, the construction of Joe Zinovief's 'race' represents a highly problematic, yet illuminating, case. Born in New York from the union between a Russian Jew (Boris's brother) and a Norwegian woman, and orphaned at an early age, Joe was raised by Americans and received an American education both at school and at university. At the beginning of the story, the narrator stresses the fact that he has barely been in contact with the Russian side of his family. Therefore, thanks both to his Nordic appearance — inherited from his mother — and his education, Joe '*could have been* mistaken for an American man' (6, my emphasis). However, in truth, he is not one of them. Despite his physical traits, his American mentality, and the fact that he was born in the United States, he is 'tainted' by his 'racial' origins: although 'he didn't look anything like the Zinovief family' his surname 'revealed his Russian Jewish origins' (6). Joe's character is fundamental to understanding the concepts of 'race' exposed in the novella. He is depicted in positive terms, as a noble young man provided with a 'good and healthy spirit' (11), psychological characteristics that seem to come from his mother's 'race' and his education. The strength of his Russian blood is, however, too powerful. Joe's contact with his original culture in the East River area — a culture that he has not learnt but naturally inherited from his ancestors — produces in him an intense effect. In a similar way to the rest of the Slavic people gathered to see Sonia's performance, he is haunted by the Russian singer's magnetism. Amidst the crowd, only Helen is not captivated by the show:

> Sólo Nell no participaba de la corriente magnética establecida por la melodía [...] También Joe parecía extasiado. La actitud de éste, que era de los suyos, fué [sic] la que más le extrañó, porque, como ella, tampoco el joven comprendía las palabras de aquella canción. Pero acaso sentía la melodía rusa; tal vez esta música, que a ella la dejaba fría, encontraba un eco en el alma del muchacho y despertaba en su sangre el calor de aquella raza. (18)

> [Only Nell did not take part in the magnetic current established by the melody [...] Joe too seemed enraptured. The attitude of the latter, who was one of her own, was what seemed oddest to her, because, like her, the young man did not understand the words of that song either. But perhaps he heard the Russian melody; maybe this music, which left her cold, found an echo in the lad's soul and stirred the warmth of that race in his blood.]

The previous extract is constructed around two oppositions that unveil the idea of 'race' developed by the narrator, namely those encapsulated by the semantic correspondence between 'frío'/'calor' ('cold'/'heat') and 'comprender/sentir' ('to understand'/'to feel'). Helen is not affected by the 'magnetic' influence exerted by the song because the music is completely alien to her, a product of an altogether different culture that she cannot understand. The warmth of this culture radically contrasts with the coldness of her intellect. On the contrary, Joe falls immediately under the spell of the Russian melody, a surprising fact for Helen, since she considers him as 'one of her own'. However, Joe is intensely conditioned by his 'racial' origins. The music produces in him a real awakening — in contrast with Helen's fake transformation — triggered by a feeling that he cannot understand and deeply rooted in his own self. The contact with his father's culture does in fact produce in Joe a decisive change. As his uncle reminds him the following day, 'de fuego es la sangre del ruso, también debes recordar, que por tus venas corre de esa misma sangre; por lo cual sería muy de temer que en ese encuentro estallara el chispazo de la pasión' [fiery is the Russian's blood, and you should also remember that this same blood runs through your veins; therefore the sparking of passion at that meeting would be something to fear] (28). Soon, and despite Boris's warnings, Joe falls in love with Sonia:

> la aventura de la víspera, que había dejado como un resquemor en el corazón del joven, era ahora una llama voraz. [...] el temperamento ardiente del ruso le abrasaba, derritiendo todo el hielo que, por su madre pudiera haber en él, y aniquilando la sangre fría, producto de una educación norteamericana. (28–29)
>
> [the adventure of the night before, which had left something like resentment in the young man's heart, was now a voracious flame [...] The ardent temperament of the Russian seared through him, melting all the ice which could have come to him through his mother, and annhilating the cold blood, the product of a North American upbringing.]

As one can see, his father's Russian blood prevails over his mother's 'racial' inheritance, implying that — following a patriarchal conception of 'race' — the paternal genetic inheritance is stronger than the maternal one. What is more, the influence of nature is more powerful than education. Whereas the latter is an artificial product of civilization that can be 'undone', the kinship established by blood is permanent and inescapable. *El crisol de las razas* concludes in fact with an explicit diatribe against miscegenation. The narrator refers to New York as

> la urbe monstruosa donde afluyen los ambiciosos, los perseguidos y desamparados por la fortuna de los países más apartados del mundo; [...] la metrópoli gigantesca donde se encuentran todas las razas y cada una de las variantes de éstas; [...] la nueva Babel donde se hablan todos los idiomas y todos los dialectos del universo; [...] ese crisol de razas, que es Nueva York, donde son lanzados unos con otros hombres y mujeres de todas las religiones y de todas las costumbres, sin que llegue a operarse esa fusión deseada, que se pretende tenga por resultado la constitución de la raza fuerte, de la raza superior por excelencia. (44)
>
> [the monstrous city where the ambitious, persecuted and those abandoned by fortune from the remotest countries in the world abound; [...] the gigantic metropolis where all races and each variant of these can be found; [...] the new Babel where all the languages and dialects of the universe are spoken; [...] this melting pot which is New York, where men and women of all religions and customs are thrown together without this desired fusion taking place, and whose desired result is the constitution of the strong race, the superior race par excellence.]

The above allusion to the mixture of different 'races', languages, cultures, and religions is preceded by a negative qualification given to the city ('monstruosa', 'gigantesca', 'nueva Babel', 'crisol de razas'), therefore implying that all these concepts are fixed and immobile 'truths', and that their alteration is a deviant act against 'the right order of things'. Although the United States is depicted as a modernizing society in terms of gender equality, it is also presented as a nation in danger due to the coexistence of different ethnic backgrounds. This view is confirmed by the final destiny of the characters. Helen is accidentally killed because she is married to a man from a different 'race' and, moreover, from a different social class. Boris is not only depicted as a member of a despicable 'race' but also as socially inferior since his current social position is not his natural place in society — in contrast with Helen's — but has been acquired thanks to allegedly murky activities. As we can see, 'race' does not only establish cultural boundaries but also a social hierarchy, and Boris has surpassed these limits with disastrous consequences. On the contrary, the relationship between Joe and Sonia has a happy ending. They share the same 'racial' origins, and therefore they are perfectly suitable for each other. Noticeably, the narrator not only simplifies Joe's polyethnicity at the end — it seems that he ends up being purely Russian — but also establishes the preponderance of 'race' over education.

The last words of the narrator convey a concern about the creation of a 'superior race' which is an expression of contradiction and confusion. European and American policies to avoid 'racial' degeneration through the implementation of eugenic programmes were not based on the mixture of 'races' but rather on the 'purification' and 'cleansing' of the white 'races' and the 'extermination' of 'degenerate races' (Moradiellos 2009: 203–04). The narrator's reference to the constitution of 'la raza fuerte, la raza superior por excelencia' (44) is therefore a misunderstanding of these policies, since such a 'superior race' would be the result of miscegenation between individuals whom the narrator depicts as 'corrupted'. The confusion and contradiction expressed in the last paragraph of the novella can be seen as a token of the increasing influence of racialist theories in Spain at the time. Nevertheless, the narrator does not criticize genetic experiments or 'racial' cleansing, but rather condemns miscegenation and the coexistence of different cultures in the same geographical territory, therefore mirroring the identification between 'nation' and 'race' promoted by ethnic nationalism. Furthermore, the emphasis placed on the negative influence of Eastern Jews not only reflects the increasing entry of modern anti-Semitism in Spain — influenced by similar attitudes in other European countries — but also perpetuate the image of the 'Jew' as Spain's archetypical 'Other'. The warnings about the alleged damaging effects of miscegenation would therefore not be limited to the dystopian image of New York's melting pot given in the text, but also to the degenerative influence that the Jewish 'race' would supposedly entail for the 'purity' of the Spanish nation.

National Identity beyond 'Race' in *Anticípolis*

As has been shown in the preceding chapters, *Anticípolis* illustrates the clash between Spanish traditionalism, embodied by Doña Jesusa, and American modernization, represented by Jesusa's children, especially Rosa. In the following pages I will show how Jesusa also encapsulates fixed notions of 'race' and 'nation', whereas her children illustrate new and fluid forms of identity that challenge the reductive views of Spanishness emanating from ethnic nationalism.

Doña Jesusa finds a way of alleviating the distress caused by New York in her conversations with Jiménez. The doctor plays the role of adviser, almost of therapist, and tries to convince the traditionalist Jesusa of the benefits of modernization. Hence, the relationship between these two characters is based on a power relation that emanates from knowledge. On the one hand, Jesusa is depicted as ignorant, stubborn, and incapable of dealing with new social challenges. Dr Jiménez, on the other hand, is an educated man who sees modernization as a necessary struggle on the way to human progress. His ideas are essential to understanding the conflicts exposed in the story; the term 'Antícípolis', which gives its name to the novel, is in fact coined by him.

The dichotomy educated man/ignorant woman seems at first to be an expression of patriarchal hierarchy. However, Jiménez is a staunch defender of women's emancipation; therefore, the opposition between these two characters is based on a different conflict. In the first pages of the novel, Jesusa describes the doctor as 'almost a fellow citizen' although he is 'a bit dark-skinned', since he speaks to her in Spanish (Jiménez is from Puerto Rico, one of the colonies lost by the Spanish empire in 1898) (Oteyza 2006: 88). Jesusa's statement follows the idea of 'la España grande' ('Greater Spain'), the Hispanic cultural and linguistic unity between Spain and the former colonies. Within the Spanish empire there were, however, first- and second-class subjects. The colonies were subdued by the power of the Spanish mainland, and the (black) colonized was ruled by the (white) colonizer. After the arrival of black slaves in the sixteenth century, social stratification in the colonies followed a 'caste system' based on racist hierarchy. At the top of this hierarchy was an elite of white Spanish born in the Peninsula, followed by the *criollo* of Spanish descent born in America, the native American, and persons of African descent (Acuña 2011: 23–24; Simms 2008: 232). This social system mirrored the earlier situation of black people in Spain, where the end of the *Reconquista* had facilitated contact with black Africans. From the fourteenth century onwards, Africans were used as slaves on the mainland, even before the colonization of the 'New World' (Manzanas 1996: 252; Kicza 1992: 231–32). The mainland is here represented by Jesusa and her patronizing attitude towards Jiménez, which echoes the colonialist archetype of the 'noble savage'. The doctor himself continues this allegory — protective motherland and naïve colonized — in one of their conversations, in which he tells Jesusa about his childhood:

> fue en mis tiempos de muchacho, cuando Puerto Rico pertenecía a España. Se trataba de una señora peninsular, de familia noble y origen provinciano. Era tan tradicionalista como usted, tan intransigente como usted y tan bondadosa como usted. Protegía a mi madre, una pobre mulata casada con un dependiente de su marido [...] A mí me protegió también, costeando mi educación. Usted me la recuerda mucho. Hasta se le parece en lo físico, siendo en lo espiritual idéntica. De aquí mi simpatía hacia usted [...] Y también el que sepa su forma de pensar, sus modos de sentir. (182)

> [it was in my boyhood years, when Puerto Rico belonged to Spain. There was a Spanish lady of noble family and provincial background. She was as traditionalist as you, as intransigent as you and as kind as you. She would protect my mother, a poor mulatta married to an employee of her husband [...] She protected me too, paying for my education. You remind me of her a lot. You even resemble her physically, and spiritually you are identical. This explains my fondness for you [...] And also because I know your way of thinking and feeling.]

In the previous extract we can see the hierarchical opposition between colonizer (white, rich, educated, strong) and colonized (mulatto, poor, ignorant, in need of protection). In the relationship between Jiménez and Jesusa, this opposition is, however, reversed. First of all, when Jesusa comes to the doctor's office, she is looking for shelter and protection from New York's 'primitiveness'. Moreover,

Jesusa's mulishness defines her as child-like, unable to understand the world around her. Jiménez, on the contrary, is the voice of modernization, and treats Jesusa with a teacher's patience when he tries to make her realize that her ideas are based on preconceptions. By empowering Jiménez, the narrator reveals the constructedness of racialist discourses of 'Otherness' at the core of nostalgic views of Spanish national identity.

This is not the only challenge posed by the novel with regard to the concept of 'race'. The notion of national and cultural identity as inherited and permanent is questioned by the contrast between Jesusa's understanding of national identity as a fixed concept and her children's adaptation to US society. Jesusa regards identity as emanating from a geographical origin; as she says after Antonio's funeral: 'now, my children, we go back to our land' (118). The spatial deictics used by Jesusa to refer to Spain and New York also show her strong attachment to her homeland. Throughout the novel, she refers to New York as 'allí' [there] (106, 145) and 'allá' [over there] (157), showing her spatial detachment from the city. For her children, on the other hand, New York is always 'aquí' ('here'). They have grown up in the city and therefore consider themselves more American than Spanish. As the narrator states:

> porque el efecto del *melting-pot*, que a la aluvial urbe ha dado tanta unidad de vecindario como cualquier aldea sin forasteros pueda tener, ese acrisolamiento de razas, que con la reunión de todas las de la Tierra forma para Nueva York una bien definida, se había producido en ellos haciéndolos perfectos neoyorquinos. No lo eran más que en potencia; pero para serlo de acción, lo cual deseaban con anhelo de sus almas y ansias de sus cuerpos, sólo les faltó, hasta entonces, que la hispana autoridad del padre dejase de pesar sobre sus conductas. (118)

> [because the melting-pot effect, which has provided as much neighbourhood unity as any village without outsiders can have for the alluvial city, this crucible process of races, which with the meeting of all those of the Earth forms a defined benefit for New York, occurred within them, making them perfect New Yorkers. They were only this potentially; but in order to be it in practice, which they desired with all their heart and souls, they only needed, up to that point, that the Spanish authority of the father ceased to weigh upon their behaviour.]

In the passage above we can recognize a terminology similar to the one used in Escoriaza's novella ('ese acrisolamiento de razas'). However, in this case the connotations are rather different. The narrator still resorts to the concept of 'race', but in his words there is no negative judgment of 'racial' mixture. Instead, identity is shown to be a fluid concept, subject to transformation, not only as a consequence of external influences, but also as the product of human will. This attitude contrasts with fixed conceptions of national identity, delimited by an inherited geographical origin and a shared language, culture, and ancestry.

Jesusa's attachment to tradition is explained by the narrator as being almost a religous faith. She is a 'devotee' of such conceptions, which are, in her view, the only legitimate possibilities (224). One of the aspects of New York to which she reacts is in fact the variety of cults practised in the city. During her husband's funeral, 'se le ocurrió de pronto que en las habitaciones contiguas se rogaba a otros dioses de otros muertos que eran herejes o acaso judíos. Dios, su Dios, el verdadero Dios, no escucharía las preces que de semejante edificio salieran' [it suddenly occurred to her that in adjoining rooms other gods of other dead people who were heretics or perhaps Jews were being called upon. God, her God, the true God, would not listen to the prayers which emerged from such a building.] (90). I suggest that the references to a 'true Catholic god' and to Jewish people are connected to the imperialist rhetoric that preceded the 1898 war. This rhetoric was later appropriated by 'a revitalized traditionalism, propagated by the Church, the Carlists, and conservative elites, which drew on the myths of the Reconquest and the conquest of the New World and emphasized the civilizing Christian mission of Spain' (Balfour 1997: 94). A few pages earlier, in a sarcastic way, the narrator significantly compares Jesusa to 'la reina Juana de Castilla' [Queen Joanna of Castile] (86), daughter of the Catholic Monarchs, the architects of Imperial Spain based on religious bigotry who were responsible not only for the conquest and domination of the American territories, but also for the expulsion of the Jews from the Peninsula. Jesusa's identification with traditionalism does therefore imply the view of Spain as a religious and 'racial' homogeneous community, and the construction of an illusory purity of the Spanish 'race' by opposition to the Jewish archenemy. In addition, one must note the sardonic comparison between Juana, known as 'the mad Queen', and Jesusa's fatal breakdown at the end of the novel.[8]

New York is seen by Jesusa as the embodiment of crude materialism, and she regards American capitalism as an attack on the 'laws of God'. She is not concerned with money but with the moral values that emanate from her religious beliefs, which in New York are disregarded thanks to the materialist nature of the metropolis. The city is therefore seen as the epitome of moral decadence, and Jesusa fears that her children will be infected by the influx of such debauchery in a city that is 'cursed by God' (109). New York is for her 'the protestant and heretic city', in opposition to 'Spain, the Catholic nation' (231). Such American 'heresy' is here directly related to money and materialism. Jesusa 'was tortured by the materialism of that way of life' (152), since 'she was hurt by unnecessary luxuries' which 'were mostly obtained against the laws of both God and men' (158). Characterized as 'archiespañola' [arch-Spanish] (85), she refuses to accept the benefits of capitalism, since they go against her Catholic values and hence against the principles of her national identity.

In stark contrast with their mother's traditionalism, Jesusa's children embrace the social changes brought about by class mobility, women's emancipation, and cultural contact. Their case shows the reader how, in Jiménez's words, 'customs change' (183), foreseeing the changes that will affect the entire world, including Spain. As Jiménez also declares, Jesusa's children are like any other New York dweller, and furthermore, like all the inhabitants of the world would be one day (191). In addition, they have all lost their Catholic faith. The most prominent case is that of Pepín, the youngest son, who enrols on a course to study theology, and eventually becomes a Protestant priest. According to Doña Jesusa, Pepín has lost his soul, for he has betrayed his origins:

> ser pecadores, ser impenitentes, ser antirreligiosos, estaba mal. Pero, al menos, en esas condiciones teníanse abiertos los caminos de la virtud y del arrepenti-

miento que vuelven a la religión. Mientras que habiéndose pasado a una religión contraria, enemiga, traidora... El que adquiere una creencia falsa para siempre pierde la verdadera. (232)

[to be sinners, to be unrepentant, to be anti-religious, was bad. But at least in those conditions the roads of virtue and regret, which lead back to religion, remained open, whereas to have passed to a different, enemy and treacherous religion... He who acquires a false belief loses the true one forever.]

By abjuring his religion, Pepín has lost his final bond with the national community, turning into a stranger and an enemy. Jesusa's children have voluntarily renounced their national language — they only speak Spanish to their mother because she barely understands English —, their culture, their geographical origins, and their religion, consciously embracing the values and customs of a foreign community. Jesusa, however, remains so attached to the fixed concept of the culture she represents that she becomes paralysed, and she dies at the end of the story.

Again, the ambiguity of the novel is manifest. On the one hand, the American nation, based on political citizenship rather than ethnic ties, and the successful adaptation of Jesusa's children to New York, challenge the identification between 'race' and nation established by ethnic nationalism in Spain. The view of New York as the city of the future also renders the identification of Spain with a 'racially' and culturally homogeneous community as an obsolete concept of nationhood. In this context, the novel promotes a more inclusive conception of national identity that goes beyond shared geographical, cultural, and 'racial' origins, and in which the 'racial' hierarchy that locates the colonized subaltern in a position of intellectual and social inferiority is unveiled as a cultural construction. However, the loss of national characteristics such as religion and language, as a consequence of the standardizing effects of New York's melting pot, also suggests a threat to the Catholic and linguistic essence of Spanish identity — not only in the Peninsula, but also in the whole Hispanic community — at the hands of the 'Big Other'. In this view, modernization is presented as a danger to the persistence of a 'natural' identification between nation, culture, religion, language, and 'race'.

'La España Grande' versus 'La España Negra' in *La ciudad automática*

In *La ciudad automática*, Julio Camba devotes three chapters to the situation of black people in New York: 'Negros' [Blacks] (1960: 22–23), 'Más negros' [More Blacks] (24–25), and 'Negros y blancos' [Blacks and Whites] (25–28). Similar to the images of 'racial contamination' developed by Moreno Villa, Camba's text especially focuses on the contact between African and white Americans. Once again, jazz music is depicted as the catalyst for the subversion of 'racial' hierarchy. Camba locates the chapter entitled 'Negros' in Harlem jazz clubs, where he argues that 'racial' hierarchy is blurred by the combined effect of black music and alcohol:

Nueva York aborrece a los negros, no cabe duda, pero los aborrece únicamente desde las ocho o nueve de la mañana hasta las doce de la noche [...] abandonando los cabarets del Broadway con su alegría mejor o peor imitada, se va al Harlem en busca del *real thing* [...] Para los americanos de estirpe puritana la alegría es una invención negra. [...] Es la hora de Harlem. La hora en que los negros más monstruosos estrechan entre sus brazos a las más áureas anglosajonas. La hora en que el alto profesorado, tipo Wilson, se pone a bailar la rumba con la servidumbre femenina de color. [...] Allí se ve bien claro que no todo son fuerzas contrapuestas entre los negros y los blancos norteamericanos, y que si los blancos odian a los negros es, en cierto modo, como el vicioso odia a su vicio. Se ve, en fin que los blancos pueden odiar a los negros durante el día y a las horas laborables, pero que, a pesar de todo, hay algo en el fondo de la raza maldita que los atrae de un modo irresistible. (22–23)

[New York despises negroes, there is no doubt, but it despises them solely from eight or nine in the morning until twelve at night [...] abandoning Broadway's Cabarets with its better or worse imitated gaiety, they go to Harlem in search of the real thing [...] For the Americans of a puritan background, gaiety is a negro invention [...] It is Harlem's time. The time when the most monstrous negroes grasp the most golden Anglo-Saxon girls in their arms. The time when college staff, of the Wilson kind, begin to dance the rumba with the coloured female serving staff. [...] There can be clearly seen that not all is contrasting forces between North American negroes and whites, and that if whites hate negroes it is, in a certain fashion, like the depraved man who hates his depravity. It can be seen, in short, that whites can hate negroes during the daytime and working hours, but that in spite of everything there is something in the depths of the accursed race which attracts them in an irresistible fashion.]

Camba does not condemn the hatred suffered by African Americans in New York, but rather focuses his criticism on the 'depraved' behaviour of Anglo-Saxons, who look for the pleasures forbidden by their puritan values in the dark and debauched clubs of Harlem. Moreover, black people are depicted as a 'vice' that white Americans cannot resist, and which leads to 'unnatural' sexual matches that destabilize 'racial' and class hierarchies. Camba strives to highlight such subversion by establishing binary oppositions between the blacks and the whites. First of all, in the couple formed by 'negros monstruosos' and 'áureas anglosajonas', the sexual and 'racial' purity suggested by the golden hair of Anglo-Saxon women — as in Moreno Villa's travelogue, 'blonde' is used to characterize the Anglo-Saxon 'race' — is opposed to the ugliness ('monstruoso') of black men. Regarding the binary opposition between white/black, Winthop Jordan points out that

> embedded in the concept of blackness was its direct opposite — whiteness. No other colors so clearly implied opposition [...] White and black connoted purity and filthiness, virginity and sin, virtue and baseness, beauty and ugliness, beneficence and evil, God and the devil. (1994: 42)

Jordan's words refer to the first encounters between the English and the Africans in the sixteenth century, yet the same racist stereotypes are still in force in Camba's text. Indeed, the portrait of African Americans given by the writer is a re-elaboration of previous discourses of 'Otherness' carried out in the West since its encounter with non-European cultures, based on binary oppositions such as sensuality/rationality, nature/civilization, and childishness/maturity. Following such oppositions, Camba defines blacks by their sensuality and musical skills, to the extent of arguing that 'bailan todos los negros [...] Dotados de una gracia de movimientos puramente animal y con un sentido extraordinario del ritmo, los negros nunca aciertan a explicar por completo un sentimiento o un deseo mientras no lo bailan' [all negroes dance [...] Blessed with a purely animal-like grace of movements and with an extraordinary sense of rhythm, negroes never succeed in completely explaining a feeling or desire if they are not dancing it] (25). Their alleged inability to articulate their feelings in words strengthens their opposition to the 'civilized' and educated white man. Furthermore, such sense of rhythm is seen by Camba as an expression of their 'primitivism' and 'racial' inferiority: in contrast with the cultural refinement of the Western man, their musical talent is 'puramente animal'. This view is confirmed later on by Camba's animalization of African Americans, who are compared to apes and dogs:

> hay negros chiquitines y muy peripuestos que se pasean por las calles de Harlem con una petulancia tan deliciosa como la de un *fox-terrier* [...] otros son enormes, como gorilas [...] bailan los negros *fox-terrier* y los negros *bulldog* [...] baila el negro gorila y el negroide chimpancé. (24–25)

> [there are tiny and very slick negroes who walk through the streets of Harlem with a petulance as delicious as that of a fox terrier [...] others are enormous, like gorillas [...] the fox-terrier negroes and the bulldog negroes dance [...] the gorilla negro and the negroid chimpanzee dance.]

Surprisingly, Camba declares himself to have 'great affection' (24) for black people. Soon we discover that this attitude is explained by his attachment to discourses of 'Otherness', in this case the infantilization of the 'racial Other':

> los niños, en especial, me encantan y, junto a un negro de seis o siete años, un blanco de tres me parece que ya está en plena senectud. En cuanto a los grandes, no hay ninguno que haya dejado enteramente de ser niño. Los negros son niños siempre por su candor y por su marrullería, por su capacidad admirativa, por sus terrores injustificados, a la par que su desconocimiento del verdadero peligro y, ante todo, por la enorme fuerza creadora de su imaginación. (24)

> [I love the children in particular, and next to a negro child of six or seven years old, a white child of three seems to me to be already in full senescence. Concerning the grown ups, no-one has stopped being a child completely. The negroes are always children because of their innocence and their cajolery, their ability to admire, their unjustified terrors, at the same time as their igorance of true danger and, above all else, the enormous creative force of their imagination.]

The distinction between whites and blacks is shown by Camba as a constant that manifests itself even in the earlier periods of human life. In his view, a white child is already older than a black one of the same age, as though the former were intellectually superior to the latter at birth. Moreover, both 'categories' remain unalterable, since blacks never overcome this state of childishness and therefore stay in a permanent condition of inferiority in relation to the white man's maturity. Camba's view of 'races' as fixed categories does certainly echo racialist theories such as those argued by Arthur de Gobineau in *The Inequality of Human Races* (1855). According to Gobineau, all 'racial differences' were permanent, since 'races' 'constitute separate branches of one of many primitive stocks' (Gobineau 1915: 133). In this regard, Camba's agreement with theories supporting 'racial' inequality is highlighted by his depiction of Harlem as a primitive and magical inner city, isolated from modernization:

> en Nueva York se habla del barrio de Harlem, donde están concentrados, como de una ciudad mágica en la que se cultivan ritos extraños y misteriosos, y hay algo de ello, no cabe duda. Harlem vive, ante todo, de artes de hechicería. Su industria principal consiste en la venta de amuletos contra el mal de ojo, filtros amorosos. (25)

> [in New York they talk of the neighbourhood of Harlem, where they are assembled, as if it were a magical city in which strange and mysterious rites are practised, and there is undoubtedly something in this. Harlem primarily lives off the art of sorcery. Its principal industry consists of the sale of amulets against the evil eye, and love potions.]

The writer insinuates that even in modern cities such as New York, blacks preserve their allegedly 'inherent' sensuality, 'animality', and superstitious character, since they are unable to become 'civilized'. Through ignorance or conscious denial, the writer ignores the booming visibility of black literature, music, and art in the 1920s and 1930s thanks to the *Harlem Renaissance* movement, which represented 'not only a golden age of African American arts but a valiant effort to remove the masks of racial stereotypes in order to put a new face on African Americans' (Buck 2010: 795). Moreover, Camba describes the Great Migration as an 'invasion', thus highlighting the position of African Americans as outsiders (26). It is precisely in the North of the United States, Camba reminds the reader, where:

> se ha libertado al negro y se ha emancipado a la mujer, a la que, a falta de equivalencia idiomática, nadie podría ahora llamar aquí, como se la llama a veces en España, 'negra de mis carnes'. Aquí, socialmente consideradas, todas las mujeres son rubias. (26)

> [the negro has been set free and woman emancipated; she who, for lack of an idiomatic equivalent, nobody could now call here as they do at times in Spain, 'black girl of my flesh'. Here, in terms of social perception, all women are fair-haired.]

In this excerpt, there is a blatant identification between women's emancipation and black people's liberation from slavery: the sentence 'socialmente [...], todas las mujeres son rubias' connects racism to social discrimination. Camba is referring to the entry of women into the public sphere, and by saying that 'todas las mujeres son rubias' he opposes blonde — and hence white — to black, implying that in the United States all women are in high social positions and thus at the same social level as men. Such a statement implies that non-blondes (blacks) belong to a lower class position. Furthermore, the reference to the expression 'negra de mis carnes', used in early twentieth-century Madrid as a sexually charged flattering comment (Díaz-Cañabate 1978: 99), refers to the change undergone by women in the United States in comparison to their situation in Spain: from sexual objects to civil subjects. Once again, 'negra' is identified with a position of inferiority, the weak element in patriarchal, classist, and racist oppositions.

The second dancing couple to which Camba refers in his description of Harlem night life, does in fact blur the 'natural' division between social classes. 'El alto profesorado, tipo Wilson, se pone a bailar la rumba con la servidumbre femenina de color' (22): the white educated man dances with the black feminine servant. Following the social elitism expressed by the writer in other sections of his travelogue, Camba reacts against the contaminating influence that black popular music has on the American highly intellectual elite. One must keep in mind that the construction of 'racial' difference in the West was parallel to the development of class ideologies (Fenton 1999: 83). As Martin Reisigl and Ruth Wodak (2001: 2) remind us, 'race' is a social construction 'used as a legitimizing ideological tool to oppress and exploit specific social groups and to deny them access to material, cultural and political resources, to work, welfare services, housing and political rights'. Camba is perfectly aware of the racist discrimination suffered by African Americans, as he openly refers to the so-called 'Negro problem' (26–27). The writer provides a list of possible 'solutions' given to such a 'problem' in the United States: 'hay quien habla de matar a todos los negros; hay quien habla de echarlos y hasta quien habla de esterilizarlos' [there are those who talk of killing all negroes; there are those who talk of removing them and even those who talk of sterilising them], and declares that 'cualquiera de estas medidas tiene cierta lógica; pero lo absurdo es eso de separar a los negros de los blancos en el tranvía, en el teatro, en la escuela y hasta en la iglesia' [any of these means has a certain logic; but what is absurd is this business of separating negroes from whites on the tramway, in the theatre, at school and even in church] (27). Given the humiliating and dehumanizing depiction of black people provided by Camba, it is unsurprising that genocide, banishment, and sterilization are seen by him as 'logical'. However, he also seems to be condemning segregation policies. The following lines clarify this first impression:

> ¿Para qué separar dos cosas de apariencia tan distinta como un líquido azul y un líquido incoloro? ¿Y para qué separar a los negros de los blancos si salta a la vista del más miope quiénes son los blancos y quiénes son los negros? [...] Por mi parte opino que el problema negro no existe, y no existe precisamente porque los negros son precisamente una raza de color [...] dentro de su piel cada negro está tan lejos de los otros ciudadanos americanos como un *paragoe* en su campo de concentración. (27–28)[9]
>
> [Why separate two things so different in appearance like a blue liquid and a colourless liquid? And why separate negroes from whites if it is blindingly obvious who is white and who is negro, even for the most short-sighted person? [...] For my part I think that the negro problem does not exist, and it does not exist precisely because negroes are precisely a coloured race [...] within their skin; each negro is as distant from other American citizens as an *paragoe* in its concentration camp.]

Black skin is compared to a concentration camp that separates African Americans from Anglo-Saxons. Camba does not even consider the possibility of egalitarianism: for him, their skin colour will always confine blacks to a position of subalternity and make visible the inferiority of their 'race'.

As in *Pruebas de Nueva York*, the emphasis is not placed on 'racial' discrimination, but on the subverting power of black culture. The writer condemns the fact that the 'natural' social boundaries established by discrimination become weaker at night, when whites become increasingly affected by the intoxicating effect of jazz, to the extent that after midnight, 'everybody feels, at least, half black' (22). The whole scene is given a carnivalesque character in which the 'right order of things' has been inverted, and the semiotic parallel between 'the night' and 'the black' strengthens the idea of temporal madness, of the dangerous and corrupting power of the African-American influence. Significantly, the explanation given by Camba for the 'irresistible' attraction that Americans feel towards blacks is explained by the supposed incompleteness of the Anglo-Saxon 'race':

> Todo lo cual tiene una explicación bien sencilla: la falta de lujuria propia en el pueblo americano. Naturalmente, yo no voy a salir en defensa de ningún pecado capital, pero opino que todos los hombres, aun los de un abolengo puritano más directo, están hechos del mismo barro, y que si se prescinde de su naturaleza o si se quiere ir brutalmente contra ella, el error será funesto. La dictadura puritana arremetió contra toda pasión carnal de un modo verdaderamente feroz, y hoy pueden ustedes ver a este pueblo que, totalmente desprovisto de sus instintos lujuriosos, no tiene más remedio que arreglárselas con la lujuria de otros pueblos. [...] Como la raza anglosajona es una de las razas menos sensuales del mundo, se consideró tarea facilísima el hacer de ella una raza enteramente virtuosa, pero al privarla de su parca sensualidad se la dejó sin defensa contra el estímulo de sensualidades extrañas, y cuando la raza elegida estaba ya a dos dedos de la pura virtud, hela aquí que se suelta el pelo y que dice: — Ahora me toca a mí... (23)

> [All of which has a fairly simple explanation: the lack of lust itself in the American people. Naturally, I am not going to come out in defence of any cardinal sin, but I believe that all men, even those with direct puritan lineage, are made of clay, and if we dispense with their nature or if we wish to go brutally against it, such a mistake would be disastrous. The puritan dictatorship lashed out against all carnal passion in a truly ferocious manner, and today you can see these people who, totally destitute of their lustful instincts, have no other choice than to make do with other peoples' lust. [...] As the Anglo-Saxon race is one of the least sensual in the world, making it an entirely virtuous race was regarded as an extremely easy task; but in being deprived of its frugal sensuality, it was left defenceless against the stimulus of foreign sensualities, and when the chosen race was already within an inch of pure virtue, there she is: she lets her hair down and says: 'Now it's my turn...]

Camba ridicules the zeal for purity of the Anglo-Saxon 'race', and its lack of sensuality is seen as an imperfection. Such an opinion reflects European views of the United States as an individualistic, materialistic, 'primitive', and dehumanized society, which led to the stereotype of Americans as cold individuals, lacking sensuality and spirituality. This is seen by Camba as precisely the 'crack' through which blacks allegedly penetrate the Anglo-Saxon 'race'. Camba's words reflect the concerns caused in Spain by theories surrounding Anglo-Saxon superiority over the Latin 'races' promoted by authors such as Edmond Demolins in *À quoi tient la supériorité des Anglo-Saxons?* (1897), translated into Spanish in 1899 as *¿En qué consiste la superioridad de los anglosajones?* [published in English as *Anglo-Saxon Superiority: To What It Is Due*] (Fox 1998: 112; Seregni 2007: 102–03). Lord Salisbury's speech 'Living and Dying Nations', delivered a few months before the end of the Spanish-American war, echoed this rhetoric of 'racial difference'. The British Prime

Minister argued that nations could be divided into two opposite groups: on the one hand, 'great countries of enormous power growing in power every year', and on the other, 'a number of communities which I can only describe as dying' (Gascoyne-Cecil 1898: 6). Although Spain was not directly mentioned, Spanish politicians understood Lord Salisbury's words as a direct allusion to the situation of their country, since it mirrored the diagnosis given by Spanish intellectuals to the decay of the empire (Seregni 2007: 96). Responses to Anglo-Saxon superiority not only dwelled on the catastrophist view of Spain developed by regenerationist writers, but in some cases also took the shape of a violent diatribe against the Americans. Polymaths such as Ramiro de Maeztu reacted strongly against theories of Anglo-Saxon superiority contained in Lord Salisbury's speech. In *Hacia otra España* [*Towards Another Spain*] (1899), Maeztzu declares:

> ¡Llámenos enhorabuena Salisbury pueblo agonizante [...]! Pienso en las muchedumbres sajonas, ebrias y brutales, sosteniendo en fuerza de alcohol una vida de animalidad dóciles al látigo de la policía, pero desenfrenadas en cuanto se les sueltan los grilletes, pienso en el color pálido del obrero de Liverpool, o de Manchester [...], en la mujer sajona, de cuerpo seco y alma enjuta, y me sonrío [...] Podrán los cañones de los yanquis cerrar el libro de nuestra historia colonial; podrán poner término provisionalmente a nuestras gloriosísimas conquistas; pero la conquista ha sido sólo uno de nuestros múltiples destinos [...] rascando un poco en la agrietada superficie social, se encuentra siempre el pueblo sano y fuerte, fecundo y vigoroso. (2007: 126–27)

> [Salisbury can happily call us a dying people [...]! I think about the Saxon horde, inebriate and brutal, sustaining their savage life with alcohol, docile with the police whip, but rampant once their shackles are loosened. I think of the pallid colour of the worker from Liverpool, or Manchester [...], of the Saxon woman, dry in body and withered in soul, and I smile [...] The Yankees' cannons might close the book of our colonial history; they might put an end provisionally to our great, glorious conquests; the conquest has been just one of our multiple destinies [...] in scratching the cracked social surface a little, one always finds that the people are healthy and strong, fertile and vigorous.]

In the decades following the war, depictions of American society as 'primitive', dehumanized, and dominated by the 'masses' also undermined the American economic, industrial, and social progress. Camba's text follows a similar logic. The writer strives to dismantle racialist theories of Anglo-Saxon superiority by showing the counterproductive effects of its excessive search for purity: the alleged suppression of sexual drives by the Protestant faith cannot contain the strength of the lowest instincts, which are attracted by the exacerbated lust of an inferior 'race' and lead Americans to fall into the 'vices' they try to avoid. In this context, the alleged supremacy of the Anglo-Saxons is turned by Camba into weakness and their 'race' as vulnerable and susceptible to degeneration.

Both Camba's racist stance regarding African Americans and his dialectical efforts to dismantle theories of Anglo-Saxon 'racial' superiority must be connected with nostalgic formulations of Spanish national identity. Significantly, Harlem reappears in a subsequent chapter entitled 'La España negra' [Black Spain] (48–51), where the writer describes the East side of this neighbourhood in the following terms:

> desde la calle 110 hasta la 116, entre las avenidas quinta y octava, puede decirse que estamos en España. Una España algo negra, desde luego, pero una verdadera España por el idioma, por el carácter y por la actitud general del hombre ante la vida [...] No hay duda de que esto es España, y sólo con espíritu mezquinamente provinciano dejaríamos de reconocerlo así. Es España en toda su enorme variedad histórica. Es la España grande, la España donde nunca se pone el sol todavía, la España hispánica, en una palabra. (48–49)

> [from 110th to 116th Street, between Fifth and Eighth Avenues, it can be said that we are in Spain. A somewhat black Spain, of course, but a true Spain because of the language, character and general attitude of man before life [...] There is no doubt that this is Spain, and only with a pettily provincial spirit would we cease to recognise it as such. It is Spain in all its enormous historical variety. It is the great Spain, the Spain where the sun still never sets. In a word, Hispanic Spain.]

Camba's account is a wistful memory of the lost Spanish Empire, of the unity between the mainland and the colonies, as he confirms some lines later:

> y si usted, lector, considerase algo bárbara esta nomenclatura, yo no podría por menos de lamentarlo, porque ello demostraría, no que es usted muy español, sino que lo es usted muy poco, que tiene usted de España un concepto peninsular exclusivamente y que carece usted de conciencia histórica nacional. Esta conciencia histórica, si en efecto le falta a usted y quiere usted adquirirla, en ninguna parte podrá lograrlo mejor que en el barrio de Nueva York a que me refiero, donde se encontrará usted, en pequeño, con una España muy grande. (49–50)

> [and if, reader, this nomenclature were considered somewhat barbaric, I could but regret it, because it would demonstrate not that you are very Spanish, but that you are not very Spanish, and that you have an exclusively peninsular concept of Spain and that you lack an historical national awareness. If in effect you lack this historical awareness and wish to acquire it, you would be able to attain it nowhere better than in the neighbourhood of New York to which I refer, where you will find, in miniature, a very large Spain.]

The writer praises the grandeur of the former 'Greater Spain', still alive in the linguistic and cultural heritage of the colonies: 'Hispanic Spain'. The success of the Spanish Empire in bonding with the colonies and creating an enduring sense of community contrasts with the Anglo-Saxon failure in the United States. The representation of New York as a city 'racially' corrupted conveyed in *La ciudad automática* suggests that Americans have failed to include their subalterns in the national unity without jeopardizing the integrity of both their 'race' and their culture. In opposition to the view of the United States as a degenerate country, Camba praises the grandeur of the former Spanish Empire, still alive in the linguistic and cultural heritage of the colonies, and presented as a colourful and joyful national community:

> en el teatro de San José no son únicamente el gallego, el catalán o el baturro quienes hacen las delicias del público con sus acentos respectivos. A la par de ellos salen a escena el jíbaro de las Antillas, el pelado mejicano, y el atorrante argentino, etcétera. Se bailan jotas y sones, sardanas y rumbas, pericones y

> muiñeiras, peteneras y jarabes. [...] Los restaurantes, por su parte, no serían considerados como restaurantes españoles si, junto al arroz valenciano o la escudella catalana, no incluyesen en la carta los tamales, el churrasco, el mole de guajalote, el chile con carne, la barbacoa, el sibiche, el chupe de camarones y demás *platillos* o *antojitos* hispanoamericanos. (49)

> [in the San José Theatre it is not just the Galician, Catalan or the Aragonese peasant who delight the public with their respective accents. Along with them there is the Jivaro from the Antilles, the Mexican oaf, the Argentinian tramp, etc. They dance jotas and sones, sardanas and rumbas, the pericón and muiñeiras, peteneras and jarabes [...] Restaurants, for their part, would not be considered Spanish restaurants if, together with Valencian rice or the Catalan escudella, they did not include tamale, grilled meat, turkey mole, chilli con carne, barbecue, ceviche, shrimp chupe and other Hispanic American dishes or snacks on the menu.]

In Camba's account, the legacy of the Spanish Empire, in the form of *Hispanidad*, shows the extent to which Spanish national identity spread through the world while absorbing the influence of colonized cultures. A Castilian-centred Spanish identity prevailed not only in the colonies, where the Castilian Spaniard maintained his position of authority over the 'primitive Others', but also in the Iberian Peninsula. The presence of representatives of different peninsular regions (Galician and Catalan), as expression of the empire's grandeur, is indeed not accidental, but mirrors the threat posed by peripheral nationalist movements to the unity of Spain. In addition, the allusion to members of the different colonies is highly misleading, as the choice of adjectives accompanying the West Indian, the Mexican, and the Argentinean unveils. The first of them is denominated 'jíbaro', thereby evoking a sense of 'primitivism', and connecting him to a particular social group, the agricultural working class.[10] Second, 'pelado' is a derogatory term used to name Mexican poor urban people.[11] Finally, in Argentinian Spanish, 'atorrante' is a term used to refer to tramps.[12] As one can see, all the representatives of the colonies are qualified according to a binary opposition that establishes their inferiority in relation to the white Spanish man of the Iberian Peninsula. Even Latin-American food is located in a subaltern position through the use of diminutives ('antojitos', 'platillos'). Although Spain's political authority over the colonies ceased after the Spanish American wars of independence, Camba's view of a Hispanic unity preserves a sense of cultural dominance. I therefore argue that the comparison between such superiority and the view of American society as 'corrupted' by the influence of black culture is aimed at disarming the racialist theories that characterized Spain as a degenerated and dying nation. On the contrary, Camba's text strives to construct a strong Spanish national identity based on 'racial' and cultural superiority over its regional and colonial 'Others'.

Following the racist nature of his portrait of African Americans, Julio Camba focuses his description of Jewish people on a series of physical characteristics that have been recurrently used in Western culture to define its archetypical 'internal Other'. In different chapters of *La ciudad automática*, the writer refers to the so-called 'Jewish nose' — 'nariz judaica' (19), 'nariz aquilina' (19), 'el judío chato' ('the snub-nosed Jew') (59), 'ángulos faciales' (119) — and to the 'Jewish beard':

> barbas vegetales de esparto, de rafia, de cáñamo, de maíz, de algodón, de buho [*sic*], de puercoespín. Barbas en forma de escoba y barbas en forma de zorros. Barbas de invierno y barbas de verano. Barbas onduladas, barbas trenzadas, barbas avirutadas [*sic*]. Barbas horizontales y barbas verticales. Barbas hirsutas, barbas lacias, barbas crespas. Barbas policromadas. Barbas lustrosas, con reflejos casi metálicos, y barbas desleídas, sin brillo ni color. Barbas de astracán, barbas de seda, barbas de pluma. (28)
>
> [vegetable beards of esparto, rafia, hemp, corn, cotton, owl and porcupine. Beards in the form of a broom and beards in the form of foxes. Winter beards and summer beards. Wavy beards, plaited beards, clipped beards. Horizontal beards and vertical beards. Hirsute beards, limp beards, curly beards. Polychrome beards. Lustrous beards with almost metallic reflection, and diluted beards without shine or colour. Astrakhan beards, silk beards and feather beards.]

In Camba's view, both the nose and the beard function as symbolical markers of the Jewish 'race'. The alleged physical distinctiveness of the 'Jew' is blatantly ridiculed by the writer in order to render this stereotypical image as expression of 'racial' and cultural inferiority. A few lines later, Camba states that

> el judío no se considera realmente dueño, sino simplemente depositario de ellas. Por eso jamás se las lava, ni se las aliña jamás. Las siembra, eso sí; las abona, las engrasa y las cultiva; pero no las altera. No verán ustedes una sola Gillette en todo Rivington Street. Las barbas están aquí en perfecto estado de Naturaleza y, al internarse entre ellas, uno tiene la sensación de internarse en una selva virgen. (29)
>
> [the Jew does not really consider himself as a proprietor, but merely the depository of them. For this reason he never washes them, nor does he ever embellish them. He sows them, of course; he fertilizes them; he greases them and tends to them; but he does not alter them. You will not see a single Gillette in all of Rivington Street. Here beards are to be found in a perfect natural state and, when going in deep amongst them, one has the impression of going deep into a virgin forest.]

The beard, seen by Camba as an indissoluble part of Jewish identity, characterizes the 'Jew' as 'uncivilized'. The references to 'una selva virgen', 'en perfecto estado de Naturaleza', take the reader immediately to the opposition between 'primitiveness' and 'civilization', which is also elaborated around the contrast between the 'Jewish beard' and the 'Gillette'. Whereas the razor blade is a symbol of modern times, the beard is constructed as a sign of archaism. According to the writer, even in the most modern city of the world, Jews still live in the Middle Ages: 'estamos en plena judería. En diez minutos de Metro nos hemos trasladado, como si dijéramos, a la Edad Media' [we are in the centre of the Jewish quarter. In ten minutes by Metro we have travelled back, we could say, to the Middle Ages] (28).

Camba's account of American Jews does not only rely on physical stereotypes, but also on psychological ones, especially the archetype of 'the avaricious Jew' so deeply ingrained in the Western imaginary. The writer describes Rivington Street as

> un mercado donde cada uno pone sobre la mesa todo lo que tiene: su ropa, su calzado, sus retratos de familia, un paraguas roto que se encontró quizás un día en el *subway*, un despertador destartalado, un rosario... Con frecuencia, sobre

la misma mesa, el judío tiene una hornilla donde cuece su comida de la noche; pero si alguien se siente con apetito, que ofrezca precio. En Rivington Street todo se vende. (28)[13]

[a market where everyone puts everything they have on the table: their clothes, footwear, family portraits, a broken umbrella which was perhaps found one day in the subway, a battered alarm clock, a rosary... Often, upon the same table, the Jew has a stove where he prepares his evening meal; but if anyone feels hungry, they can offer a price. In Rivington Street everything is for sale.]

Following Camba's parodistic style, the stereotype is exaggerated. According to the writer, everything is for sale in the 'Jewish market'. For the 'Jew', money is more important than family ('sus retratos de familia') and religion ('un rosario'). Furthermore, since the rosary is a religious object used for the homonymous prayer that commemorates the fifteen Mysteries of the life of Jesus, the allusion to this item can also be related to the 'Christ killer' stereotype: in Camba's text, the 'Jew' sells the rosary — which metaphorically symbolizes Christ — therefore recalling Judas's treason. Moreover, the reference to broken objects is used not only to highlight the alleged greed of the 'Jew' but also to ridicule and humiliate him. In Camba's depiction, the 'Jew's' irrational greed has no limits, and he tries to sell objects that nobody would buy. A similar image is used in the chapter entitled 'La España negra', in which the writer argues that during a walk in the Bowery (East Harlem), 'habiéndome detenido, por pura curiosidad a la puerta de una ropavejería, cuatro o cinco judíos se abalanzaron simultáneamente sobre mí. — ¿Le gusta a usted este gabán? — me dijeron enseñándome un gabán muy grande' [having stopped out of pure curiosity in the doorway of an old-clothes shop, four or five Jews simultaneously pounced upon me. 'Do you like this overcoat?', they said, showing me a very large overcoat.] (50). As the story develops, Camba is harassed by the Jewish peddlers, who insist on trying to sell him an old and excessively big coat in a malicious manner:

toda mi resistencia fue inútil. Quieras o no, no tuve más remedio que probarme aquel gabán que, en opinión de los judíos, me sentaba muy bien. Yo me daba perfecta cuenta de que varias manos recogían a mis espaldas la tela sobrante y de que, en cuanto yo me quedase a solas con el gabán, desaparecería por completo dentro de él; pero esta convicción no me servía de nada. Los judíos, simulando una súbita afección por mí, dijeron que aquel gabán valía lo menos cincuenta dólares, pero que, en vista del interés que yo tenía en llevármelo, harían un sacrificio y me lo dejarían en veinte.
 — Vengan quince dólares — me replicaban. — Vengan diez solamente. Vengan ocho. Vengan siete y medio. Vengan cinco...
 Total, que me llevé el gabán de los judíos y casi todos mis dólares, y que ésta es la hora en que no comprendo todavía aquel negocio [...] (50)

[all my resistance was futile. Like it or not, I had no other choice than to try on that overcoat which, in the Jews' opinion, fitted me very well. I realized perfectly that several hands pulled the surplus cloth behind me and that as soon as I was alone with the overcoat, I would completely disappear within it; but this conviction would be of no use to me. The Jews, feigning sudden affection towards me, said that that overcoat was worth at least fifty dollars, but that in light of the interest that I had in taking it with me, they would make a sacrifice and they would let me have it for twenty.

'That'll be fifteen dollars', they replied. 'That'll be just ten. That'll be eight.

That'll be seven and a half. That'll be five...'

In short, I took the overcoat from the Jews and almost all my dollars, and even now I still do not understand that transaction.]

Camba's story follows a modern stereotype that described Jewish inhabitants of early twentieth-century European metropolises, such as London, as old clothes dealers, often 'portrayed carrying under one arm a bag or sack to put his stack of second hand clothes' (Felsenstein 1995: 78). As Felsenstein states, 'the lowly social status of such an occupation and the importunity of some of these traders were sometimes put forward as further evidence of the debased condition of the Jews since biblical times' (1995: 78). I suggest that the episode narrated by Camba follows the same objective, namely to render Jewish people as 'corrupt' and 'primitive', and therefore inferior to white Europeans. The coincidence with the stereotype suggests that Camba is consciously recreating and therefore perpetuating Western stereotypes of the 'Jew'. At the beginning of the travelogue, he declares that 'from my point of view, verisimilitude is always more important than the truth' (13). Resemblance to the truth is based on the reader's horizon of understanding, on what s/he expects from the text. As I have argued throughout this book, the perception of social constructs such as 'class', 'race', 'gender', and 'nation' relies on the re-elaboration of a series of discursive formations based on the binary opposition between 'Us' and 'Them'. Literary works help to promote and keep such discursive formations alive in the social imaginary. Camba's description of Jewish people in New York, rather than referring to facts, is elaborated by using old stereotypes available in the discursive archive of the West. Furthermore the location of this anti-Semitic fable in a chapter devoted to praising the cultural grandeur of the Spanish Empire responds to the intention of reinforcing a nostalgic view of Spanish national identity. By combining medieval stereotypes of the 'Jew' and modern reinventions of this archetype, Camba creates an oppositional image of Spain's 'internal Other' that preserves the view of a Spanish national identity rooted in Catholicism and cultural homogeneity. The closing paragraphs of 'La España negra' cast a new light on the writer's choice of title for this chapter, which intertwines nostalgic views of Spain with racist and anti-Semitic stereotypes:

> Pero ya no quedan judíos en Harlem. Los negros de Puerto Rico, al invadir Nueva York, iniciaron una ofensiva realmente sangrienta contra ellos. Hubo tiros y puñaladas, y como a pesar de todo, los judíos se resistían, a veces, para desalojarlos fue necesario comprarles todos los gabanes que tenían en venta, hecho histórico que explica en gran parte la pintoresca elegancia de los llamados aquí negros latinos. Hoy ya no se habla *yiddish* más que en la calle 110. Desde la 111 en adelante hasta la 120 [...] se habla el español con todas sus modalidades. Se habla, se reza, se canta y hasta se baila. (51)

> [But there are no longer any Jews left in Harlem. The negroes of Puerto Rico, with their invasion of New York, began a truly bloody offensive against them. There were shootings and stabbings, and because the Jews resisted in spite of all

that, at times it was necessary to buy all the overcoats that they had on sale in order to get them out, a historic event which largely explains the picturesque elegance of so-called Latin negroes here. Today, Yiddish is not spoken except on 100 Street. From 111 onwards up to 120 [...] Spanish in all its variety is spoken. It is spoken, prayed, sung and even danced in.]

Here, Camba narrates a new expulsion of the Jews from a Hispanic territory, in this case carried out by the black colonized subaltern from Puerto Rico, who has interiorized the culture of the colonizer. 'The Jewish enemy' has once more been defeated by the strength of the Empire, still alive in the Spanish language and, significantly, in the Catholic religion. One must also note the insistence on 'the avaricious Jew' trope, since the text implies that the way to fight against the stubbornness of the Jews is to resort to their greed and materialism.

Probably echoing the interest in Sephardic Jews in early twentieth-century Spain, Camba refers to an alleged encounter with a Jew of Spanish origin in Rivington Street:

> a veces, en una esquina de Rivington Street se congregan seis o siete barbas tan diferentes entre sí como si sus portadores no hubieran tenido otro objeto al reunirse que el de cotejar las unas con las otras. Estas barbas vienen directamente de Amsterdam, aquéllas llegan del fondo de Polonia, las de más allá son, sin duda alguna, unas barbas españolas del siglo XV, y, por el olor que despiden, parecen haber estado hasta ahora conservadas en naftalina. Los judíos sefarditas no escasean por aquí, y yo recuerdo una tarde en la que observando la gracia, puramente oriental, con que hacía sus compras una chica, me dijo uno de ellos:
> — Fermosa doncella, ¿no piensa lo mismo vuesa merced?
> A lo que no pude menos de replicar:
> — Lo mismo pienso, amigo, y cristiana o infiel, una doncella tan fermosa merece los mayores acatamientos. (29)
>
> [at times, on a corner of Rivington Street, six or seven beards congregate, so different between themselves as if their wearers had no other purpose in meeting than to compare them against each other. These beards come directly from Amsterdam, those others hail from the depths of Poland, and those from elsewhere are, without a doubt, some Spanish beards from the fifteenth century. With the smell that they exude, they seem to have been preserved until now in napthalene. Sephardic Jews are not scarce around here, and I remember one afternoon when, observing the purely oriental charm with which a girl did her shopping, one of them said to me:
> 'Beautiful Maiden, does Sir not agree?'.
> To which I could but reply:
> 'I agree, my friend, and Christian or Infidel, such a beautiful Maiden merits the greatest respect.'.]

At the beginning of the previous extract, Camba seems to be alluding to the stereotype of 'the wandering Jew'. By referring to the different origins of the metonymic Jewish beard, the writer highlights the nomadic existence of the Jewish people, who never become — allegedly — a legitimate part of the national community. Moreover, this purported encounter brings forward a nostalgic recollection of medieval Spain, the golden age of Spanish nationalism. The persistence of the

Judeo-Spanish language centuries after the expulsion is here used in order to show the greatness of Spanish culture, of its endurance even in the antagonistic 'race' par excellence. However, the use of the adjective 'infiel' reminds the reader that despite linguistic similarities, the 'Jew' cannot be really considered as an 'amigo' and a 'true' Spaniard. The reference to religion therefore reinforces a traditionalist stand that identifies the essence of Spanish identity not only with past imperial glories, but also with Catholicism. The blatantly sexist remark made by the writer also suggests the dominant position of the 'male Spaniard'. Whether Christian or Jew, the 'oriental' woman must comply with male authority ('acatamientos'). Camba might be even playing with the etymology of this verb. 'Acatar' — to obey — comes from 'catar', meaning 'to see' in its archaic form. The 'observed woman' is hence constructed through the male gaze as a sexual object.

Finally, Camba differentiates between the Jews of Rivington Street and those living on Park Avenue:

> ¡Qué diferencia entre los judíos de Rivington Street y los de Park Avenue! Los judíos de Park Avenue son hijos de los de Rivington Street, pero carecen totalmente de carácter. Tienen Picassos y Rolls Royces, cebellinas y sillones metálicos, *solariums* y piscinas de natación, pero no tiene barbas. Rivington Street es el Oriente, el mundo antiguo, la Biblia. Park Avenue, en su parte judaica, es tan sólo Nueva York, ya posguerra y, a lo sumo, el *Times*. (30)

> [What difference there is between the Jews of Rivington Street and those of Park Avenue! The Jews of Park Avenue are the children of those of Rivington Street, but completely lack character. They have Picassos and Rolls Royces, sables and metallic armchairs, solariums and swimming pools, but they do not have beards. Rivington Street is the Orient, the ancient world, the Bible. Park Avenue, in its Jewish area, is just New York, now postwar and, at most, *The Times*.]

The writer opposes two antithetical, yet equally recurrent stereotypes: that of 'Jewish primitivism' and that of 'the Jew as symbol of modernization'. The result of such an opposition renders the Jews from Rivington Street almost harmful, a vestige of an archaic culture that has bent to the authority of the white European. However, the Jews of Park Avenue represent the arrival of a new era dominated by technology (embodied by the car as a symbol of modern times), by avant-garde art (Picasso), ruled by American power (a country that has shown its military potential in the First World War) and its new capitalist system and society of mass production ('no tienen carácter'). This new American Jew poses a real threat to white-European supremacy, since it represents the strength of the 'Big Other'. When confronted with these two contrary archetypes of the 'Jew', Spanish national identity is therefore aligned by Camba with the idea of European civilization, finding in the two contrary archetypes of the 'Jew' a double paradigm of 'Otherness': internal — in relation to the history of Jewry in Spain and Europe — and external, in the form of the American 'Big Other'.

The concept of 'race' around which New York's incipient multiculturalism is set in *Pruebas de Nueva York*, *El crisol de las razas*, and *La ciudad automática* reveals a particular conception of Spanish national identity as the result of a common ancestry, language, culture, and religion, as an eternal category that provides the illusion of a stable and immutable identity. This cultural construction is the result of hierarchical binary oppositions in which the white Spanish man occupies a position of superiority over both (black) external and (Jewish) internal 'Others'. The image of African Americans as 'racially' inferior — therefore confined to the lowest rungs of the social ladder — and corrupting, stems from colonialist discourses that are in turn a re-elaboration of ancient prejudices against the 'Other'. The archetype of the 'Jew' developed in these texts can be analysed in similar terms: the view of Jews as the embodiment of capitalism and of the dangers of modernization is in fact a re-elaboration of a stock of anti-Jewish images.

The racist attitudes shown in the New York narratives of Julio Camba and Teresa de Escoriaza are a response to the challenge posed by the increasing multiculturalism of American society to the stability of the concept of national identity promoted by ethnic nationalism. In the particular case of Spain, a country undergoing a necessary redefinition of its national identity after the fall of its colonial Empire, the reactions expressed in these texts show a special interest in highlighting the need of preserving a stable ethnic community based on 'racial' hierarchy. The views of African Americans and Jewish people provided in these works confirm the oppositional nature of identity formation in the nationalist sense, by establishing an asymmetrical relationship between the national representation of Peninsular Spain and both its subordinates (the black colonized) and its religious and cultural antagonists (the 'Jew' and the Protestant or atheist American). The efforts to preserve the stability of national identity fall, however, into continuous contradictions, showing the constructedness of such a concept as well as the inadequacy of racialist arguments and pseudo-scientific theories of 'race' to which the view of polyethnicity given in these texts often resort. Furthermore, efforts to dismantle the theories of Anglo-Saxon 'racial' superiority in vogue at the time reflect contemporary concerns about the degeneration of the Spanish 'race'.

Moreno Villa's travelogue offers a more empathic view of African Americans as humble and hardworking servants. However, such position of subalternity is never questioned by the writer, who prefers not to discuss the dominant racism of American society at the time. Moreno Villa's attitude reflects widespread reactions to primitive art by the European avant-garde, which turned black people into fascinating and often mysterious objects of contemplation, without engaging with the problems caused by the discrimination and segregation suffered by these individuals in the United States and the long history of colonization and domination of the 'Other' at the core of Western civilization. As for his depiction of Jewish people, his initial identification between Judaism and American capitalism falls repeatedly into pervasive discourses of Jews as 'Others', which overlap with the negative portrayal of the United States as a country solely moved by greed and materialism developed in Spain before the war against this country in 1898. However, the contrast with

Spain's poverty leads the writer to question his initially negative opinions about US society and to consider some of the positive effects of its economic system for the improvement of the living conditions of its citizens.

A different perspective is suggested in *Anticípolis*, in which identity is rendered a fluid, mutable category, not dependent on limiting conceptions of ethnic membership. Oteyza's novel presents a challenge to essentialist views of national identity, considering culture not as an immovable entity, but rather as a permeable concept in constant change. The novel also 'anticipates' the need for Spain to embrace new identitarian principles and overcome the cultural stagnation caused by a monolithic view of the Spanish nation. New York's multiculturalism, presented in *Anticípolis* as an unavoidable consequence of progress and modernization, represents therefore the need to leave behind the almost religious faith in 'ethnic' homogeneity promoted by Spanish nationalism. Nevertheless, the polyphonic structure of the novel leaves the reader uncertain as to whether such a challenge represents a threat to the unity of the Hispanic community. The essentialist view of Spanishness represented by Jesusa could be considered endangered in this case, and therefore — following traditionalist notions of Spanish national identity — in need of protection from pernicious foreign influences.

Notes to Chapter 4

1. In this regard, Carlos Taibo (2008) offers a relevant distinction between different (and sometimes opposed) ways of understanding nationalism.
2. See Robert Goldwater (1986), Susan Miller (ed.) (1991), Colin Rhodes (1994), Frances Connelly (1999), Jack Donald Flam and Miriam Deutch (eds) (2003), and Carol Sweeney (2004). Jed Rasula also mentions specific studies on the fascination exerted by jazz music on the European avant-garde: Jody Blake (1999); Bernard Gendron(2002); Glenn Watkins (1994).
3. I borrow the term 'primitivist modernism' from Sieglinde Lemke (1998).
4. Although it is outside the scope of this book, a postcolonial reading of *Poeta en Nueva York* seems necessary and would shed new light on García Lorca's text.
5. See also Baltasar Fra Molinero (1995).
6. For a study of the literary concept of *Hispanismo* at the turn of the century, see John E. Englekirk (1940).
7. *En el país de los Bubis*, recently re-issued by Ediciones del Viento in 2010, narrates the author's experiences in Africa.
8. For a comprehensive study of literary representations of Juana de Castilla, see María A. Gómez, Santiago Juan-Navarro, and Phyllis Zatlin (eds) (2008).
9. I have not been able to find the meaning of the word 'paragoe'. I can only deduce that Camba is misspelling 'arapahoe' and he is referring to Indian reservations.
10. Paul Allatson (2007: 133) points out that 'traditionally, the term jíbaro conveyed a sense of rural-based island character as poor, humble, fatalistic, unknowledgeable about the wider world, and yet stoic and endearing'.
11. According to Heather Levi (2001: 342), 'the term pelado, which literally means "baldie" or "stripped", identifies a poor (man) with (his) lack: of possessions, of culture, of everything'.
12. Jason Wilson (1999: 33) argues that 'the *atorrante* was an immigrant who hadn't made it, who lived homeless in the gutter'. The RAE Dictionary defines this adjective as 'vago' [lazy] and 'persona desfachatada, desvergonzada' [shameless person], both meanings used in Argentina and Uruguay.
13. Rivington Street is part of the Lower East Side neighbourhood, a multicultural area of New York with a prominent Jewish population. For a detailed history of this neighbourhood see Hasia R. Diner (2002).

CONCLUSION

❖

This book has studied the role played by New York as a symbol of modernization in early twentieth-century Spanish narrative, and how literary representations of the city reflected the crisis of Spanish national identity triggered by the end of the Empire in 1898. In particular, I have focused on the view of New York developed in two little-studied pieces of narrative fiction (*El crisol de las razas* by Teresa de Escoriaza and *Anticípolis* by Luis de Oteyza) and in two travelogues (*Pruebas de Nueva York* by José Moreno Villa and *La ciudad automática* by Julio Camba), all written between 1927 and 1932. Although the interest of Spanish writers in this American city has not gone completely unnoticed in Hispanic literary and cultural studies, analysis of this phenomenon has mostly focused on poetry, and non-canonical works have conventionally been dismissed because of their perceived lack of literary value. Departing from this approach, I have argued that the study of mass-produced narratives and travelogues provides a more complete and inclusive understanding of Spain's struggle for modernity in the early twentieth century. The canon of Spanish narrative works of the 1920s and 1930s has mainly included texts belonging to the so-called avant-garde novel. Studies of Spanish narrative based on this premise have therefore reduced the corpus of narrative texts to one literary genre and to a specific set of stylistic characteristics, such as formal experimentation. On a thematic level, a unifying feature of the corpus of canonical works is the presence of the increasingly visible effects of modernization in Spain: the urban space and the city, technology, the 'masses', and the 'modern woman'. As I have shown, all these themes are an essential part of the narrative works studied in this book, therefore revealing key concomitances between the so-called 'high' and 'low' literature. In addition, drawing on Beatriz Barrantes's analysis of the Spanish narrative written in the 1920s and 1930s, the limiting term 'avant-garde novel' not only hides the similarities between experimental and 'popular' genres, but also overlooks the variety of narrative genres coexisting in this period. Building on the term 'novela de la modernidad' proposed by Barrantes, I have suggested a more overarching concept, that of 'narrativa de la modernidad' or 'Spanish narratives of modernity', to include all Spanish narrative forms produced in this period, such as the novel, the novella, and the travelogue. These narrative genres are embedded in the tensions and contradictions brought about by modernizing process in Spain, and this is precisely the characteristic of the Spanish New York narratives of the 1920s and 1930s which has traditionally been overlooked. Sometimes openly (*Pruebas de Nueva York, Anticípolis, La ciudad automática*) or more subtly (*El crisol de las razas*), the chosen texts engage with the debates around traditional and modernizing views of Spanish national identity. Recurrent images of 'Otherness' highlight the challenge posed by modernization to monolithic views of Spanish national identity based on fixed notions of class, gender, and 'race'. In that sense, following similar attitudes in other European literary systems, New York — functioning as an often reductive epitome of the United States — is an ambivalent symbol in the narratives of Moreno Villa, Camba, Escoriaza, and Oteyza: on the one hand, an image of 'Otherness' which serves the purpose of reinforcing the Spanish 'Self' by opposing images of 'Us' versus 'Them'; on the other, a threatening 'Big Other', whose growing power and influence seems to foretell the inexorable worsening of similar modernizing processes already budding in Europe. In this regard, I have argued that Spanish responses to modernization must be contextualized within the context of the crisis of Western modernity. This book aims to dismantle the theoretical pigeonholing of the Spanish crisis as an isolated phenomenon, epitomized within Spanish literary studies by the opposition between Generation of 1898 and Spanish *Modernismo*. My work is indebted to studies such as those by Gullón (1992), Bretz (2001), Larson and Woods (2005), Soufas (2010), and Delgado, Mendelson and Vázquez (2007), which have located the literary production of the period within the broader scope of international modernism. However, these studies have mostly focused on the texts of the so-called Generation of 1898 and the Hispanic avant-garde, whereas this book has aimed to show how other non-canonical narrative forms also respond to the challenges and anxieties that are key to understanding Modernity and the effects of modernization processes in Spain. Themes such as the 'masses', technology, dehumanization, the rise of the 'modern woman', and the destabilization of ethnocentric views of the nation, do indeed connect the Spanish New York narratives to similar reactions in other European literary works. As the analysis of the case studies has shown, the discourses of 'Otherness' developed in these texts are connected to similar and pervasive discourses used in the West in order to create a European identity that opposes civilization, rationality, culture, and 'racial' superiority to primitivism, irrationality, nature, and 'racial' inferiority. The similarities between European and Spanish discourses of the 'masses', women, and non-white ethnicities reveal the role played by Spain in the construction of archetypes of the 'Other' since the early years of colonial expansion in America, as well as the perpetuation of patriarchy through a biosocial conception of gender, and the social and cultural elitism promoted by both the establishment and the intellectual elite in the first decades of the twentieth century.

The starting point of my analysis was the confrontation between two apparently conflicting projects of national regeneration, namely traditionalist and liberal, and their opposing reactions to Spain's increasing modernization. However, despite the contrast between nostalgic claims for the Catholic and monarchic essence of the Spanish nation and liberal attempts to move forward towards a secular, modern, and republican state, both projects share similar views of the 'masses', women, and non-white ethnicities as 'Others'. This is highlighted by the use of similar discourses in the different case studies, in which authors associated with liberal and republican positions such as Moreno Villa, Escoriaza, and Oteyza have points in common with the view of 'Otherness' given by Camba, a writer who has been connected to traditionalism and even Francoism. In my view, this fact strengthens the idea that discourses of 'Otherness' work as a grid or system of representation which shapes the author's perception of the 'Self' and the 'Other'. Consequently, the interest of the case studies examined in this book lies not only in the way such discourses are perpetuated through cultural products, but also in the difficulty presented to the author by these discourses, which resist being broken. It is precisely when the challenge to this prevalent world view creates a crack in the discourse that contradictions and tensions arise, showing the constructedness of concepts such as class, gender, and 'race'. All four texts studied in this book are party to these tensions to varying degrees.

The view of the 'masses', mass society, and technology given in the New York narratives of Moreno Villa, Oteyza, and Camba is reminiscent of similar attitudes in both European literary works and the Spanish narrative of the period. In these texts, the modernization and constant movement towards the future represented by the American city clashes with a view of Spanish identity based on nostalgic memories of a past in ruins. The skyscraper and the increasing presence of the machine contrast with the veneration of ancient monuments, representatives of the attachment to a mythicized view of Spanish identity. In addition, these texts show concerns about how modernization has created a new type of civilization in which the individual has been enslaved by the vociferous and primitive power of the 'masses'. Consequently, the United States is depicted as a dehumanized society and a primitive country. These attitudes show the threat posed by capitalism and mass society to social and cultural elitism. The messianic role assumed by intellectuals at the beginning of the twentieth century is challenged by a society where class mobility and capitalist consumerism blurs social difference, and where democratic and egalitarian ideals empower the 'masses' and diminish the impact of the intelligentsia. When this society is compared to Spain, the initial response in both Moreno Villa's and Camba's travelogues is that of resisting modernization. However, both texts evolve in different ways, and whereas in *Pruebas de Nueva York* there is a change of perspective and an eventual critique of the project of *Regeneracionismo*, Camba's chronicles strengthen an elitist view of society which is increasingly threatened by the rise of the 'masses', in Spain as well as America. Oteyza's novel, for its part, overlaps with both a positive and a negative view of modernization. On the one hand, it can be interpreted as a critique of Spain's stagnation. On the other, New York's unstoppable movement towards the future can also be read as a warning of the dangers posed by the unavoidable influence of modernization on a traditionalist view of Spanish national identity.

The reactions to women's emancipation displayed in the case studies can be grouped into three different positions. First of all, both Moreno Villa's and Camba's travelogues show a strong resistance to the entrance of women in the public sphere and to the challenges posed by female economic and emotional independence from male authority. This view is in tune with patriarchal and biosocial gender constructions not only promoted by traditionalist positions and the Catholic church in Spain, but also by liberal intellectuals such as José Ortega y Gasset. Female rebelliousness is portrayed in these two texts as violence and chaos. However, women still remain in a position of patriarchal subjugation, depicted as 'niñas' and 'chicas', irrational beings in need of male protection. The persistent identification between woman and the home/family as well as the role ascribed to womanhood as reproducer of the nation, confirms the patriarchal gaze behind the construction of Spanish national identity. Reactions to the increasing visibility of the 'modern woman', embodiment of dynamism and a challenge to biosocial constructions of gender, shows the discomfort caused in both conservative and liberal Spanish male intellectuals by the dismantling of gender categories prompted by modernization. Secondly, *El crisol de las razas* represents a change of perspective from a male to a female point of view. Following the ideas of Spanish female intellectuals of the time such as Carmen de Burgos and Rosa Chacel, in Escoriaza's novella women are depicted as essential actors in modernization processes. Consequently, whereas Helen's reluctance to embrace her life as an independent woman is punished at the end of the narrative by her accidental death, Sonia's final escape from patriarchy is rewarded with Joe's love. Of the male characters in the narrative, Boris embodies the archetype of patriarchal domination. Joe however represents a new type of masculinity that respects women's independence. Finally, *Antícipolis* confronts two opposing voices: traditional motherhood (Jesusa) and the rebelliousness of the young 'modern woman' (Rosa). Jesusa's attachment to religious and social conventions reveals the role played by women as cultural reproducers as well as the power exerted by symbolic violence — to borrow Bourdieu's term — on women. Rosa, on the other hand, fully embraces the freedom and independence given by modernization to women in New York. The symbolism of Jesusa's death at the end of the novel remains, however, ambiguous. The ultimate paralysis and fatal fit suffered by this traditionalist woman can be read either as the need to embrace modernization in order to overcome the weight of the past and move forward, or as a warning against the devastating effects of modernization on the essence of Spanish national identity.

The final aspect analysed in this book has been the reaction to New York's cultural diversity and the challenge posed by polyethnic societies to the ethnocentric concept of national identity promoted in Spain at the time. In particular, I have examined the depiction of both black and Jewish people — the traditional external and internal 'Others' of the West — and the connection of such depictions to the re-assessment of Spanish national identity in the first decades of the twentieth century. The racist bias shown in *La ciudad automática* and *El crisol de las razas* reveals the similarities between the pervasive racist stand of Western constructions of 'Otherness' and the Spanish case. On the one hand, both anti-Semitic discourses and the construction of the 'black' as subaltern in Camba's travelogue echo nostalgic views of Spain's imperial past, which relies on the construction of the 'Other' as 'racially' inferior. I have argued that Camba's appraisal of the concept of *Hispanidad* responds to contemporary concerns about the degeneration of the Spanish 'race' as opposed to the alleged superiority of Anglo-Saxon 'races', as argued for example in Lord Salisbury's speech 'Living and Dying Nations' (1898) and discussed by Edmond Demolins in *Anglo-Saxon Superiority: To What It Is Due* (1897). In *La ciudad automática*, New York's incipient multiculturalism is turned into a oppositional device used to highlight the supposed pernicious effects of miscegenation and 'racial' diversity for the Anglo-Saxon 'race' in the United States. The aim of this strategy is to construct an image of the Spanish 'race' as protected against 'racial' degeneration, creating the illusion of a national community in which the 'Other' remains in a position of subalternity, which responds to an alleged 'natural' hierarchy, and therefore does not threat the authority of the colonial master. *El crisol de las razas*, a text that challenges the patriarchal nationalism defended in *Pruebas de Nueva York* and *La ciudad automática*, paradoxically shares with these two texts an anti-Semitic bias. Escoriaza's novella associates patriarchy with a racist view of Eastern Jews as a primitive and degenerate 'race', which in this case not only poses a threat to 'racial' purity, but also to the social advances of US society in relation to gender equality. Therefore, in spite of the attempt to destabilize biosocial conceptions of gender, this text remains strongly attached to racist stereotypes of the 'Jew'. Whereas the novella strives to challenge the construction of woman as an inferior 'Other', the influence of Jewish culture and 'race' in New York is demonized, to the extent of considering miscegenation as a threat to American modernization. The confusing terminology used in the novella — where 'racial' mixture is seen as an attempt to create a superior 'race' in the United States — highlights, similarly to Camba's text, the increasing fear of 'racial' degeneration in both Europe and Spain, and the pervasiveness of racist stereotypes of the 'Jew' as an internal and corrupting 'Other'. On the contrary, José Moreno Villa's depiction of black and Jewish people in *Pruebas de Nueva York* offers a revealing contrast with the openly racist bias expressed in Camba's and Escoriaza's texts, although it yet shares some of the assumptions and stereotypes developed in these two works. Whereas the view of African Americans provided in Moreno Villa's travelogue shows a greater appreciation towards this ethnic community, the writer never challenges the idea of the black 'race' as a naturally subaltern one. Such apparent contradiction is explained by the widespread modernist approach to blacks in aesthetic terms, in which although the so-called primitive art was praised by its authenticity and naturalness, the discrimination suffered by these individuals was rarely addressed. Similarly, the depiction of Jewish people carried out by Moreno Villa perpetuates a series of discourses of 'Otherness' used since antiquity to characterize Jews as a malignant influence on the health of Western nations. At the same time, the writer combines such stereotypes with images of American society as governed by materialism and greed, thus identifying Judaism with capitalism. As happens several times in *Pruebas de Nueva York*, Moreno Villa's view evolves from rejection and even disdain to a more appreciative opinion of the United States and of the benefits that Spanish society could enjoy thanks to modernization. Finally, in tune with the ambiguity deriving from its polyphonic nature, *Antícipolis* offers two opposing views of 'race' and national identity simultaneously. On the one hand, the embracing of American culture and modernizing social values such as capitalism, class mobility, and women emancipation by Jesusa's children, as well as the unstoppable influence of modernizing processes represented by New York in Spain, suggest a flexible view of national identity, not dependent on essentialist values, but rather open to negotiation. Moreover, the archetype of the 'subaltern black' is subverted by presenting Jiménez — a Puerto Rican mulatto — as the voice of modernization. The advanced ideas articulated by this educated doctor are in stark contrast with Jesusa's ignorance and irrational attachment to traditionalism, therefore undermining the authority of the Spanish colonizer over the 'primitive' colonized. On the other hand, the potential disintegration and disappearance of Spanish national identity at the hands of modernization is represented not only by the conscious rejection of the Spanish language, religion, and classist values by Jesusa's children, but also by her own final paralysis and demise. The novel therefore presents two hegemonic responses to modernization in Spain, revealing the direct connection between modernization and the reassessment of Spanish national identity.

New York as a symbol of modern times, the embodiment of modernization and 'Otherness', functions in all these four texts as a contrasting image that is continuously questioned, sometimes feared, sometimes admired, but always projecting the concerns, tensions, and anxieties brought about by modernization in Spain. The challenge to class, gender, and 'race' constructions catalysed by this discovery of a 'new world' in New York reveals the contradictions and fissures of the elitist, patriarchal, and ethnocentric foundations of the projects of national regeneration promoted in early twentieth-century Spain.

AFTERWORD

❖

New York in Spanish Narrative: A Constant Presence in the Twentieth and Twenty-First Centuries

Although the restricted scope of this book (1898–1936) was aimed at providing a thorough analysis of the reactions towards New York in Spanish narrative emerging during a specific period of Spanish history, such an approach does not fully reflect the constant presence of this city in Spanish letters in the twentieth and twenty-first centuries. As Julio Neira has extensively studied in *Historia poética de Nueva York en la España contemporánea* (2012), the references to New York in Spanish poetry did not wane after the Civil War, and have been especially significant since the end of Franco's regime. Similarly, the city has been a recurrent location for both Spanish travel literature and fictional narrative from 1939 to the present day.

During the dictatorship, New York appears especially in travel books. To name a few: *Nueva York: un español entre rascacielos* [*New York: a Spaniard amidst Skyscrapers*] (1945) by Gaspar Tato Cumming, *Nueva York en retales* [*A Patchwork of New York*] (1946) by Joaquín Calvo Sotelo, *Nueva York: impresiones de un español del siglo XIX que no sabe inglés* [*New York: Impressions of a Nineteenth Century Spaniard Who Doesn't Speak English*] by Diego Hidalgo (1946), *Nueva York* (1947) by Agustín del Saz, *Reportaje a Nueva York: las Naciones Unidas* [*New York Reportage: the United Nations*] (1950) by José Blanco Amor, *De Nueva York a California* [*From New York to California*] (1953) by Antonio Heras, *Manhattan de refilón: Nueva York contado por un español* [*Manhattan at a Glance: New York Told by a Spaniard*] (1955) by Manuel Tovar, *Nueva York, ida y vuelta: los Estados Unidos vistos por un español* [*A Round Trip to New York: the United States Seen by a Spaniard*] (1961) by Gregorio Marañón and *Nueva York: nivel de vida, nivel de muerte* [*New York: Standard of Living, Standard of Dying*] (1970) by Ramón Carnicer. The examination of this body of works, which remains 'forgotten' by literary and cultural studies, would provide an excellent insight into post-Civil War views of the United States, as well as into the image of Spain projected by the literature of the period. We may also ask whether we would still find in these texts similar discourses to those expressed in early twentieth-century Spanish New York narratives. It is outside the scope of this book to address such a question; however, it is worth noting that a cursory look at these travelogues unveils some thematic similarities. For example, José Blanco Amor's account of New York includes chapters entitled 'Materialismo', 'La american girl', 'Compañera y tirana' [Partner and Tyrant], 'La danza de las razas' [The Dance of Races], and 'Negros'. Another significant case is Ramón Carnicer's travelogue, in which, although published in 1970, we still find titles such as 'El presidente de la Universidad. Los judíos' [The President of the University. Jews] and 'Negros y otras yerbas' [Blacks and Other Weeds]. Moreover, in texts such as Joaquín Calvo Sotelo's *Nueva York en retales*, there are direct references to the situation in Spain at the time, in this case justifying the military uprising that led to the Spanish Civil War and criticizing the negative views of Franco's Spain expressed in US newspapers such as *The New York Times*.

By contrast, the Spanish New York narratives published since the end of the dictatorship offer a more empathetic view of the United States, both in travel literature and narrative fiction. Some examples of travel accounts of this city (which often combine travel narrative with other genres such as journalism) written since 1978 include: *Nueva York* (1986) by Eduardo Mendoza, *Ventanas de Manhattan* [*Windows of Manhattan*] (2004) by Antonio Muñoz Molina, *Historias de Nueva York* [*New York Stories*] (2006) by Enric González, *Visión de Nueva York* [*Vision of New York*] (2005) by Carmen Martín Gaite, *Nueva York: el deseo o la quimera* [*New York: Desire or Chimera*] (2007) and *Diccionario de Nueva York* [*New York Dictionary*] (2010) by Alfonso Armada, and *Nueva York Hipster* (2014) by Mario Suárez. The city has also had a prominent presence in multiple forms of narrative fiction, for example: a novel written in English by Felipe Alfau, *Chromos* (1990), young-adults' literature in *Caperucita en Manhattan* [*Red Riding Hood in Manhattan*] (1990) by Carmen Martín Gaite, collected short stories from different authors in *Líneas Urbanas: Lectura de Nueva York* [*Urban Lines: Reading New York*] (2002) edited by José Luis García Martín, the postmodern collection of short stories *El hombre que inventó Manhattan* [*The Man Who Invented Manhattan*] (2004) by Ray Loriga, the irreverent pulp novel *New York Shitty* (2005) by Germán Sánchez Espeso, and the award-winning novels *Llámame Brooklyn* [*Call me Brooklyn*] (Nadal Prize 2006) by Eduardo Lago and *Mitología de Nueva York* [*New York Mythology*] (Ateneo de Sevilla Prize 2010) by Vanessa Montfort Écija. The list grows every year. Nowadays, the amazement expressed by the Spanish writers who travelled to New York in previous eras and the discontent they often showed in their literary accounts, is replaced by instances of some identification with the city through the encounter with familiar images of New York that had been previously experienced by the traveller in photographs, films, and music. In some cases, as in Muñoz Molina's text, the identity of the writer becomes blurred after his return to Spain:

> Ahora, en las calles de Madrid, soy como el fantasma rezagado y sin sustancia de la parte de mí mismo que se quedó en la otra ciudad, tan lejana en los mapas, tan próxima en el tiempo, tan inmediata y asidua en el recuerdo, en la sensación de aturdimiento y extranjería que llevo conmigo y que no se alivia ni cuando han desaparecido los trastornos de sueño provocados por el viaje de vuelta. (2004: 376)
>
> [Now, in the streets of Madrid, I'm like the straggler and empty ghost of the part of myself that stayed in the other city; a city so far away in the maps but so close in time, so immediate and frequent in my memories, in the feeling of

bewilderment and in the impression of being a foreigner that I carry with me and that is not alleviated even when the sleep disorder caused by the return trip has disappeared.]

The influence of American culture is also reflected in the literary style employed in narrative fiction and by the presence of American main characters in these texts. This is the case, for example in the fictional Spanish New York narratives by Loriga, Lago, and Sánchez Espeso.

The novel *Chromos* by Alfau, a Catalan writer who emigrated to the United States at an early age (during World War I), is an unusual and fascinating case. Written in the 1940s and only published almost fifty years later, his novel tells the story of a group of 'Americaniards', the term used by the narrator for Spanish people living in New York. This definition, which clearly shows a sense of hybrid identity as opposed to previous expressions of national homogeneity, was also introduced by Lago in *Llámame Brooklyn* to refer to a group of writers established in the city. The parallels between both novels go even further, as Alfau also appears as a character in Lago's text. The influence of Alfau's work on Lago's novel and the thematic similarities between both have been recently studied by Reginna Galasso (2010). However, although some of these texts captured the attention of literary critics (especially those written by widely acclaimed authors such as Muñoz Molina, Loriga, and Lago), there has not been, to the best of my knowledge, a complete study of this body of works as a whole. When compared to previous Spanish New York narratives written in the periods 1898–1936 and 1939–1978, the examination of this group of texts would shed light into the growing influence of American culture in Spain and Spanish literature.

Finally, in order to provide a complete approach to the narrative representations of New York published by authors born in the Spanish state, we should also consider similar cases written in Galician, Basque, and Catalan literatures, for example Josep Pla's *Week-end d'estiu a Nova York* [*Summer Weekend in New York*] (Catalan, 1995) and Harkaitz Cano's *El puente desafinado: baladas de Nueva York* [*The Bridge Out of Tune: New York Ballads*] (Basque, 2003). In the past decade, the presence of New York has been especially prominent in Galician narrative, including the collection of short stories, *Ratas en Manhattan* [*Rats in Manhattan*] (2007) by Francisco Álvarez 'Koki', the novels *Xelamonite* [*Gelignite*] (2006) by Luís Paradelo and *O home inédito* [*The Unpublished Man*] by Carlos G. Meixide (2007), and Inma López Silva's fictionalized diary *New York, New York* (2007). The views of New York, Spain, and Galicia given in these texts provide an excellent understanding of issues of national identity in contemporary Spain, within the context of minority cultures and the tension between centre and periphery.

BIBLIOGRAPHY

❖

ACUÑA, RODOLFO FRANCISCO. 2011. *Occupied America: A History of Chicanos* (Boston: Longman)
ADAMS, PERCY G. 1983 *Travel Literature and the Evolution of the Novel* (Lexington: University Press of Kentucky)
ALARCÓN, MARIANO. 1918. *Impresiones de un viaje a New-York* (Madrid: Gráficas Excelsior)
ALARCÓN SIERRA, RAFAEL. 2005. 'Los libros de viaje en la primera mitad del siglo XX: Julio Camba: "La rana viajera"', in Patricia Almarcegui Elduayen and Leonardo Romero Tobar (eds), *Los libros de viaje: realidad vivida y género literario* (Madrid: Akal), pp. 158–95
ALBERCA SERRANO, MANUEL. 1989. 'La estrategia vital (a propósito de *Vida en claro* de José Moreno Villa)', in Cristóbal Cuevas García (ed.), *José Moreno Villa en el contexto del 27* (Barcelona: Anthropos), pp. 235–42.
ALEC-TWEEDIE, ETHEL. 1913. *America as I Saw It; or, America Revisited* (New York: Macmillan)
ALEXANDER, GERARD. 1999. 'Women and Men at the Ballot Box: Voting in Spain's Two Democracies', in Victoria Enders and Pamela Radcliff (eds), *Constructing Spanish Womanhood: Female Identity in Modern Spain* (Albany: State University of New York Press), pp. 349–74
ALFAU, FELIPE. 1991. *Chromos* (London: Viking)
ALLATSON, PAUL. 2007. *Key Terms in Latino/a Cultural and Literary Studies* (Oxford: Blackwell)
ALONSO, CECILIO. 2007. 'El Cuento Semanal en la continuidad literaria y periodística de su tiempo', *Monteagudo: revista de literatura española, hispanoamericana y teoría de la literatura*, 12: 27–50
——2008. 'Sobre la categoría canónica de "raros y olvidados"', *Anales de literatura española*, 20: 11–38
ÁLVAREZ CASTAÑO, EMILIO JOSÉ. 2004. *Nueva York en los escritores españoles del siglo XX* (Seville: Edición Digital@tres)
ÁLVAREZ CHILLIDA, GONZALO. 2002. *El Antisemitismo en España. La imagen del judío (1812–2002)* (Madrid: Marcial Pons)
——2007. 'La eclosión del antisemitismo español: de la II República al Holocausto', in Gonzalo Álvarez Chillida and Ricardo Izquierdo Benito (eds), *El Antisemitismo en España* (Cuenca: Universidad de Castilla-La Mancha), pp. 181–206
ÁLVAREZ DOMÍNGUEZ, MÓNICA, and ÁNGELES ABUÍN PRIETO. 2003. 'Julio Camba en Nova Iorque: Impresións dun xornalista visionario', in Ofelia Requejo (ed.), *Xornadas sobre Julio Camba* (Santiago de Compostela: Xunta de Galicia), pp. 29–45
ÁLVAREZ JUNCO, JOSÉ. 1995. 'Education and the Limits of Liberalism', in Helen Graham and Jo Labanyi (eds), *Spanish Cultural Studies, an Introduction* (Oxford: Oxford University Press), pp. 45–52
——1999. 'History, Politics and Culture (1875–1936)', in David T. Gies (ed.), *Modern Spanish Culture* (Cambridge: Cambridge University Press), pp. 67–85
ÁLVAREZ 'KOKI', FRANCISCO. 2007. *Ratas en Manhattan* (Santiago de Compostela: Sotelo Blanco)

ANDERSON, BENEDICT. 2006. *Imagined Communities: Reflections on the Origin and Spread of Nationalism* (London: Verso)

ANONYMOUS. 1933. 'El aniversario de la República', *El Radical, órgano de la juventud republicana radical*, 36 (10 April 1933)

ARANGO, MANUEL ANTONIO. 1995. *Símbolo y simbología en la obra de Federico García Lorca* (Madrid: Fundamentos)

ARAQUISTÁIN, LUIS. 1921. *El peligro yanqui* (Madrid: Publicaciones España)

ARCE PINEDO, REBECA. 2008. *Dios, Patria y Hogar. La construcción social de la mujer española por el catolicismo y las derechas en el primer tercio del siglo XX* (Santander: Universidad de Cantabria)

ARENAL, CONCEPCIÓN. 1993. *La mujer del porvenir* (Madrid: Castalia)

ARENDT, HANNAH. 1979. *The Origins of Totalitarianism* (London: Harcourt Brace)

ARMADA, ALFONSO. 2007. *Nueva York: el deseo o la quimera* (Madrid: Espasa)

—— 2010. *Diccionario de Nueva York* (Barcelona: Península)

ARRANZ, LUIS, and MERCEDES CABRERA FERNANDO DEL REY. 2000. 'The Assault on Liberalism, 1914–1923', in José Álvarez Junco and Adrian Shubert (eds), *Spanish History Since 1808* (London: Arnold), pp. 191–206.

AUBERT, PAUL. 2006. 'Hacia la modernización', in Carlos Serrano and Serge Salaün (eds), *Los felices años veinte. España, crisis y modernidad* (Madrid: Marcial Pons)

AYALA, FRANCISCO. 1929. 'Josefina Baker'. *Indagación del cinema* (Madrid: Iberoamericana), pp. 148–51.

AZORÍN. 1975. *Obras Completas*, Volume 1 (Madrid: Aguilar)

BAKHTIN, MIKHAIL. 1984. *Problems of Dostoevsky's Poetics* (Manchester: Manchester University Press)

BALFOUR, SEBASTIAN. 1995. 'The Loss of Empire: Regenerationism and the Forging of a Myth of National Identity', in Helen Graham and Jo Labanyi (eds), *Spanish Cultural Studies, an Introduction* (Oxford: Oxford University Press), pp. 25–31

—— 1996. '"The Lion and the Pig": Nationalism and National Identity in the Fin-de-Siècle Spain', in Clare Mar-Molinero and Angel Smith (eds), *Nationalism and the Nation in the Iberian Peninsula* (Oxford: Berg), pp. 107–17.

—— 1997. *The End of the Spanish Empire, 1898–1923* (Oxford: Clarendon Press)

—— 2000. 'Spain from 1931 to the Present', in Raymond Carr (ed.), *Spain: A History* (New York: Oxford University Press), pp. 243–82

BALLESTEROS, RAFAEL, and JULIO NEIRA. 2000. 'Introducción', in José Moreno Villa, *Jacinta la pelirroja* (Madrid: Castalia), pp. 7–60

BAROJA, PÍO. 1972. *Camino de perfección (Pasión mística)* (Madrid: Editorial Caro Raggio)

BARRANTES MARTÍN, BEATRIZ. 2001. 'Luis de Oteyza: visionario de la modernidad', *Hibris. Revista de Bibliofilia*, 44: 5–16

—— 2006. 'Introducción', in Luis de Oteyza, *Anticípolis* (Madrid: Cátedra), pp. 11–74

—— 2007. *Ciudad y modernidad en la prosa hispánica de vanguardia* (Valladolid: Universidad de Valladolid)

BELDA, JOAQUÍN. 1926. *En el pais del bluff: veinte dias en Nueva York* (Madrid: Biblioteca Hispania)

BELLER, STEVEN. 2007. *Antisemitism: A Very Short Introduction* (Oxford: Oxford University Press)

BENBASSA, ESTHER. 2010. 'Otherness, Openness and Rejection in Jewish Context', *Journal of the Interdisciplinary Study of Monotheistic Religions*, 5: 16–25

BERMAN, MARSHALL. 1999. *All that is Solid Melts into Air*, 10th edn (London: Verso)

BERMEJO, JOSÉ MARÍA. 1978. 'Vida en claro de un retraído: José Moreno Villa', *Cuadernos Hispanoamericanos*, 331: 115–25

BERNAL, DIEGO. 1997. *Julio Camba* (Santiago de Compostela: Xunta de Galicia)

BLAKE, JODY. 1999. *Le Tumulte Noir: Modernist Art and Popular Entertainment in Jazz-Age Paris, 1900–1930* (University Park: Pennsylvania State University Press)

BLANCO AGUINAGA, CARLOS. 1999. 'On Modernism from the Periphery', in Anthony L. Geist and José B. Monleón (eds), *Modernism and Its Margins: Reinscribing Cultural Modernity from Spain and Latin America* (London: Garland), pp. 3–16

BLANCO AMOR, JOSÉ. 1950. *Reportaje a Nueva York: las Naciones Unidas* (Buenos Aires: Bell)

BOURDIEU, PIERRE. 2001. *Masculine Domination* (Cambridge: Polity Press)

BRETZ, MARY LEE. 2001. *Encounters Across Borders: The Changing Visions of Spanish Modernism, 1890–1930* (Lewisburg : Bucknell University Press)

BRITT ARREDONDO, CHRISTOPHER. 2005. *Quixotism: The Imaginative Denial of Spain's Loss of Empire* (Albany: State University of New York Press)

BUCK, CHRISTOPHER. 2010. 'Harlem Renaissance', in Leslie M. Alexander and Walter C. Rucker (eds), *Encyclopaedia of African American History* (Santa Barbara: ABC-CLIO), pp. 795–99

BUCKLEY, RAMÓN, and JOHN CRISPIN. 1973. *Los vanguardistas españoles (1925–1935)* (Madrid: Alianza)

BURGOS, CARMEN DE. 2007. *La mujer moderna y sus derechos* (Madrid: Biblioteca Nueva)

BURKE, PETER. 2007. *Historia y teoría social* (Madrid: Amorrortu Editores)

BURROW, J.W. 2000. *The Crisis of Reason: European Thought, 1848–1914* (London: Yale University Press)

CALATRAVA, JUAN. 2007. 'Leopoldo Torres Balbas. Architectural Restoration and the Idea of "Tradition" in Early Twentieth-Century Spain', *Future Anterior*, IV (2): 41–49

CALLE, JOSÉ DE LA. 1990. 'Jacinta la pelirroja: lírica de evidencias', in Cristóbal Cuevas García (ed.), *Investigaciones Filológicas* (Málaga: Departamento de Filología Española II y Teoría de la Literatura), pp. 55–65

CALVO SOTELO, JOAQUÍN. 1946. *Nueva York en retales* (Madrid: Dossat)

CAMBA, JULIO. 1960. *La ciudad automática* (Madrid: Espasa Calpe)

——— 1960. *Alemania, impresiones de un español* (Madrid: Espasa Calpe)

——— 1973. *Londres* (Madrid: Espasa Calpe)

——— 2007. *Aventuras de una peseta* (Barcelona: Alhena Media)

——— 2008. *La rana viajera* (Barcelona: Alhena Media)

——— 2009. *Un año en el otro mundo* (Madrid: Rey Lear)

CAÑAS, DIONISIO. 1994. *El poeta y la ciudad. Nueva York y los escritores hispanos* (Madrid: Cátedra)

CANO, HARKAITZ. 2003. *El puente desafinado: baladas de Nueva York* (Donostia: Erein)

CANO, JOSÉ LUIS. 1970. *La poesía de la Generación del 27* (Madrid: Labor/Guadarrama)

——— 1976. 'José Moreno Villa: Vida en claro', *Ínsula*, 377: 361

CANSINOS ASSENS, RAFAEL. 1995. *La novela de un literato, 3. 1923–1936* (Madrid: Alianza)

CARMONA MATO, EUGENIO. 1985. *José Moreno Villa y los orígenes de las vanguardias artísticas en España (1909–1936)* (Málaga: Universidad de Málaga/Colegio de Arquitectos)

CARNERO, GUILLERMO. 1977. 'Recuperación de Moreno Villa', *Ínsula*, 378: 368–69

——— 1989. 'José Moreno Villa y las orientaciones de la Vanguardia española', in Cristóbal Cuevas García (ed.), *José Moreno Villa en el contexto del 27* (Barcelona: Anthropos), pp. 13–29

CARNICER, RAMÓN. 1970. *Nueva York: nivel de vida, nivel de muerte* (Barcelona: Taber)

CEASER, JAMES W. 1997. *Reconstructing America: The Symbol of America in Modern Thought* (New Haven: Yale University Press)

CÉLINE, LOUIS-FERDINAND. 2013. *Journey to the End of the Night*, trans. by Ralph Manheim (London: Alma Classics)

CHACEL, ROSA. 1931. 'Esquema de los problemas prácticos y actuales del amor', *Revista de Occidente*, 31: 129–80

CHILLÓN ASENSIO, LLUIS ALBERT. 1999. *Literatura y periodismo: una tradición de relaciones promiscuas* (Barcelona: Universidad Autónoma de Barcelona)

CIRRE, JOSÉ FRANCISCO. 1963. *La poesía de José Moreno Villa* (Madrid: Ínsula)

CIXOUS, HÉLÈNE, and CATHERINE CLÉMENT. 1996. *The Newly Born Woman* (London: I. B. Tauris)

CONNELLY, FRANCES. 1999. *The Sleep of Reason: Primitivism in Modern European Art and Aesthetics, 1725–1907* (University Park: Pennsylvania State University Press)

COSTA, MARÍA DOLORES. 1996. 'The Travel Writing of Julio Camba', *Monographic Review*, 12: 154–65

CRIADO REQUENA, EDUARDO. 2004. *La ciudad de los rascacielos* (Seville: Alfar)

CUEVAS GARCÍA, CRISTÓBAL. 1991. 'Civilización artística y civilización comercial: *Pruebas de Nueva York* de José Moreno Villa', *Analecta malacitana: Revista de la Sección de Filología de la Facultad de Filosofía y Letras*, 14(2): 301–14

DALY, NICHOLAS. 2004. *Literature, Technology and Modernity 1860–2000* (Cambridge: Cambridge University Press)

DAVIES, CATHERINE. 1998. *Spanish Women's Writing 1849–1996* (London: Athlone Press)

DELANTY, GERARD. 1995. *Inventing Europe: Idea, Identity, Reality* (London: St Martin's Press)

DELGADO, ELENA, JORDANA MENDELSON and ÓSCAR VÁZQUEZ. 2007. 'Introduction: Recalcitrant Modernities — Spain, Cultural Difference and The Location of Modernism', *Journal of Iberian and Latin American Studies*, 13(2–3): 105–19

DEMOLINS, EDMOND. 1899. *Anglo-Saxon Superiority: To What It Is Due* (Toronto: The Musson Book Company)

DÍAZ-CAÑABATE, ANTONIO. 1978. 'María la de Postas', *ABC* (9 June 1978), 99

DÍAZ DE CASTRO, FRANCISCO JAVIER. 1989. 'La poesía vanguardista de Moreno Villa', in Cristóbas Cuevas García (ed.), *José Moreno Villa en el contexto del 27* (Barcelona: Anthropos), pp. 30–67

DÍAZ ECHARRI, EMILIANO, and JOSÉ MARÍA ROCA FRANQUESA. 1962. *Historia General de la literatura Española e Hispanoamericana* (Madrid: Aguilar)

DÍAZ-PLAJA, GUILLERMO. 1979. *Modernismo frente a Noventa y Ocho: una introducción a la literatura española del siglo XX* (Madrid: Espasa Calpe)

DÍEZ DE REVENGA, FRANCISCO JAVIER. 2001. '*Jacinta la Pelirroja*, de José Moreno Villa. Entre Modernismo y Vanguardia', *Monteagudo*, 6: 129–32

DINER, HASIA R. 2002. *Lower East Side Memories: A Jewish Place in America* (Princeton: Princeton University Press)

DOMINGO, JOSÉ. 1982. 'La prosa narrativa hasta 1936', in José M. Díez Borque (ed.), *Historia de la literatura española*, Volume 4 (Madrid: Taurus), pp. 203–48

DOMINGUEZ BURDALO, JOSÉ. 2006. 'Del ser (o no ser) hispano: Unamuno frente a la negritud', *Modern Language Notes (Hispanic Issue)*, 121.2: 322–42

DOUGHERTY, DRU, and MARÍA FRANCISCA VILCHES DE FRUTOS. 1990. *La escena madrileña entre 1918 y 1926: análisis y documentación* (Madrid: Fundamentos)

DUHAMEL, GEORGES. 1974. *America the Menace: Scenes from the Life of the Future* (New York: Arno Press)

EATON TRAVIS, DORIS. 2003. *The Days We Danced: The Story of My Theatrical Family from Florenz Ziegfeld to Arthur Murray and Beyond* (Norman: University of Oklahoma Press)

EISENSTEIN, ZILLAH. 2000. 'Writing Bodies on the Nation for the Globe', in Sita Ranchod-Nilsson and Mary Ann Tétreaut (eds), *Women, States and Nationalism* (London: Routledge), pp. 35–53

ENGLEKIRK, JOHN E. 1940. 'El Hispanoamericanismo y la Generación del 98', *Revista Iberoamericana*, 2: 321–51

EPPS, BRAD, and LUIS FERNÁNDEZ CIFUENTES (eds). 2005. *Spain Beyond Spain: Modernity, Literary History, and National Identity* (Lewisburg: Bucknell University Press)

ESCORIAZA, TERESA DE. 1921. *Del dolor de la guerra (crónicas de la campaña de Marruecos)* (Madrid: Pueyo)

—— 1924. 'La primera conferencia feminista. Teresa de Escoriaza habla a las radioescuchas' (transcript of the original radio broadcast), *T.S.H, Revista semanal órgano de "Radio Madrid" y portavoz de la federación nacional de aficionados*, 1 (25 May 1924), 13–14

——. 1929. *El crisol de las razas, Los novelistas*, year 2, number 43 (Madrid: Prensa Moderna)

FELSENSTEIN, FRANK. 1995. *Anti-Semitic Stereotypes: A Paradigm of Otherness in English Popular Culture, 1660–1830* (Baltimore: Johns Hopkins University Press)

FENTON, STEVE. 1999. *Ethnicity, Racism, Class and Culture* (London: Macmillan)

FERNÁNDEZ, PURA. 2002. 'Vías y desvíos en la codificación literaria del erotismo español finisecular (siglos XIX-XX)', in Tomás Facundo (ed.), *En el país del arte: literatura y arte en el entresiglos XIX-XX* (Valencia: Biblioteca Valenciana), pp. 117–50

FERNÁNDEZ CIFUENTES, LUIS. 1982. *Teoría y mercado de la novela en España del 98 a la República* (Madrid: Gredos)

—— 1993. 'Fenomenología de la vanguardia: el caso de la novela', *Anales de literatura española*, 9: 45–60

FISCHER, KLAUS P. 2006. *America in White, Black, and Grey: The Stormy 1960s* (New York: Continuum)

FITZPATRICK, SHEILA. 1994. *The Russian Revolution*, 2nd edn (Oxford: Oxford University Press)

FLAM, JACK DONALD, and MIRIAM DEUTCH (eds). 2003. *Primitivism and Twentieth-century Art: A Documentary History* (California: University of California Press)

FLESLER, DANIELA, TABEA ALEXA LINHARD and ADRIÁN PÉREZ MELGOSA. 2011. 'Introduction: Revisiting Jewish Spain in the Modern Era', *Journal of Spanish Cultural Studies*, 12(1): 1–11

FORNAS, JOHAN. 1995. *Cultural Theory and Late Modernity* (London: Sage)

FOX, INMAN. 1998. *La invención de España* (Madrid: Cátedra)

—— 1999. 'Spain as Castile: Nationalism and National Identity', in David T. Gies (ed.), *Modern Spanish Culture* (Cambridge: Cambridge University Press), pp. 21–36

FRA MOLINERO, BALTASAR. 1995. *La imagen de los negros en el teatro del Siglo de Oro* (Madrid: Siglo XXI)

FRENK, SUE, CHRIS PERRIAM and MIKE THOMSON. 1995. 'The Literary Avant-Garde: A Contradictory Modernity', in Helen Graham and Jo Labanyi (eds), *Spanish Cultural Studies, an Introduction* (Oxford: Oxford University Press), pp. 63–69

FRIEDMAN, MICHAL. 2011. 'Reconquering "Sepharad": Hispanism and Proto-Fascism in Giménez Caballero's Sephardist Crusade', *Journal of Spanish Cultural Studies*, 12(1): 35–60

FUCHS, ANNE. 2002. 'A Psychoanalytic Reading of *The Man who Disappeared*', in Julian Preece (ed.), *The Cambridge Companion to Kafka* (Cambridge: Cambridge University Press), pp. 25–42

FUENTES, VÍCTOR. 1984. 'La narrativa española de vanguardia (1923–1931)', in Víctor García de la Concha (ed.), *Historia y crítica de la literatura española, Volumen 7, Tomo 1 (Época Contemporánea: 1914 -1939)* (Madrid: Crítica), pp. 561–67

FUENTES, VÍCTOR, and MANUEL TUÑÓN DE LARA. 2006. *La marcha al pueblo en las letras españolas, 1917–1936* (Madrid: Ediciones de la Torre)

FUSI, JUAN PABLO. 1997. 'La sociedad española en los años veinte', in Rosario de la Torre and Helena Fernández Sandoica (eds), *Siglo XX. Historia Universal (8). Los felices años veinte. Entre la Gran Guerra y la crisis* (Madrid: Historia 16)

GALASSO, REGINNA. 2010. 'The Lifeline of *Chromos*: Translation and Felipe Alfau' *TranscUlturAl*, 1(3): 43–55.

GALINDO ARRANZ, FERMÍN. 2002. *Julio Camba, unha lección de xornalismo* (Santiago de Compostela: Ediciones Lea)

——2004. 'Julio Camba, y a los cuarenta años resucitó', in José Luis Valero (ed.), *El periodismo, motor de cultura y de paz*, VIII Congrés de la Societat Espanyola de Periodística, pp. 231–44

GAMBER, FRANCESCA. 2010. 'American Anti-Slavery Society (AASS)', in Leslie M. Alexander and Walter C. Rucke (eds), *Encyclopedia of African American History* (Santa Barbara: ABC-CLIO), pp. 304–06

GANIVET, ÁNGEL. 1996. *Idearium Español* (Madrid: Biblioteca Nueva)

GARCÍA BARRANCO, MARGARITA. 2010. 'Correlaciones y divergencias en la representación de dos minorías: negroafricanos y moriscos en la literatura del Siglo de Oro', in Aurelia Martín Casares and Margarita García Barranco (eds), *La esclavitud negroafricana en la historia de España. Siglos XVI y XVII* (Granada: Comares), pp. 151–71

GARCÍA JAMBRINA, LUIS. 2004. 'Nueva York, género literario', *ABC, Suplemento 'Blanco y Negro Cultural'* (27 March 2004), 16

——2006. 'El poeta y la ciudad', *ABC, Suplemento 'ABCD de las Artes y las Letras'* (18 February 2006), 20

GARCÍA LORCA, FEDERICO. 1978. 'Escribe a su familia desde Nueva York y La Habana [1929–1930]', *Poesía, Revista Ilustrada de Información Poética* 23/24, ed. by Christopher Maurer (Madrid: Ministerio de Cultura)

—— 1997. *Poeta en Nueva York* (Barcelona: Lumen)

—— 1998. *Poeta en Nueva York* (Madrid: Cátedra)

GARCÍA MARTÍN, JOSÉ LUIS (ed.). 2002. *Líneas Urbanas: Lectura de Nueva York* (Gijón: Libros del Pexe)

GARCÍA-MONTÓN, ISABEL. 2000. 'Agentes de una aproximación cultural: viajeros españoles en los Estados Unidos tras la Guerra Finisecular', in Constante González Groba et al. (eds), *Travelling Across Cultures/ Viaxes interculturais: The Twentieth-Century American Experience* (Santiago de Compostela: Universidade de Santiago de Compostela), pp. 237–47

——2002. *Viaje a al modernidad: la visión de los Estados Unidos en la España finisecular* (Madrid: Verbum)

GARCÍA PÉREZ, RAFAEL. 2008. 'Interpretaciones del tópico de la ciudad muerta en la poesía francesa y española', *Çedille. Revista de Estudios Franceses*, 4: 119–30

GARCÍA POSADA, MIGUEL. 1990. 'Pruebas de Nueva York', *ABC Literario* (20 January 1990), 47

GASCOYNE-CECIL, ROBERT ARTHUR TALBOT (3rd Marquess of Salisbury). 1898. 'Living and Dying Nations', *The New York Times* (18 May 1898), 6

GEIST, ANTHONY L., and JOSÉ B. MONLEÓN (eds). 1999. *Modernism and Its Margins: Reinscribing Cultural Modernity from Spain and Latin America* (New York: Garland)

GELLNER, ERNEST. 1983. *Nation and Nationalism* (Oxford: Blackwell)

GENDRON, BERNARD. 2002. *Between Montmartre and the Mudd Club: Popular Music and the Avant-Garde* (Chicago: University of Chicago Press)

GIES, DAVID T. (ed.). 1999. *The Cambridge Companion to Modern Spanish Culture* (Cambridge: Cambridge University Press)

GIL GASCÓN, FÁTIMA, and SALVADOR GÓMEZ GARCÍA. 2010. 'Al oído de las mujeres españolas. Las emisiones femeninas de Radio Nacional de España durante el primer franquismo (1937–1959)', *Estudios sobre el Mensaje Periodístico*, 16: 131–43

GIRÓN, SOCORRO. 1984. *Julio Camba, escritor novecentista* (Pontevedra: Ayuntamiento de Vilanova de Arosa)

GIRÓN Y ARCAS, JOAQUÍN. 1906. *La cuestión judaica en la España actual y en la universidad de Salamanca* (Salamanca: Andrés Iglesias)

GOBINEAU, ARTHUR DE. 1915. *An Essay on the Inequality of Human Races* (New York: Putnam)

GOLDWATER, ROBERT. 1986. *Primitivism in Modern Art* (Cambridge, MA: Harvard University Press)

GÓMEZ, MARÍA A., SANTIAGO JUAN-NAVARRO and PHYLLIS ZATLIN (eds). 2008. *Juana of Castile: History and Myth of the Mad Queen* (Danvers: Rosemont)
GÓMEZ DE LA SERNA, RAMÓN. 1931. *Ismos* (Madrid: Biblioteca Nueva)
GÓMEZ-SANTOS, MARIANO. 2003. 'La soledad de Julio Camba', in Ofelia Requejo (ed.), *Xornadas sobre Julio Camba* (Santiago de Compostela: Xunta de Galicia), pp. 47–54
GONZÁLEZ, ENRIC. 2006. *Historias de Nueva York* (Barcelona: RBA)
GONZÁLEZ LÓPEZ-BRIONES, CARMEN. 2000. 'Some 20th Century Spanish Views on the U.S', in González Groba et al. (eds), *Travelling Across Cultures / Viaxes interculturais: The Twentieth-Century American Experience* (Santiago de Compostela: Universidade de Santiago de Compostela), pp. 269–81
GONZÁLEZ RUIZ, NICOLÁS. 1943. *La literatura española* (Madrid: Ediciones Pegaso)
GONZÁLEZ SALINERO, RAÚL. 2000. *El anti judaísmo cristiano occidental (siglos IV y V)* (Madrid: Editorial Trotta)
GORKY, MAXIM. 2001. *In America* (Honolulu: University Press of the Pacific)
GRACIA GARCÍA, JORDI and DOMINGO RÓDENAS DE MOYA. 2008. *El ensayo español del siglo XX* (Madrid: Crítica)
GRAHAM, HELEN, and JO LABANYI (eds). 1995a. *Spanish Cultural Studies: An Introduction: The Struggle for Modernity* (Oxford: Oxford University Press)
—— 1995B. 'Editors' Preface', in Helen Graham and Jo Labanyi (eds), *Spanish Cultural Studies: An Introduction: The Struggle for Modernity* (Oxford: Oxford University Press), pp. v–viii.
—— 1995C. 'Culture and Modernity: The Case of Spain', in Helen Graham and Jo Labanyi (eds), *Spanish Cultural Studies: An Introduction: The Struggle for Modernity* (Oxford: Oxford University Press), pp. 1–19
GRANT MEYER, STEPHEN. 2001. *As Long as They Don't Move Next Door: Segregation and Radical Conflict in American Neighborhoods* (Boston: Rowman & Littlefield)
GUERRERO, SALVADOR. 1999. 'Arquitectura y arquitectos en la Residencia de Estudiantes', *Boletín Residencia*, 8: 14–16
GUIBERNAU, MONTSE. 2007. *The Identity of Nations* (Cambridge: Polity Press)
GULLÓN, GERMÁN. 1992. *La novela moderna en España (1885–1902): los albores de la modernidad* (Madrid: Taurus)
HALL, STUART. 1992. 'The West and the Rest: Discourse and Power', in Stuart Hall and Bram Gieben (eds), *Formations of Modernity* (Oxford: Polity Press), pp. 275–320
HARRIS, DEREK (ed.). 1995. *The Spanish Avant-Garde* (Manchester: Manchester University Press)
HARRISON, JOSEPH. 1979. 'The Regenerationist Movement in Spain after the Disaster of 1898', *European History Quarterly*, 9(1): 1–27
HASTINGS, ADRIAN. 1997. *The Construction of Nationhood: Ethnicity, Religion, and Nationalism* (Cambridge: Cambridge University Press)
HAWKINS, MIKE. 1997. *Social Darwinism in European and American Thought, 1860–1950* (Cambridge: Cambridge University Press)
HEMMING, JOHN. 1993. *The Conquest of the Incas* (London: Macmillan)
HERAS, ANTONIO. 1953. *De Nueva York a California* (Madrid: Espasa-Calpe)
HERNÁNDEZ LES, JUAN A. 2006. 'Julio Camba, individuo y creatividad', *Estudios sobre el Mensaje Periodístico*, 17: 317–29.
HERNÁNDEZ RUIGÓMEZ, ALMUDENA. 1988. 'La abolición de la esclavitud en Puerto Rico: Introducción al estudio de las mentalidades anti-esclavistas', *Quinto centenario*, 14: 27–42
HERNÁNDEZ SÁNCHEZ-BARBA, MARIO. 1985. 'Las cortes españolas ante la abolición de la esclavitud en las Antillas (Opinión institucional ante un tema de política social)', *Quinto Centenario*, 8: 15–36
HIDALGO, DIEGO. 1949. *Nueva York: impresiones de un español del siglo XIX que no sabe inglés*, 2nd edn (Madrid: Aguilar)

HOBSBAWM, ERIC J. 1990. *Nations and Nationalism Since 1780* (Cambridge: Cambridge University Press)
HUERGO CARDOSO, HUMBERTO. 1996. 'Lo sublime y la vanguardia. Forma y finalidad en Jacinta la Pelirroja', *Nueva Revista de Filología Hispánica*, 4(2): 489–549
——2001. 'Moreno Villa por Moreno Villa. Cronología y Etopeya', *Temas de arte. Selección de escritos periodísticos sobre pintura, escultura arquitectura y música (1916–1954)*, ed. by Humberto Huergo Cardoso (Valencia: Pre-Textos), pp. 59–122
——2001A. 'Los artículos de arte de Moreno Villa. A vista de pájaro'. *Temas de arte. Selección de escritos periodísticos sobre pintura, escultura arquitectura y música (1916–1954)*, ed. by Humberto Huergo Cardoso (Valencia: Pre-Textos), pp. 19–56
——2010. 'La ironía y la adhesión', in José Moreno Villa, *Función contra forma y otros escritos sobre arquitectura madrileña, 1927–1935* (Valencia: Iseebooks), pp. 19–77
HUYSSEN, ANDREAS. 1988. *After the Great Divide: Modernism, Mass Culture and Postmodernism*, 2nd edn (London: Macmillan)
IÑIGUEZ BARRENA, MARÍA LOURDES. 2005. *El Cuento Semanal, 1907–1912: estudio y análisis de una colección de novelas cortas* (Barcelona: Grupo Editiorial Universitario)
IZQUIERDO, LUIS. 1978. 'El vanguardismo innato de Moreno Villa', *Ínsula*, 382: 3
——1989. 'En el umbral de la poesía nueva', in Cristóbas Cuevas García (ed.), *José Moreno Villa en el contexto del 27* (Barcelona: Anthropos), pp. 68–91
JERVIS, JOHN. 1999. *Transgressing the Modern: Explorations in the Western Experience of Otherness* (Malden, MA: Blackwell)
JIMÉNEZ, JUAN RAMÓN. 1994. *Diario de un poeta reciencasado* (Madrid: Visor)
JIMÉNEZ FAJARDO, SALVADOR. 1996. 'José Moreno Villa, the "Residencia" and *Jacinta la pelirroja*', *Anales de la Literatura Española Contemporánea*, 19(1–2): 67–83
JIMÉNEZ URDIALES, EDUARDO. 1998. *La narrativa de José Moreno Villa: Evoluciones y Patrañas* (Málaga: Centro Cultural de la Generación del 27)
JOHNSON, ROBERTA. 2003A. *Gender and the Nation in the Spanish Modernist Novel* (Nashville: Vanderbilt University Press)
——2003B. 'From the Generation of 1898 to the Vanguard', in Harriet Turner and Adelaida López de Martínez (eds), *The Cambridge Companion to the Spanish Novel: From 1600 to the Present* (Cambridge: Cambridge University Press), pp. 155–71
JOHNSTON JUSTIN, MARCUS. 2010. 'Miscegenation', in Leslie M. Alexander and Walter C. Rucker (eds), *Encyclopaedia of African American History* (Santa Barbara: ABC-CLIO), pp. 229–31
JORDAN, WINTHROP. 1994. 'First Impressions: Libidinous Blacks', in Ronald Takaki (ed.), *From Different Shores: Perspectives on Race and Ethnicity in America* (Oxford: Oxford University Press), pp. 41–51
JOUINI, KHEMAIS. 2007. 'Circunstancias y quehacer poético en Jacinta la pelirroja, de José Moreno Villa', *Espéculo: Revista de Estudios Literarios*, 35, <http://www.ucm.es/info/especulo/numero35/jmvilla.html> [accessed 18 March 2011]
JULIÁ, SANTOS. 2004. *Historia de las dos Españas* (Madrid: Taurus)
KAFKA, FRANZ. 2012. *The Man who Disappeared (America)*, trans. and intro. by R. Robertson (Oxford: Oxford University Press)
KAPLAN, E. ANN. 1992. *Motherhood and Representation: The Mother in Popular Culture and Melodrama* (London: Routledge)
KEDOURIE, ELIE. 1993. *Nationalism*, 4th edn (Oxford: Blackwell)
KEENE, JUDITH. 1999. '"Into the Clear Air of the Plaza": Spanish Women Achieve the Vote in 1931', in Victoria Enders and Pamela Radcliff (eds), *Constructing Spanish Womanhood: Female Identity in Modern Spain* (Albany: State University of New York Press), pp. 325–47
KICZA, JOHN E. 1992. 'Patterns in Early Spanish Overseas Expansion', *The William and Mary Quarterly*, 49(2): 229–53

KIRKPATRICK, SUSAN. 1995. 'Gender and Difference in Fin de Siglo Literary Discourse', in José Colmeiro et al. (ed.), *Spain Today: Essays on Literature, Culture and Society* (Hanover, NH: Dartmouth College), pp. 95–101
——2003. *Mujer, modernismo y vanguardia en España (1898–1931)* (Madrid: Catedra)
LABANYI, JO. 2000. *Gender and Modernization in the Spanish Realist Novel* (Oxford: Oxford University Press)
——(ed.). 2002. *Constructing Identity in Contemporary Spain: Theoretical Debates and Cultural Practice* (Oxford: Oxford University Press)
——2005. 'Relocating Difference: Cultural History and Modernity in Late Nineteenth-Century Spain', in Brad Epps and Luis Fernández Cifuentes (eds) *Spain Beyond Spain. Modernity, Literary History and National Identity* (Lewisburg: Bucknell University Press), pp. 168–86
LAGO, EDUARDO. 2001. 'El español y sus autores en EEUU', *El País* (10 November 2001), <http://www.elpais.com/articulo/semana/espanol/autores/EE/UU/elpbabese/ 20011110elpbabese_17/Tes> [accessed 16 September 2011]
——2006. *Llámame Brooklyn* (Barcelona: Destino)
LAHEY, LAURIE. 2010. 'The Great Migration', in Leslie M. Alexander and Walter C. Rucker (eds), *Encyclopedia of African American History* (Santa Barbara: ABC-CLIO), pp. 787–90
LAÍN ENTRALGO, PEDRO. 1993. *La generación del noventa y ocho* (Madrid: Espasa Calpe)
LARRÍNAGA RODRÍGUEZ, CARLOS. 2002. 'El paisaje nacional y los literatos del 98. El caso de Azorín', *Lurralde: Investigación y espacio*, 25: 183–96
LARSON, SUSAN, and EVA WOODS (eds). 2005. *Visualizing Spanish Modernity* (Oxford: Berg)
LEIRO, BENITO. 1986. *El hombre que no quería ser nada* (Aranguren: El Paisaje)
LEMIRE, ELISE. 2002. *Miscegenation: Making Race in America* (Philadelphia: University of Pennsylvania Press)
LEMKE, SIEGLINDE. 1998. *Primitivist Modernism: Black Culture and the Origins of Transatlantic Modernism* (Oxford: Oxford University Press)
LEÓN GROSS, TEODORO, and BERNARDO GÓMEZ CALDERON (eds). 2009. *Diez articulistas para la historia de la literatura española* (Madrid: Ediciones APM, Fundación Manuel Alcántara, Asociación de la Prensa de Cádiz and Fragua Libros)
LINDSAY, BEN B., and WAINWRIGHT EVANS. 1925. *The Revolt of Modern Youth* (New York: Boni & Liveright)
——1927. *The Companionate Marriage* (New York: Garden City)
LLAVADOR, JOSÉ MARÍA TOMÁS. 2010. 'Prólogo', in José Moreno Villa, *Función contra forma y otros escritos sobre arquitectura madrileña, 1927–1935* (Valencia: Iseebooks), pp. 9–16
LLERA RUIZ, JOSÉ ANTONIO. 2002. 'Perspectivismo y contraste en las crónicas humorísticas de Julio Camba', *Revista Hispánica Moderna*, 55(2): 320–41
——2003. 'La literatura de Julio Camba ante los géneros periodísticos', *Bulletin Hispanique*, 1: 159–74
——2004. *El humor en la obra de Julio Camba. Lengua, estilo e intertextualidad* (Madrid: Biblioteca Nueva)
LODGE, DAVID. 1990. *After Bakhtin: Essays on Fiction and Criticism* (London: Routledge)
LOOMBA, ANIA. 1998. *Colonialism/Postcolonialism* (London: Routledge)
LÓPEZ, SIRO. 2003. 'Julio Camba. Humorista galego', in Ofelia Requejo (ed.), *Xornadas sobre Julio Camba* (Santiago de Compostela: Xunta de Galicia), pp. 9–17
LÓPEZ FRÍAS, MARÍA ANTONIA. 1989. 'Aspectos biográficos de José Moreno Villa antes del exilio', in Cristóbal Cuevas García (ed.), *José Moreno Villa en el contexto del 27* (Barcelona: Anthropos), pp. 282–29
——1990. *José Moreno Villa: Vida y poesía antes del exilio (1887–1937)* (Málaga: Diputación Provincial de Málaga)
LÓPEZ GARCÍA, PEDRO. 2003. *Julio Camba: El solitario del Palace* (Madrid: Espasa Calpe)

López-Luaces, Marta. 2008. 'Nueva York como motivo de ruptura en la poesía española: Juan Ramón Jiménez, Federico García Lorca y José Hierro', in Alfonso Gamo (ed.), *Nombres Propios* (Madrid: Fundación Carolina), pp. 127–32

López Silva, Inma. 2007. *New York, New York* (Vigo: Galaxia)

Loriga, Ray. 2004. *El hombre que inventó Manhattan* (Barcelona: El Aleph)

Lozano, Miguel. 2000. *Imágenes del pesimismo. Literatura y arte en España, 1898–1930* (Alicante: Universidad de Alicante)

Luengo López, Jordi. 2008. 'Entre la "Maja Goyesca" y la frívola demi-vierge. Idealidades comparativas en el "Serenismo Literario" del umbral del siglo XX', *Çedille. Revista de estudios franceses*, 4: 203–36

Luna Sellés, Carmen. 2002. *La exploración de lo irracional en los poetas modernistas hispanoamericanos. Literatura onírica y poetización de la realidad* (Santiago de Compostela: Universidade de Santiago de Compostela)

Maeztu, Ramiro de. 2007. *Hacia otra España*, ed. by Javier Varela (Madrid: Biblioteca Nueva)

Magnien, Brigitte. 1986. *Ideología y texto en el Cuento Semanal 1907–1912* (Madrid: Ediciones de la Torre)

Mainer Baqué, José Carlos, and Luis Granjel. 1984. 'La novela corta y Wenceslao Fernández Flórez', in Víctor García de la Concha (ed.), *Historia y crítica de la literatura española, Volumen 7, Tomo 1 (Época contemporánea: 1914–1939)* (Madrid: Crítica), pp. 143–55

Manzanas, Ana. 1996. 'Conversion Narratives: Othello and Other Black Characters in Shakespeare's and Lope de Vega's Plays', *Calvo Sederi*, 7: 231–36

Marañón, Gregorio. 1961. *Nueva York, ida y vuelta: los Estados Unidos vistos por un español* (Madrid: Magerit)

Martín Casares, Aurelia, and Margarita García Barranco. 2008. 'Popular Literary Depictions of Black African Weddings in Early Modern Spain', *Renaissance and Reformation*, 31(2): 107–21

Martín Gaite, Carmen. 1990. *Caperucita en Manhattan* (Madrid: Siruela)

—— 2005. *Visión de Nueva York* (Madrid: Siruela)

Mártinez Arnaldos, Manuel. 2007. '"El Cuento Semanal": presentación, proyecto y proyección', *Monteagudo: Revista de literatura española, hispanoamericana y teoría de la literatura*, 12: 11–26

Martínez Góngora, Mar. 2005. 'La invencion de la "blancura": el estereotipo y la mímica en "Boda de negros" de Francisco de Quevedo', *Modern Language Notes (Hispanic Issue)*, 120(2): 262–86

Martínez Martín, Jesús A. 2001. 'La edición moderna', in Jesús A. Martínez Martín (ed.), *Historia de la edición en España, 1836–1936* (Madrid: Marcial Pons), pp. 167–207

Más, José. 2010. *En el país de los Bubis* (Corunna: Ediciones del Viento)

McCulloch, John A. 2007. *The Dilemma of Modernity: Ramón Gómez de la Serna and the Spanish Modernist Novel* (New York: Lang)

Meixide, Carlos G. 2007. *O home inédito* (Pontevedra: Rinoceronte)

Memmi, Albert. 2003. *The Colonizer and the Colonized* (London: Earthscan)

Mendoza, Eduardo. 1986. *Nueva York* (Barcelona: Destino)

Menéndez Bueyes, Luis Ramón. 2001. *Reflexiones críticas sobre el origen del Reino de Asturias* (Salamanca: Ediciones Universidad de Salamanca)

Mermall, Thomas. 1999. 'Culture and the Essay in Modern Spain', in David T. Gies (ed.), *Modern Spanish Culture* (Cambridge: Cambridge University Press), 163–72

Mill, John Stuart. 1970. 'The Subjection of Women', in *Essays on Sex Equality*, ed. by Alice S. Rossi (Chicago: University of Chicago Press), pp. 123–242

Millard Rosenberg, S.L. (1932). 'Antícípolis por Luis de Oteyza', *Hispania*, 15(3): 307–08

Miller, Susan (ed.). 1991. *The Myth of Primitivism* (New York: Routledge)

MIQUELARENA, JACINTO. 1930. ...*Pero ellos no tienen bananas: el viaje a Nueva York* (Madrid: Espasa Calpe)
MONSALVO ANTÓN, JOSÉ MARÍA. 1985. *Teoría y evolución de un conflicto social. El antisemitismo en la Corona de Castilla en la Baja Edad Media* (Madrid: Siglo Veintiuno Editores)
MONTFORT ÉCIJA, VANESSA. 2010. *Mitología de Nueva York* (Seville: Algaida)
MORA, RÓMULO DE. 1922. *Los cauces. Novela de vida norteamericana* (Madrid: Imprenta Clásica Española)
MORA VALCÁRCEL, CARMEN DE. 1978. 'Sobre la poesía de José Moreno Villa', in *Andalucía en la generación del 27* (Seville: Universidad de Sevilla), pp. 149–87
MORADIELLOS, ENRIQUE. 2000. 'Spain in the World: from Great Empire to Minor European Power', in José Álvarez Junco and Adrian Shubert (eds), *Spanish History Since 1808* (London: Arnold, 110–20)
—— 2009. *La semilla de la barbarie: antisemitismo y holocausto* (Barcelona: Península)
MORALES GUINALDO, LUCÍA. 2008. *El indio y el indiano según la visión de un conquistador español de finales del siglo XVI: Bernardo de Vargas Machuca (1555–1622)* (Bogotá: Universidad de Los Andes)
MORAND, PAUL. 1931. *New York* (London: Heinemann)
MORENO VILLA, JOSÉ. 1930. *Locos, enanos, negros y niños palaciegos: gente de placer que tuvieron los Austrias en la Corte española desde 1563 a 1700* (México: Editorial Presencia)
—— 1989. *Pruebas de Nueva York* (Valencia: Pre-Textos)
—— 2000. *Jacinta la pelirroja*, Madrid: Castalia.
—— 2001. *Temas de arte. Selección de escritos periodísticos sobre pintura, escultura arquitectura y música (1916–1954)*, ed. by Humberto Huergo Cardoso (Valencia: Pre-Textos)
—— 2001A. 'Artistas y mercaderes', in *Temas de arte. Selección de escritos periodísticos sobre pintura, escultura arquitectura y música (1916–1954)*, ed. by Humberto Huergo Cardoso (Valencia: Pre-Textos), pp. 315–17
—— 2001B. 'Fisonomía del caserío malagueño', in *Temas de arte. Selección de escritos periodísticos sobre pintura, escultura arquitectura y música (1916–1954)*, ed. by Humberto Huergo Cardoso (Valencia: Pre-Textos), pp. 307–13
—— 2001C. 'Temas de arte. El arte negro, factor moderno', in *Temas de arte. Selección de escritos periodísticos sobre pintura, escultura arquitectura y música (1916–1954)*, ed. by Humberto Huergo Cardoso (Valencia: Pre-Textos), pp. 273–79
—— 2006. *Vida en claro. Autobiografía* (Madrid: Visor Libros)
—— 2010. *Función contra forma y otros escritos sobre arquitectura madrileña, 1927–1935* (Valencia: Iseebooks)
—— 2010A. 'Casa "honesta" en Madrid', in José Moreno Villa, *Función contra forma y otros escritos sobre arquitectura madrileña, 1927–1935* (Valencia: Iseebooks), pp. 127–31
—— 2010B. 'Casa y casada', in José Moreno Villa, *Función contra forma y otros escritos sobre arquitectura madrileña, 1927–1935* (Valencia: Iseebooks), pp. 119–21
—— 2010C. *Medio mundo y otro medio. Memorias escogidas*, ed. by Humberto Huergo Cardoso (Valencia: Pre-Textos)
—— 2010D. 'Magisterio de los criados', in *Medio mundo y otro medio. Memorias escogidas*, ed. by Humberto Huergo Cardoso (Valencia: Pre-Textos), pp. 97–101
—— 2010E. 'Mi españolismo y mi mexicanismo', in *Medio mundo y otro medio. Memorias escogidas*, ed. by Humberto Huergo Cardoso (Valencia: Pre-Textos), 233–35
—— 2010F. 'La enseñanza de los pobres', in *Medio mundo y otro medio. Memorias escogidas*, ed. by Humberto Huergo Cardoso (Valencia: Pre-Textos), pp. 167–69
—— 2010G. 'Los años tienen su música', in *Medio mundo y otro medio. Memorias escogidas*, ed. by Humberto Huergo Cardoso (Valencia: Pre-Textos), pp. 329–31
—— 2010H. 'Primeras nociones del mundo', in *Medio mundo y otro medio. Memorias escogidas*, ed. by Humberto Huergo Cardoso (Valencia: Pre-Textos), 187–89

——2011. *Memoria*, ed. by Juan Pérez de Ayala (El colegio de México/Residencia de Estudiantes)
——2011A. 'Vida en claro. Autobiografía', in *Memoria*, ed. by Juan Pérez de Ayala (El colegio de México/Residencia de Estudiantes), pp. 31–241
MULLIN, KATHERINE. 2006. 'Modernism and Feminisms', in Ellen Rooney (ed.), *The Cambridge Companion to Feminist Literary Theory* (Cambridge: Cambridge University Press), pp. 136–52
MUÑOZ MOLINA, ANTONIO. 2004. *Ventanas de Manhattan* (Barcelona: Seix Barral)
MUÑOZ OLIVARES, CARMEN. 2000. 'Concepción Gimeno de Flaquer y Sofía Casanova: novelistas olvidadas de principios de siglo', in Marina Villalba Álvarez (ed.), *Mujeres novelistas en el panorama literario del siglo XX: I Congreso de narrativa española (en lengua castellana)* (Cuenca: Ediciones de la Universidad de Castilla-La Mancha)
MUSI, AURELIO. 2007. 'The Kingdom of Naples in the Spanish Imperial System', in Thomas James Dandelet and John A. Marino (eds), *Spain in Italy: Politics, Society and Religion 1500–1700* (Leiden: Brill), pp. 73–98
NASH, MARY. 1999. 'Un/Contested Identities: Motherhood, Sex Reform and the Modernization of Gender Identity in Early Twentieth-Century Spain', in Victoria Lorée Enders and Pamela Beth Radcliff (eds), *Constructing Spanish Womanhood. Female Identity in Modern Spain* (Albany: State University of New York Press), pp. 25–49
NAVARRO DOMÍNGUEZ, ELOY. 2004. 'Introducción', in Eduardo Criado Requena, *La ciudad de los rascacielos* (Seville: Alfar), pp. 9–53
NEIRA, JULIO. 2012. *Historia poética de Nueva York en la España contemporánea* (Madrid: Cátedra)
NEVILLE, EDGAR. 1998. *Don Clorato de Potasa* (Madrid: Espasa Calpe)
NEVINS, ALLAN. 1968. *America through British Eyes* (Gloucester, MA: P. Smith)
NODDINGS, NEL. 1991. *Women and Evil* (Berkeley: University of California Press)
NORA, EUGENIO DE. 1958. *La novela española contemporánea* (Madrid: Gredos)
NORTON, MICHAEL I., and SAMUEL R. SOMMERS. 2011. 'Whites See Racism as a Zero-Sum Game That They Are Now Losing', *Perspectives on Psychological Science*, 6: 215–18
OLEZA, JUAN. 1995. 'Introducción', in Leopoldo Alas 'Clarín', *La Regenta*, Volume 1 (Madrid: Cátedra), pp. 11–102
ORTEGA, JOSÉ. 1981. 'Juan Ramón Jiménez y Federico García Lorca: dos poetas andaluces en Estados Unidos', *Cuadernos Hispano-Americanos*, 376–78: 875–85
——1995. 'Periodismo, literatura y compromiso', *La Palabra y el Hombre*, 96: 111–37
ORTEGA Y GASSET, JOSÉ. 1987. *La deshumanización del arte y otros ensayos de estética* (Madrid: Espasa Calpe)
——1995. 'La poesía de Ana de Noualles', in *Obras Completas*, Volume 4 (Madrid: Revista de Occidente), pp. 432–33
——2007A. *La España invertebrada: bosquejo de algunos pensamientos históricos* (Madrid: Espasa Calpe)
——2007B. *La rebelión de las masas*, 43rd edn (Madrid: Espasa Calpe)
OTEYZA, LUIS DE. 1993. *El Diablo Blanco*, ed. by José A. Pérez Bowie (Badajoz: Diputación de Badajoz)
——2000. *Abd-El-Krim y los prisioneros*, ed. by María Rosa de Madariaga (Melilla: Consejería de Cultura)
——2000. *Obras selectas* (Caracas: Universidad Católica Andrés Bello)
——2006. *El Diablo Blanco* (Caracas: Universidad Católica Andrés Bello)
——2006. *Anticípolis*, ed. by Beatriz Barrantes Martín (Madrid: Cátedra)
PALENQUE, MARTA. 2006. 'Ni ofelias ni amazonas, sino seres completos: aproximación a Teresa de Escoriaza', *Arbor: Ciencia, pensamiento y cultura (Ejemplar dedicado a escritoras españolas del siglo XX)*, 719: 363–76

Pao, Marta T., and Rafael Hernández-Rodríguez (eds). 2002. *Agítese Bien: A New Look at the Hispanic Avant-Gardes* (Newark: Juan de la Cuesta)

Papachristophorou, Madrilena. 2008. 'Sleeping Beauty', in Donald Hasse (ed.), *The Greenwood Encyclopedia of Folk Tales and Fairy Tales*, Volume 3 (Westport: Greenwood Publishing), pp. 881–83

Paradelo, Luís. 2006. *Xelamonite* (Vigo: Galaxia)

Pardo Bazán, Emilia. 1999. *La mujer española y otros escritos* (Madrid: Cátedra)

Pateman, Carol. 1988. *The Sexual Contract* (Stanford: Stanford University Press)

Patmore, Coventry. 1905. *The Angel in the House; together with the Victories of Love* (London: Routledge)

Peckler, Ana María. 2003. *Historia del Arte Universal de los Siglos XIX y XX* (Madrid: Editorial Complutense)

Pérez Firmat, Gustavo. 1993. *Idle Fictions: The Hispanic Vanguard Novel, 1926–1934* (Durham, NC: Duke University Press)

Pérez-Villanueva Tovar, Isabel. 1990. *La Residencia de Estudiantes: grupo universitario y de señoritas, Madrid, 1910–1936* (Madrid: Ministerio de Educación y Ciencia)

Peters Hasty, Olga, and Susanne Fusso. 1988. *America through Russian Eyes, 1874–1926* (New Haven: Yale University Press)

Peterson, V. Spike. 2000. 'Sexing Political Identities/Nationalism as Heterosexism', in Sita Ranchod-Nilsson and Mary Ann Tétreaut (eds), *Women, States and Nationalism* (London: Routledge), pp. 54–80

Pick, Daniel. 1989. *Faces of Degeneration: A European Disorder* (Cambridge: Cambridge University Press)

Pino, José María del. 1995. *Montajes y fragmentos: una aproximación a la narrativa española de vanguardia* (Amsterdam: Rodopi)

Pla, Josep. 1995. *Week-end d'estiu a Nova York* (Barcelona: Destino)

Porter, Eric. 2002. *What Is This Thing Called Jazz: African American Musicians as Artists, Critics, and Activists* (Los Angeles: University of California Press)

Pulido, Ángel. 1905. *Españoles sin patria y la raza sefardí* (Madrid: Establecimiento tipográfico de E. Teodoro)

Punter, David. 2007. *Modernity* (New York: Palgrave Macmillan)

Rasula, Jed. 2004. 'Jazz as Decal for the European Avant-Garde', in Heike Raphael-Hernandez (ed.), *Blackening Europe: The African American Presence* (New York: Routledge), pp. 13–33

Rattansi, Ali. 1994. '"Western" Racisms, Ethnicities and Identities in a "Postmodern" Frame', in Ali Rattansi and Sallie Westwood (eds), *Racism, Modernity, Identity on the Western Front* (Cambridge: Polity Press), pp. 15–86

Read, Hollis. 1864. *The Negro Problem Solved, or, Africa as She Was, as She Is, and as She Shall Be: Her Curse and Her Cure*, Volume 2 (New York: A. A. Constantine)

Rebollo Sánchez, Félix. 1998. *Periodismo y movimientos literarios contemporáneos españoles (1900–1939)* (Madrid: Huerga y Fierro)

Rehrmann, Norbert. 1998. 'Los sefardíes como "anexo" de la hispanidad: Ernesto Giménez Caballero y "La Gaceta Literaria"', in Mechthild, Albert (ed.), *Vencer no es convencer: literatura e ideología del fascismo español* (Frankfurt: Vervuert; Madrid: Iberoamericana)

Reisigl, Martin, and Ruth Wodak. 2001. *Discourse and Discrimination: Rhetorics of Racism and Antiseminism* (London: Routledge)

Requejo, Ofelia (ed.). 2003. *Xornadas sobre Julio Camba* (Santiago de Compostela: Xunta de Galicia)

Revilla Guijarro, Almudena. 2002. *Periodismo y literatura en la obra de Julio Camba* (Pontevedra: Servicio de Publicaciones, Diputación Provincial de Pontevedra)

Rhodes, Colin. 1994. *Primitivism and Modern Art* (New York: Thames and Hudson)

Ricci, Christian H. 2010. 'Breve recorrido por la bohemia hispana: mal vino, champaña y ajenjo', *Journal of Hispanic Modernism*, 1: 151–68

Rodríguez Fischer, Ana. 1999. *Prosa Española de Vanguardia* (Madrid: Castalia)

——2004. 'Julio Camba, coleccionistas de países', *Cuadernos Hispanoamericanos*, 651–52: 183–94

Rohr, Isabelle. 2007. *The Spanish Right and the Jews, 1898–1945: Antisemitism and Opportunism* (Eastbourne: Sussex Academic Press)

——2011. '"Spaniards of the Jewish Type": Philosephardism in the Service of Imperialism in Early Twentieth-Century Spanish Morocco', *Journal of Spanish Cultural Studies*, 12(1): 61–75.

Romero Chamorro, María José. 1988. 'Sobre la autobiografía *Vida en claro*', *Poesía del 27*, 2: 36–38

Romero Jodar, Andrés. 2009. 'Simbolismo temporal en *Garba* de José Moreno Villa', *Revista de Literatura*, 71(142): 627–36

Romojaro, Rosa. 1991. 'La segunda poética de José Moreno Villa (*Jacinta la pelirroja*, *Carambas*, *Puentes que no acaban*, *Salón sin muros*)', *Analecta Malacitana* 14(1): 129–40

Rother, Bernd. 1999. 'Españoles filosefardíes and primeros falangistas', in Judit Targarona Borrás and Ángel Sáenz-Badillos (eds), *Jewish Studies at the Turn of the Twentieth Century: Judaism from the Renaissance to Modern Times* (Leiden: Brill), pp. 616–22

Said, Edward. 1995. *Orientalism* (London: Penguin)

Sainz de Robles, Federico Carlos. 1952. *La novela corta en España. Promoción de "El Cuento Semanal" (1901–1920)* (Madrid: Aguilar)

——1971. *Raros y olvidados (La promoción de El Cuento Semanal)* (Madrid: Prensa Española)

——1975. *La promoción de "El Cuento Semanal" 1907–1925 (un interesante e imprescindible capítulo de la historia de la novela española)* (Madrid: Espasa Calpe)

Salas Moreno, Ada. 1992. 'Prosaísmos en la poesía de José Moreno Villa', in Manuel Ariza Viguera (ed.), *Actas del II Congreso Internacional de Historia de la Lengua Española 2*, pp. 853–66

Salazar y Acha, Jaime de. 1991. 'La limpieza de sangre', *Revista de la Inquisición: (intolerancia y derechos humanos)*, 1: 289–308

Salvador, Álvaro. 1978. 'José Moreno Villa, un hombre del 27. Jacinta, la pelirroja o la erótica moderna', *Cuadernos Hispanoamericanos*, 335: 352–58

Sambricio Rivera-Echegaray, Carlos. 2000. 'La normalización de la arquitectura vernacular (Un debate en la España de los veinte)', *Revista de Occidente*, 235: 21–44

Sánchez Álvarez-Insúa, Alberto. 1996. *Bibliografía e historia de las colecciones literarias en España (1907–1957)* (Madrid: Libris)

——2007. 'La colección literaria *Los Contemporáneos*. Una primera aproximación', *Monteagudo* (3ª época), 12: 91–120

Sánchez Espeso, Germán. 2005. *New York Shitty* (Barcelona: Debolsillo)

Sánchez Suárez, María Ángeles. 2004. *Mujeres en Melilla* (Granada: SATE-STES/Grupo Editorial Universitario)

Santonja, Gonzalo. 1989. *La República de los libros: el nuevo libro popular de la II República* (Barcelona: Anthropos)

Santos Morillo, Antonio. 2011. 'Caracterización del negro en la literatura española del XVI', *Lemir*, 15: 23–46

Saz, Agustín del. 1947. *Nueva York* (Barcelona: Seix)

Segura, Pedro. 1935. *Nueva York 1935: impresiones de un viaje a los Estados Unidos* (Barcelona: Nuñez)

Seregni, Alessandro. 2007. *El antiamericanismo español* (Madrid: Síntesis)

Serrano Acosta, Pura, and José A. Fortes. 1989. 'Las escrituras del exilio (Moreno Villa y Vida en claro)', in Cristóbal Cuevas García (ed.), *José Moreno Villa en el contexto del 27* (Barcelona: Anthropos), pp. 243–54

SERVERA BAÑO, JOSÉ. 1978. 'Clasicismo y modernidad en la figura de Jacinta la Pelirroja de Moreno Villa', *Mayurqa: revista del Departament de Ciències Històriques i Teoria de les Arts*, 17: 261–64

SHOWALTER, ELAINE. 1996. *Sexual Anarchy: Gender and Culture at the Fin de Siècle* (London: Virago)

SIEBURTH, STEPHANIE. 1990. *Reading 'La Regenta': Duplicitous Discourse and the Entropy of Structure* (Amsterdam: Benjamins)

—— 1994. *Inventing High and Low: Literature, Mass Culture, and Uneven Modernity in Spain* (Durham, NC: Duke University Press)

SIMMEL, GEORGE. 2002. 'Metropolis and Mental Life', in Gary Bridge and Sophie Watson (eds), *The Blackwell City Reader* (Oxford: Wiley-Blackwell), pp. 11–19

SIMMONS, CHRISTINA. 2009. *Making Marriage Modern: Women's Sexuality from the Progressive Era to World War II* (Oxford: Oxford University Press)

SIMMS, ELLEN YVONNE. 2008. 'Miscegenation and Racism: Afro-Mexicans in Colonial New Spain', *The Journal of Pan African Studies*, 3(2): 228–54

SINGLETON, THERESA A. 2001. 'Slavery and Spatial Dialectics on Cuban Coffee Plantations', *World Archaeology*, 33(1): 98–114

SMERDOU ALTOLAGUIRRE, MARGARITA. 1988. 'José Moreno Villa y su voz en vuelo a su cuna', *Anuario de la Sociedad Española de Literatura General y Comparada*, 6–7: 65–69

SMITH, ANTHONY D. 1998. *Nationalism and Modernism* (London: Routledge)

SOUFAS, CHRISTOPHER. 2007. *The Subject in Question: Early Contemporary Spanish Literature and Modernism* (Washington, DC: Catholic University of America Press)

—— 2010. 'Modernism and Spain: Spanish Criticism at the Crossroads', *Anales de la literatura española contemporánea*, 35: 7–16

SPENGLER, OSWALD. 1926. *The Decline of the West*, Volume 1 (London: Allen & Unwin)

—— 1928. *The Decline of the West*, Volume 2 (London: Allen & Unwin)

SPIRES, ROBERT C. 2000. 'New Art, New Woman, Old Constructs: Gómez de la Serna, Pedro Salinas, and Vanguard Fiction', *Modern Language Notes (Hispanic Issue)*, 115(2): 205–23

SPOERRI, WILLIAM T. 1937. *The Old World and the New: A Synopsis of Current European Views on American Civilization* (Zurich: Max Niehans)

STURROCK, JOHN. 1990. *Louis-Ferdinand Céline: Journey to the End of the Night* (Cambridge: Cambridge University Press)

SUÁREZ, MARIO. 2014. *Nueva York Hipster* (Barcelona: Lunwerg)

SUÁREZ MIRAMÓN, ANA. 1980. *Modernismo y 98. Rubén Darío* (Madrid: Cincel)

SWEENEY, CAROL. 2004. *From Fetish to Subject: Race, Modernism and Primitivism, 1919–1935* (Westport: Greenwood Publishing)

SWINGEWOOD, ALAN. 1998. *Cultural Theory and the Problem of Modernity* (Basingstoke: Palgrave)

TAIBO, CARLOS. 2008. *Fendas abertas. Seis ensaios sobre a cuestión nacional* (Vigo: Xerais)

TATO CUMMING, GASPAR. 1945. *Nueva York: un español entre rascacielos* (Madrid: Febo)

THOMPSON, CARL. 2011. *Travel Writing* (New York: Routledge)

TODOROV, TZVETAN. 1989. *La conquista de América: el problema del otro* (Buenos Aires: Siglo XXI)

—— 2000. 'Race and Racism', in *Theories of Race and Racism: A Reader*, ed. by Les Back and John Solomos (London: Routledge), pp. 64–70

TORRE, GUILLERMO DE. 1965. *Historia de las literaturas de vanguardia* (Madrid: Guadarrama)

TORRES BALBÁS, LEOPOLDO. 1918. 'Mientras labran los sillares. Las nuevas formas de la arquitectura', *Arquitectura: órgano de la Sociedad Central de Arquitectos*, 2: 31–34

TOVAR, MANUEL. 1955. *Manhattan de refilón: Nueva York contado por un español* (Barcelona: Iberia)

TURNER-SADLER, JOANNE. 2009. *African American History: An Introduction* (New York: Lang)

UCELAY DA CAL, ENRIC. 2000. 'The Restoration. Regeneration and the Clash of Nationalisms, 1875–1914', in José Álvarez Junco and Adrian Shubert (eds), *Spanish History Since 1808* (London: Arnold), pp. 121–36

UNAMUNO, MIGUEL. 2005. *En torno al casticismo*, ed. by Jean-Claude Rabaté (Madrid: Cátedra)

VALBUENA PRAT, ÁNGEL. 1950. *Historia de la literatura española*, Volume 3 (Barcelona: Gustavo Gili)

VALENDER, JAMES. 1999. 'A propósito de las *Poesías completas* de José Moreno Villa', in *Nueva Revista de Filología Hispánica*, 472: 385–98

VEGA, GARCILASO DE LA. 2009. *Selected Poems of Garcilaso de la Vega: A Bilingual Edition*, trans. by John Dent-Young (Chicago: University of Chicago Press)

VENEGAS, JOSÉ LUIS. 2009. 'Unamuno, Epistolarity, and the Rhetoric of Transatlantic Hispanism', *Modern Language Notes (Hispanic Issue)*, 124(2): 438–59

VILLENA, LUIS ANTONIO DE. 1999. 'Un moderno muy olvidado: Luis de Oteyza', in Javier Barreiro et al. (eds), *Oscura turba de los más raros escritores españoles* (Saragossa: Xordica), pp. 161–70

VINCENT, MARY. 2007. *Spain 1833–2002: People and State* (Oxford: Oxford University Press)

WAGNER, PETER. 2001. *Theorizing Modernity* (London: Sage)

WARNER, MARINA. 1996. *Monuments and Maidens: The Allegory of the Female Form* (London: Vintage)

WATKINS, GLENN. 1994. *Pyramids at the Louvre: Music, Culture, and Collage from Stravinsky to the Postmodernists* (Cambridge: Harvard University Press)

WELLS, H. G. 1906. *The Future in America* (London; New York: Harper Brothers)

—— 1921. *The Salvaging of Civilization* (London: Cassell)

—— 1935. *The New America, the New World* (New York: Macmillan)

WHITE, SARAH L. 1999. 'Liberty, Honour, Order: Gender and Political Discourse in Nineteenth-Century Spain', in Victoria Enders and Pamela Radcliff (eds), *Constructing Spanish Womanhood: Female Identity in Modern Spain* (Albany: State University of New York Press), pp. 233–57

WILLIAMS, PATRICK. 2000. '"Simultaneous Uncontemporaneities": Theorising Modernism and Empire', in Howard J. Booth and Nigel Rigby (eds), *Modernism and Empire* (Manchester: Manchester University Press), pp. 13–38

WILSON, JASON. 1999. *Buenos Aires: A Cultural and Literary Companion* (Oxford: Signal Books)

WOHL, ROBERT. 1979. *The Generation of 1914* (Cambridge, Massachusetts: Harvard University Press)

WOOLF, VIRGINIA. 1979. 'Professions for Women', in *Women and Writing* (London: The Women's Press), pp. 57–63

YUVAL-DAVIES, NIRA. 1997. *Gender and Nation* (London: Routledge)

ZARO, JUAN JESÚS. 2007. *Shakespeare y sus traductores: análisis crítico de siete traducciones españolas de obras de Shakespeare* (New York: Lang)

ZIPES, JACK DAVID. 1993. *The Troubles and Tribulations of Little Red Riding Hood* (London: Routledge)

INDEX

❖

African American 110, 115, 119, 120, 121, 123, 124, 127, 128, 143, 144, 145, 146, 147, 148, 149, 151, 157, 163
Alec-Tweedie, Ethel 73
Alfau, Felipe 166, 167
Álvarez Chillida, Gonzalo 117, 118, 119
Andrés Álvarez, Valentín 33
Ángel del hogar 70, 71, 82, 93, 102, 107, 108
Angel in the House 47, 67, 68, 69, 70, 79, 93, 100, 107, 108
anti–Semitic 87, 91, 108, 116, 117, 118, 119, 124, 154, 162, 163
anti–Semitism 116, 118, 139
Araquistáin, Luis 4, 31, 74, 122
Arenal, Concepción 71
avant–garde 6, 12, 13, 14, 18, 19, 20, 32, 33, 36, 37, 52, 72, 112, 113, 118, 130, 156, 157, 158 n. 2, 159, 160
Ayala, Francisco 112, 113
Azorín 22, 27, 36

Balfour, Sebastian 3, 11, 142
Baroja, Pío 27, 29, 36
Barrantes Martín, Beatriz 10, 13, 14, 17, 18, 19, 33, 45, 71, 72, 159
Belda, Joaquín 4, 31, 122, 123
black 5, 8, 23, 24, 32, 112, 113, 114, 115, 119, 120, 121, 122, 123, 124, 125, 126, 127, 128, 129, 130, 131, 140, 143, 144, 145, 146, 147, 148, 149, 150, 151, 155, 157, 162, 163, 166
Bourdieu, Pierre 75, 76, 78, 98, 162
Bretz, Mary Lee 11, 69, 70, 72, 117, 160
Burgos, Carmen de 15, 16, 71, 74, 80, 97, 117, 162

Camba, Julio:
  Alemania, impresiones de un español 21
  Aventuras de una peseta 21
  El destierro 21
  El matrimonio de Restrepo 21
  La ciudad automática 3, 6, 7, 8, 9, 10, 19, 21–23, 24, 25, 55–64, 65, 102–06, 108, 110, 143–56, 157, 159, 162, 163
  La rana viajera 21
  Londres 21
  Un año en el otro mundo 21,23
Cañas, Dionisio 5
capitalism 5, 7, 8, 15, 21, 25, 28, 29, 30, 31, 33, 38, 40, 51, 60, 63, 65, 73, 91, 101, 110, 116, 117, 124, 131, 132, 133, 142, 157, 161, 163

casticismo 34, 48, 66 n. 1
casticista 34, 45, 47, 54, 62, 63, 100, 108, 134
Céline, Louis-Ferdinand 30, 31
Chacel, Rosa 71, 72, 97, 162
Cixous, Hélène 93
class 9, 14, 17, 26, 27, 29, 30, 38, 40, 41, 48, 63, 64, 69, 75
colonial 109, 110, 113, 114, 115, 121, 129, 149, 151, 157, 160, 163
colonialist 112, 119, 123, 124, 127, 131, 140, 157
Costa, Joaquín 27, 41, 44
Criado Requena, Eduardo 4, 6, 31, 73, 122

Davies, Catherine 14, 70
degeneration 26, 27, 47, 54, 66 n. 1, 69, 107, 111, 116, 118, 121, 124, 139, 149, 157, 162, 163
Duhamel, Georges 1, 29, 58, 72, 120, 121

El cuento semanal 14, 21
Escoriaza, Teresa de:
  Del dolor de la guerra (crónicas de la campaña de Marruecos) 15
  El crisol de las razas 3, 5, 8, 9, 10, 12, 14, 15–17, 25, 83–93, 94, 99, 107, 110, 134–39, 157, 159, 162, 163
  'La primera conferencia feminista. Teresa de Escoriaza habla a las radioescuchas' 15
Espina, Antonio 33

Fuentes, Víctor 33, 90

Ganivet, Ángel 41, 66 n.1
García Lorca, Federico 1, 4, 5, 6, 12, 30, 66, 112, 114, 130, 158 n. 4
gender 9, 14, 17, 23, 25, 38, 67, 68, 70, 72, 74, 75, 77, 78, 79, 85, 86, 93, 95, 99, 100, 102, 103, 104, 107, 109, 114, 129, 138, 154, 160, 161, 162, 163, 164
Generation of 27: 11, 12, 20, 23
Generation of 98: 11, 12, 160
Giménez Caballero, Ernesto 118
Gobineau, Arthur de 145
Gómez de la Serna, Ramón 12, 32, 33, 112, 113
Gorky, Maxim 1, 29, 30, 31
Gramsci, Antonio 98
Guibernau, Montse 111
Gullón, Germán 11, 160

Hall, Stuart 115

Hispanidad 118, 126, 151, 162
Hobsbawm, Eric 111
Huyssen, Andreas 10, 14, 70, 78

Institución Libre de Enseñanza 20, 34, 70, 71

Jarnés, Benjamín 33
jazz 6, 21, 112, 113, 128, 129, 130, 143, 147, 158 n. 2
Jew 17, 23, 24, 83, 85, 110, 115, 116, 117, 118, 119, 123, 124, 131, 132, 133, 134, 135, 136, 139, 142, 151, 153, 154, 155, 156, 157, 163, 166
Jewish 8, 17, 21, 40, 86, 87, 89, 93, 107, 110, 115, 116, 117, 118, 119, 122, 123, 124, 131, 132, 133, 134, 135, 136, 137, 139, 142, 151, 152, 153, 154, 155, 156, 157, 158 n. 13, 162, 163
Jiménez, Juan Ramón 5, 6, 21, 114
Judaism 15, 21, 87, 91, 108, 116, 127, 131, 132, 133, 157, 163

Kafka, Franz 1, 29
Kaplan, E. Ann 69, 97, 101
Kirkpatrick, Susan 70, 71, 72, 80, 85

Lago, Eduardo 166, 167
Laín Entralgo, Pedro 11
Loriga, Ray 166, 167

Maeztu, Ramiro de 41, 149
Martín Gaite, Carmen 166
'masses' 2, 3, 5, 8, 9 n. 2, 18, 21, 25, 26, 27, 28, 36, 38, 40, 42, 49, 58, 59, 60, 61, 64, 65, 69, 70, 78, 105, 109, 122, 149, 159, 160, 161
McCulloch, John 3, 12, 32
mechanization 2, 7, 8, 12, 21, 23, 24, 25, 26, 28, 29, 30, 31, 33, 39, 55, 57, 60, 64, 65, 72, 104, 114
melting pot 3, 110, 138, 139, 141, 143
Miquelarena, Jacinto 4, 32, 74, 123
miscegenation 17, 93, 110, 115, 120, 121, 129, 134, 135, 136, 138, 139, 162, 163
modernism 2, 3, 4, 5, 9 n. 3, 10, 11, 12, 20, 69, 160
Modernismo 9 n. 3, 11, 12, 160
modernity 1, 2, 3, 4, 7, 8, 11, 12, 13, 14, 17, 18, 19, 21, 29, 33, 34, 45, 55, 64, 67, 68, 70, 72, 75, 94, 100, 111, 112, 114, 115, 116, 117, 124, 131, 159, 160
modernization 1, 2, 3, 9, 10, 12, 14, 18, 19, 21, 23, 24, 28, 30, 31, 33, 38, 43, 45, 51, 53, 55, 56, 57, 63, 65, 67, 69, 71, 72, 75, 82, 83, 97, 99, 100, 102, 107, 108, 110, 116, 132, 133, 134, 139, 141, 143, 146, 156, 157, 158, 159, 160, 161, 162, 163, 164
modern woman 8, 17, 19, 21, 23, 66, 67, 69, 70, 71, 72, 73, 74, 75, 78, 80, 81, 83, 84, 85, 87, 93, 94, 95, 100, 106, 107, 108, 109, 159, 160, 162
Morand, Paul 1, 39, 72, 73, 119
Moreno Villa, José:
  'Casa "honesta" en Madrid' 36
  'Casa y casada' 76
  Función contra forma y otros escritos sobre arquitectura madrileña, 1927–1935: 66 n. 4

Jacinta la Pelirroja 21, 24 n. 7, 130
'La enseñanza de los pobres' 125
Locos, enanos, negros y niños palaciegos: gente de placer que tuvieron los Austrias en la Corte española desde 1563 a 1700: 127
'Magisterio de los criados' 125
'Mi españolismo y mi mexicanismo' 127
'Primeras nociones del mundo' 125
Pruebas de Nueva York 3, 6, 8, 9, 10, 20–21, 25, 33–45, 57, 64, 75–83, 84, 107, 110, 124–34, 147, 157, 159, 161, 163
'Temas de arte. El arte negro, factor moderno' 113
Vida en claro 21, 130
multiculturalism 2, 6, 8, 12, 18, 21, 23, 24, 109, 110, 111, 120, 157, 158, 162
Muñoz Molina, Antonio 22, 166, 167

national identity 6, 7, 8, 9, 10, 11, 14, 19, 25, 33, 34, 36, 41, 44, 45, 50, 54, 62, 63, 64, 65, 66, 67, 68, 75, 100, 102, 107, 108, 109, 110, 111, 117, 119, 124, 126, 132, 133, 134, 141, 142, 143, 149, 151, 154, 156, 157, 158, 159, 160, 161, 162, 163, 164, 167
nationalism 17, 22, 110, 111, 139, 143, 155, 157, 158, 163
Navarro Domínguez, Eloy 6, 7, 31
Neira, Julio 5, 6, 21, 24 n. 7, 113, 165
Neville, Edgar 5, 123, 124
novela de vanguardia 13

Obregón, Antonio de 33
Ortega y Gasset, José 8, 22, 25, 27, 28, 36, 41, 47, 49, 58, 59, 61, 62, 64, 65, 69, 72, 102, 161
  La España invertebrada 27
  La rebelión de las masas 28, 49, 59
Oteyza, Luis de:
  Abd-El-Krim y los prisioneros 18
  Anticípolis 3, 4, 5, 7, 8, 9, 10, 12, 17–19, 25, 45–55, 65, 93–102, 108, 110, 139–43, 158, 159, 162, 163
  El diablo blanco 18
  Obras selectas 18
  Picaresca Puritana 5
'Otherness' 17, 24, 41, 47, 64, 65, 111, 112, 113, 114, 115, 117, 130, 141, 144, 145, 156, 159, 160, 161, 162, 163, 164

Pardo Bazán, Emilia 15, 17, 71
Pateman, Carol 68
patriarchal 8, 23, 47, 54, 64, 66, 67, 68, 70, 72, 73, 74, 76, 77, 81, 82, 83, 85, 86, 88, 90, 91, 93, 94, 95, 99, 100, 103, 104, 106, 107, 108, 109, 136, 138, 140, 146, 161, 162, 163, 164
patriarchy 2, 17, 47, 48, 53, 67, 68, 69, 71, 72, 75, 76, 77, 82, 83, 86, 87, 88, 90, 91, 93, 94, 95, 97, 98, 99, 101, 102, 103, 105, 107, 108, 109, 160, 162, 163
Pino, José María del 36
primitive 8, 25, 28, 31, 40, 41, 42, 47, 48, 49, 53, 55, 57, 59, 60, 64, 65, 69, 81, 82, 85, 87, 89, 93, 94,

96, 105, 107, 112, 113, 114, 115, 123, 127, 145, 146, 148, 149, 151, 154, 157, 161, 163, 164
primitivism 9, 25, 27, 42, 43, 46, 49, 53, 57, 63, 64, 65, 80, 96, 105, 112, 113, 115, 119, 135, 145, 151, 156, 160
primitivist modernism 122, 113, 158 n. 3

'race' 9, 16, 17, 25, 26, 28, 40, 48, 61, 62, 70, 77, 80, 81, 91, 107, 110, 111, 112, 115, 116, 117, 118, 119, 120, 121, 122, 123, 124, 125, 126, 128, 129, 132, 133, 134, 135, 136, 137, 138, 139, 141, 142, 143, 144, 145, 147, 148, 149, 150, 152, 154, 156, 157, 160, 161, 162, 163, 164, 166
racialism 8, 110, 111, 112
racism 111, 112, 118, 120, 121, 123, 128, 146, 157
Regeneracionismo 33, 51, 83, 161
regeneration 2, 28, 41, 45, 47, 65, 66 n. 1, 71, 107, 112, 117, 130, 160, 164
Residencia de Estudiantes 20, 21, 34, 113
Revista de Occidente 62

Rohr, Isabelle 117, 118

Simmel, George 54, 72
Social Darwinism 26, 27
Soufas, Christopher 11, 160
Spengler, Oswald 2, 26, 33, 59, 60, 65
subaltern 98, 121, 124, 125, 126, 127, 128, 143, 147, 150, 151, 155, 157, 162, 163
symbolic violence 98, 101, 162

travel writing 19, 22, 23

Unamuno, Miguel de 41, 66 n. 1, 114, 115, 117

Wagner, Peter 2, 29
Wells, H. G. 1, 26, 28, 121, 122
Woolf, Viginia 12, 69, 100

Yuval-Davies, Nira 68, 95, 129